Meditations on the Hero

Meditations on the Hero

A Study of the Romantic Hero
in Nineteenth-Century Fiction

Walter L. Reed

New Haven and London, Yale University Press

1974

Published with assistance from the
Mary Cady Tew Memorial Fund.

Library of Congress catalog card number: 74-77068
International standard book number: 0-300-01735-9

Designed by John O. C. McCrillis
and set in Baskerville type.
Printed in the United States of America by
The Vail-Ballou Press, Binghamton, New York.

Published in Great Britain, Europe, and Africa by Yale University Press,
Ltd., London. Distributed in Latin America by Kaiman & Polon, Inc.,
New York City; in Australasia and Southeast Asia by John Wiley & Sons
Australasia Pty. Ltd., Sydney; in India by UBS Publishers' Distributors
Pvt., Ltd., Delhi; in Japan by John Weatherhill, Inc., Tokyo.

FOR LOREE

Contents

Preface

This study began with a graduate school paper that attempted to elucidate Melville by referring to Kierkegaard's doctrine of the three stages of existence. In the course of reading more widely in Kierkegaard I discovered that his works could not be so easily plundered for abstract schemes, that they had imaginative forms of their own. The comparison led to a dissertation that included chapters on Melville, Kierkegaard, and Carlyle. The present study is a further outgrowth of this investigation, which has crystallized around the ambiguous figure of the Romantic hero as he appears in works of prose fiction in the nineteenth century.

I have written on Kierkegaard and Lermontov in translation, with no firsthand knowledge of Danish or Russian; I have avoided, I hope, the kind of precise verbal analysis that translation inevitably defies. I have ventured this far afield in the conviction that literary history transcends the barriers of language, and that the works in question are not only particularly relevant to the problem of the hero but deserve to be better known among English-speaking readers and critics.

My greatest intellectual debt is to Charles Feidelson, who countenanced, supervised, and supported this project from its start. Without his generosity and incisiveness, his singular ability to help another's thinking nearer the clarity and depth of his own, this book would never have been. I also owe much to my friend Michael Holquist, whose wide learning and genius for discussion have frequently expanded my horizons and sharpened my views. Other friends and mentors read portions of the study and provided inspiration along the way: Geoffrey Hartman, whose effect on my thinking about Romanticism is I hope clear; James McIntosh, who read the dissertation and encouraged it to persevere; George Fayen, who offered much food for thought and a number of useful suggestions; and William Oram, Michael Rubinovitz, Howard Felperin, and Priscilla Clark, who all read and queried shrewdly. I would like to thank Merle Spiegel, formerly of Yale Press, for the generous reception the manuscript was given, and Judy Metro for her care in its retailoring.

My deepest debt has been to my wife Loree, for her loyalty, support, and patience. Her purity of heart through my will to one thing is acknowledged, inadequately, by the dedication.

W.L.R.

London
January 1974

I

Prolegomenon: The Romantic Hero and the Dialectical Form

The imaginative revolution of Romanticism, contemporary with but by no means determined by the political revolution in France, gave rise to a great many changes in literary form and theme. One of the most obvious changes, and the one least studied in a sympathetic way, was the revival of interest in the hero, that singular and energetic individual whose character contains his fate, who dominates as well as represents the society around him. The hero's domination may take a political form—he may be a leader of men—but it is also an aesthetic phenomenon. The hero stands above and beyond the common range of human experience, even though he is ultimately human and not a god. Like Melville's Billy Budd, the hero is the "cynosure" of those around him; he evokes the response that Thomas Greene has called "heroic or epic awe." [1]

Speaking in 1840 Thomas Carlyle said: "For myself in these days, I seem to see in this indestructibility of Hero-worship the everlasting adamant lower than which the confused wreck of revolutionary things cannot fall. . . . That man, in some sense or other, worships Heroes; that we all of us reverence and must ever reverence Great Men: this is, to me, the living rock amid all rushings-down whatsoever;—the one fixed point in modern revolutionary history, otherwise as if bottomless and shoreless." [2] Carlyle's words show how the ideal of the hero

1. *The Descent from Heaven* (New Haven, 1963), p. 15.
2. *Carlyle's Lectures On Heroes, Hero-Worship, and the Heroic in History*, ed. P. C. Parr (Oxford, 1920), p. 14.

1

could be made to transcend the imaginative upheavals that
brought it back into prominence after its decline in the Enlightenment, but they also reveal the political dimensions of
the Romantic hero that have brought him into disrepute
in this century. In his 1930 lecture "Carlyle and Hitler"
H. J. C. Grierson drew attention to the gathering political
consequences of hero worship, not only in Germany, but in
Italy, Russia, and the United States as well. Eric Bentley,
writing toward the end of World War II, proclaimed in *A
Century of Hero-Worship*, "The Heroic Vitalists are dead.
The Gordian knot of their ambiguity was cut by the hero with
the folkish banner, Adolf Hitler." [3] Though both Grierson
and Bentley are reasonable in the way they judge the culpa-
bility of earlier writers on the hero, they link the Romantic
revival of the hero with the rise of totalitarian government
and the advent of world war. Subsequent discussions of the
hero, Romantic or otherwise, tend to be critical of the concept of heroism per se,[4] or to concentrate on the phenomenon
of "the hero in eclipse" in the nineteenth and twentieth
centuries.[5]

There have, of course, been significant attempts in this
century in the fields of psychology and mythology to redeem
the notion of the hero. C. G. Jung, Otto Rank, and Joseph
Campbell are only the most distinguished names. But in all
these interpretations the hero is displaced from his higher

3. *A Century of Hero-Worship* (Philadelphia, 1944), p. 285.
4. See, e.g., Maurice Blanchot, "Le Héros," *Nouvelle Revue Française*
25 (1965): 90–104; Raney Stanford, "The Romantic Hero and That Fatal
Selfhood," *Centennial Review* 12 (1968): 430–54; and Edith Kern, "The
Modern Hero: Phoenix or Ashes?" *Comparative Literature* 10 (1958): 325–
34, reprinted in Victor Brombert, ed., *The Hero in Literature* (New York,
1969), pp. 266–77.
5. Mario Praz, *The Hero in Eclipse in Victorian Fiction*, trans. Angus
Davidson (Oxford, 1956); Raymond Giraud, *The Unheroic Hero in the
Novels of Stendhal, Balzac and Flaubert* (New Brunswick, N.J., 1957);
Sean O'Faolain, *The Vanishing Hero* (London, 1956); and Harry Levin,
"From Priam to Birotteau," *Yale French Studies* 6 (1950): 75–82 (also in
idem, *The Gates of Horn* [New York, 1963], pp. 56–64).

level above and beyond the common man. Otto Rank is explicit: "We feel justified in analogizing the ego of the child with the hero of the myth. . . . The hero should always be interpreted merely as a collective ego, which is equipped with all the excellences." Jung also reduces the hero to a manifestation of the ego, though he emphasizes the "collective" nature of the psyche more than Rank. Both Jung and Campbell approach the hero archetypally: a specific hero is significant as he participates in a mythical ur-identity and pattern of action. The individual hero is part of a larger composite figure, "The Hero with a Thousand Faces," as Campbell calls him. But one may object, as William Gilman does, that "a hero is distinguished first of all by being himself, not by the resemblances he may bear to someone else." The archetypal view distorts the hero, though it need not involve a reduction to the psychological. The hero may be seen as a displaced image of a god, as in Northrop Frye's scheme of literary evolution. "In romance," Frye says, "the hero is still half a god," while in what Frye calls high mimetic tragedy he is "balanced midway between godlike heroism and all-too-human irony." [6] Whether identified as a projection of the psyche, grounded in myth, or defined in terms of his divine antecedents, the hero loses his peculiar heroic identity.

For many of the Romantics and their successors, however, the hero in and of himself exercised a special fascination. The idea of a hero presented unique possibilities, even though it presented problems as well. Byron justifies his famous Childe Harold when he describes and addresses his creation:

6. Otto Rank, *The Myth of the Birth of the Hero,* trans. Robbins and Jelliffe (New York, 1952), p. 68; William Gilman, "The Hero and the Heroic in American Literature: An Essay in Definition," in *Patterns of Commitment in American Literature,* ed. Marston LaFrance (Toronto, 1967), p. 4; Northrop Frye, *Anatomy of Criticism* (Princeton, 1957), pp. 36, 37. For accounts of the emergence of the hero from the divine and mythic background that are more solidly based in cultural history than Frye's and that stress the emergence as a complete differentiation, see G. R. Levy, *The Sword from the Rock* (New York, 1953) and C. M. Bowra, *Heroic Poetry* (London, 1952).

'Tis to create, and in creating live
A being more intense that we endow
With form our fancy, gaining as we give
The life we image, even as I do now—
What am I? Nothing: but not so art thou,
Soul of my thought! with whom I traverse earth,
Invisible but gazing, as I glow
Mixed with thy spirit, blended with thy birth,
And feeling still with thee in my crushed feelings' dearth.

The hero is a more passionate and imaginative projection of
the poet's self. Kierkegaard seeks the solution to the problems
of the age in heroes of the past:

> Let others complain that the age is wicked; my complaint
> is that it is paltry; for it lacks passion. Men's thoughts
> are thin and flimsy like lace, they are themselves pitiable
> like the lace-makers. . . . This is the reason my soul al-
> ways turns back to the Old Testament and to Shakespeare.
> I feel that those who speak there are at least human be-
> ings: they hate, they love, they murder their enemies, and
> curse their descendants throughout all generations, they
> sin.

Nietzsche sounds a similar note but places his hero in the
revolutionary future instead of the traditional past: "Verily,
a polluted stream is man. One must be a sea, to receive a
polluted stream without becoming impure. Lo, I teach you the
Superman: he is that sea; in him can your great contempt be
submerged." [7]
There are two common themes in these characteristic Romantic attitudes. The first is that the hero is not heroic because of any moral excellence; he may well be a wrongdoer

7. *Childe Harold's Pilgrimage*, Canto 3, stanza 6, in *The Works of Lord
Byron*, ed. E. H. Coleridge (London, 1904), 2 : 219–20; Kierkegaard, *Either /
Or*, vol. 1, trans. David and Lillian Swenson, rev. Howard A. Johnson
(Garden City, N.Y., 1959), p. 27; Nietzsche, *Thus Spake Zarathustra*, trans.
Thomas Common, in *Complete Works*, ed. Oscar Levy (New York, 1924),
11 : 8.

but is in some sense "beyond good and evil," beyond the
common categories of morality. The definition of the hero as
one who "represents . . . a socially approved norm, for rep-
resenting which to the satisfaction of society he is decorated
with a title" does not apply at all here.[8] The Romantic hero is
never simply an antisocial being; his conflicts always involve
some germ or vestige of social concern, and he may be pictured
as an eventual redeemer of society.[9] But he clearly feels free to
reject most social norms. The second theme in these quotations
is more positive. The hero is presented as the solution to a
major problem of the age, the modern problem of an overly
developed reflective thought. I am referring here to Geoffrey
Hartman's crucial insight in his "Romanticism and Anti-
Selfconsciousness":

> Two trials or perils of the soul deserve special mention.
> We learn that every increase in consciousness is accom-
> panied by an increase in self-consciousness, and that
> analysis can easily become a passion that "murders to
> dissect." These difficulties of thought in its strength ques-
> tion the ideal of absolute lucidity. The issue is raised of
> whether there exist what might be called *remedia intellec-
> tus:* remedies for the corrosive power of analysis and the
> fixated self-consciousness.[10]

As Hartman shows, the Romantics saw art as a primary source
of these remedies and used a variety of artistic means or strategies in attempting to cure this disease of the age. One such
strategy was meditation on the figure and ideal of the hero—
a hero who seemed to possess wholeness, unselfconscious passion, and the ability to act.

Our modern view of Romanticism tends to slight the preoccupation with heroes, as a useful study of Byron's heroes

8. O'Faolain, *The Vanishing Hero,* p. 14.

9. See especially Frederick Garber, "Self, Society, Value, and the
Romantic Hero," *Comparative Literature* 19 (1967) : 321–33, reprinted in
Brombert, *The Hero in Literature,* pp. 213–27.

10. *Beyond Formalism* (New Haven, 1970), p. 299.

points out.[11] We stress the personal voice of lyric poetry in Wordsworth, Keats, and Shelley; we stress the communal and social vision of the Victorian novel. But behind these individual consciousnesses and social panoramas there often lurks the specter of a heroic existence, whether as possibility or as fact. Keats dreams of an epic mode where he may find "the agonies, the strife / Of human hearts" and defines poetry in the heroic, sculpturesque image of "might half slumb'ring on its own right arm." [12] Both Keats and Shelley write poems of heroic conflict in a mythopoeic mode, while Wordsworth tries his hand at a revival of Shakespearean heroism and villainy in *The Borderers.* As far as the English novel is concerned, one need only think of Thackeray's subtitle to *Vanity Fair,* elegiac as well as satiric—*A Novel without a Hero.* Or there is the prefatory model of Saint Theresa in *Middlemarch,* the romantic and religious ideal to which Dorothea Brooke unconsciously aspires and is measured against in Eliot's "home epic."

More obvious, of course, are the poetic romances and poetic dramas of Byron and Scott, which focus on the figure of the hero, not to mention the works of Goethe and Schiller, of Chateaubriand and Hugo, and of Pushkin abroad. The significance of the hero is perhaps least evident in England and most evident in Germany, "the home of the mystical worship of the Hero," as Grierson calls it.[13] The heroes of French Romanticism are more prone to self-consciousness themselves, more passive than active. As with Constant's Adolphe and Musset's *enfant de notre siècle,* they exhibit the disease of the age rather than provide its remedy.[14]

11. Peter L. Thorslev, Jr., *The Byronic Hero: Types and Prototypes* (Minneapolis, 1962), pp. 14–19.

12. "Sleep and Poetry," ll. 124–25, 237, in *Poetical Works,* ed. H. W. Garrod (London, 1956), pp. 45, 48.

13. *Carlyle and Hitler* (Cambridge, 1933), p. 42. See, however, the chapter "Hero-Worship" in Walter Houghton's *The Victorian Frame of Mind, 1830–1870* (New Haven, 1957), pp. 305–40, for evidence of the English preoccupation with the hero in this period; Houghton discusses the social and political aspects of hero worship more than the literary.

14. See George Ross Ridge, *The Hero in French Romantic Literature* (Athens, Ga., 1959), pp. 11–14.

In this study I am concerned with the figure of the hero in certain works of prose fiction of the mid-nineteenth century, works that take a single, active heroic figure as their central concern and adopt various narrative strategies to present this figure in his mastery and complexity. The works to be considered are diverse: Kierkegaard's *Fear and Trembling* and *Repetition,* Lermontov's *A Hero of Our Time,* Emily Brontë's *Wuthering Heights,* and Melville's *Moby-Dick* and *Pierre.* In all of them the hero is explored by a narrator or series of narrators who are both attracted to and repelled by the enigmatic presence before them. The hero is the object of epic awe and admiration, but he is also an imaginative problem as his narrator tries to present him to the contemporary world. The narrator's world is a common, prosaic one, and the narrator appropriately works in the medium of prose. This medium is not entirely appropriate for the hero himself, however. The heroes of poetry, drama, or pure romance are less of a problem in this respect; their forceful and commanding presence is more sanctioned by literary tradition. In the novel the true, active hero is something of an outsider.

This generic distinction is expressed most clearly by Goethe in *Wilhelm Meister,* when the theatrical troupe is considering a production of *Hamlet:*

> In the novel, it is chiefly *sentiments* and *events* that are exhibited; in the drama, it is *characters* and *deeds.* The novel must go slowly forward; and the sentiments of the hero, by some means or another, must restrain the tendency of the whole to unfold itself and to conclude. The drama, on the other hand, must hasten, and the character of the hero must press forward to the end; it does not restrain, but is restrained. The novel-hero must be suffering, at least he must not in a high degree be active; in the dramatic one, we look for activity and deeds. Grandison, Clarissa, Pamela, the Vicar of Wakefield, Tom Jones himself, are, if not suffering, at least retarding personages; and the incidents are all in some sort modelled by their sentiments. In the drama the hero models nothing by

himself; all things withstand him, and he clears and casts away the hindrances from off his path, or else sinks under them.[15]

In fact, there are two different senses of "hero" in this passage, and it would be best to resolve this ambiguity at the start. Toward the end of the seventeenth century in France and England, as Edith Kern has shown, a new sense of the term "hero" emerges from the older Renaissance and classical sense. "The hero of a book no longer has to be heroic. He may be, indeed, the very opposite. He owes his designation as hero solely to the fact that he is the book's leading character." [16] Kern notes how Thackeray, somewhat facetiously, refuses the title of hero in this older sense to Tom Jones. Indeed, Fielding can be seen as writing in a specifically mock-heroic tradition, the tradition of *Don Quixote* rather than of *Hamlet,* where the incongruity between the archaic, public image of the hero and the modern literary protagonist is stressed.[17] It is this older, public sense of the hero as a figure of strength and stature, not the more modern literary sense of the hero as the main charac-

15. *Wilhelm Meister's Apprenticeship,* trans. Thomas Carlyle, ed. Victor Lange (New York, 1962), pp. 288–89. Cf. Jean Paul Friedrich Richter's essay "On Character" in his *Vorschule der Aesthetik:* "The prosaic author takes a real being from his circle and tries to raise it to an ideal through poetic appendages; the poet endows, inversely, his ideal creature with the individualizing properties of reality" (translation from a dissertation by Margaret Hale, "Jean Paul Friedrich Richter's *Vorschule der Aesthetik:* Fulcrum for Its Period," Yale University, 1970). The idea that the novel was ideally a mixture of genres was F. Schlegel's, who also said, "I detest the novel as far as it wants to be a separate genre" (*Dialogue on Poetry and Literary Aphorisms,* trans. Ernst Behler and Roman Struc [University Park, Pa., 1968], p. 101).

16. "The Modern Hero," *The Hero in Literature,* p. 276.

17. It is tempting, though beyond the scope of this chapter, to consider Romanticism as taking the mock-heroic structure of the Augustan Age and standing it back on its feet; this inversion is evident in a comparison of eighteenth- and nineteenth-century interpretations of *Don Quixote.* The Augustan Age, conversely, may be seen as inverting an earlier Renaissance sense of positive heroic values; Milton's Satan would be a transitional figure here.

ter, that Kierkegaard, Lermontov, Brontë, and Melville are concerned with. The heroes of their works are in fact not native to the traditions of the novel, and this is one of the problems that as heroes they present. They are literary revivals or imports from drama or epic or poetic romance, often of an earlier age, and are felt to be such by narrators who try to present them to their modern audience. They are positive heroes in a negative field.[18]

The four authors I have chosen may seem at first to form an unlikely company in the diversity of their nationalities and literary traditions. In fact, the lack of direct relation among them is significant for the purposes of my study.[19] All these writers are reacting separately to a common Romantic concern, and in showing the parallel themes and forms of their disparate works I hope to be able to show something about a more general structure of the Romantic imagination. I do not mean to imply that the heroes of these works share a common identity; they are separate and distinct characters. It is rather the generic concern with the hero qua hero that these works share, along with a common narrative form for exploring this concern. All these works are informed by a structure that I have called the "meditation on the hero." The hero's acts comprise a story in their own right, but a more complex fate is described in the interaction of the heroic presence and the narrative point of view—curious, skeptical, interested, and detached by turns. The meditation on the hero is not a genre in the common sense of the term, a formal system of publicly recognized conventions; it is rather an imaginative structure of thought, more implicitly than explicitly evolved. I shall re-

18. As a corollary of this status of the hero as generic outsider, there is little sense of a generic specificity about the hero himself, e.g., an epic hero rather than a tragic one.

19. Barriers of language (translations coming too late) would have kept Lermontov and Kierkegaard from reading Brontë and Melville, as well as Lermontov from Kierkegaard. Although Lermontov read English, he died before any of the other three authors published. The only possibility is that Melville read *Wuthering Heights* before writing *Moby-Dick,* but there is no evidence that he did so.

turn to the question of genre in a concluding chapter. In this introductory chapter I am concerned with tracing the philosophical significance and the historical emergence of this peculiar imaginative form.

The Romantic hero is not a simple being, but one involved in a set of relationships both dialectical and dynamic. The hero is first of all a figure related to a ground. He is not himself divine or immortal but, like Achilles or Odysseus, he has a privileged relation with the supernatural, whether this is the supernatural of the gods or, as is more usual in Romanticism, the natural supernaturalism of the created world. The heroic existence, in other words, must define its special relation to a metaphysical or ontological ground. The hero is secondly related as an actor is to an audience, as an extraordinary person is to the ordinary members of his society. The social audience is often represented by a sociable narrator, someone like Ishmael in *Moby-Dick,* who survives to tell the tale. It is not merely a question here of a foil to the hero, the "opposing voice," as Maynard Mack calls the Horatios and Edgars of Shakespeare's tragedies, whom the audience may compare and contrast with the hero.[20] Audience and society themselves are drawn into the drama of the Romantic hero; the social norm itself is out of joint and the society is actively in search of heroism—even as it is skeptical of its possibility. Finally, the Romantic hero is involved in a relationship to himself, that is, to his own heroic identity. He is not a simple unified self but must live up to, or decline from, an inherited heroic ideal. The Romantic hero, in other words, finds his being organized along historical lines. His identity is never completely fixed but is in a process of evolution or devolution. I would like to consider these three relationships in this order, filling out the dialectic with historical examples that will show how the total structure develops in the Romantic era and beyond.

20. "The Jacobean Shakespeare," in *Jacobean Theatre* (New York, 1960), p. 15.

The hero of the older epics emerged, it has been argued, from the divine beings of myth, but his heroic acts were only possible when his human activity was differentiated from the recurrent cyclical patterns of a mythic world view.[21] This is not to say that the hero is a "faded god" or that there is a simple historical progression from god to hero to common man in literary history. It is rather to say that the notion of a hero is only possible when the human figure has emerged as a symbolic form in art, when the protagonist of a story is no longer fully divine. On the other hand, if the protagonist is too distant from this mythic background, too isolated in his mortality, he is in danger of losing his heroic identity altogether. Jung expresses this tension in psychological terms; for him the hero is a "self-representation of the longing of the unconscious, of its unquenched and unquenchable desire for the light of consciousness. But consciousness, continually in danger of being led astray by its own light and of becoming a rootless will o' the wisp, longs for the healing power of nature, for the deep wells of being and for unconscious communication with life in all its countless forms."[22]

The Romantic hero tends to find his "deep wells of being" neither in the pantheon of divinity nor in the psychic unconscious, but in the world of nature.[23] In *Dichtung und Wahrheit* Goethe discusses the demoniacal individual as the manifestation of a principle of nature. The passage is an important one, as it constitutes in miniature a meditation on a heroic type. "He thought he could detect in nature—both animate and inanimate, with soul or without soul—something which manifests itself only in contradictions, and which, therefore, could not be comprehended under any idea, still less under

21. See Levy, *The Sword from the Rock* and Bowra, *Heroic Poetry*. Carlyle's *Heroes and Hero-Worship* begins with "The Hero as Divinity" and then moves on to more humanized forms.

22. "The Origin of the Hero," *Symbols of Transformation*, trans. R. F. C. Hull, in *Collected Works of C. G. Jung* (Princeton, 1950), 5 : 205.

23. The most magisterial treatment of this theme, the replacement of the Christian deity and the created world by Nature alone, is in M. H. Abrams, *Natural Supernaturalism* (New York, 1971), esp. pp. 88–94.

one word. It was not godlike, for it seemed unreasonable; not
human, for it had no understanding. . . . To this principle
. . . I gave the name of Demoniac. . . ." Goethe finds this
principle most compelling when it appears in human form:

> The most fearful manifestation of the demoniacal is when
> it is seen predominating in some individual character.
> During my life I have observed several instances of this,
> either more closely or remotely. Such persons are not
> always the most eminent men, either morally or intellec-
> tually; and it is seldom that they recommend themselves
> to our affections by goodness of heart: a tremendous
> energy seems to be seated in them; and they exercise a
> wonderful power over all creatures, and even over the
> elements; and indeed, who shall say how much farther
> such influence may extend? All the moral powers com-
> bined are of no avail against them: in vain does the more
> enlightened portion of mankind attempt to throw suspi-
> cion upon them as deceived if not deceivers,—the mass is
> still drawn on by them. Seldom if ever do the great men
> of an age find their equals among their contemporaries,
> and they are to be overcome by nothing but the universe
> itself. . . .[24]

This sense of the proximity of the hero to primal conflicts
of nature provides a rationale for the close relation between
the Romantic hero and the natural landscape. Such a use of
landscape is easily dismissed as a pathetic fallacy or as a piece
of stage scenery for grand heroic gestures. But in a more profound sense it is related to the Romantic hero in much the
same way that the Olympian gods are related to Achilles—
sometimes as a partial source, sometimes as an analogue, but
never as a total determinant or a simple projection of the
hero's actions and resolve. Werther, the man of sensibility in

24. *Truth and Fiction Relating to My Life,* trans. J. Oxenford
(Boston, 1882), 1 : 323. I am indebted to my colleague James McIntosh for
pointing out the relevance of this passage.

the process of becoming a hero, is closely attuned to the trees and the clouds. Faust, as Erich Heller puts it, is involved in a struggle against nature even as he himself is a part of it.[25] And Faust periodically returns to this well of being in the form of a landscape, as in the haunting "Forest and Cavern" scene in Part One. Childe Harold is continually fading out into different continental landscapes, and Manfred's Alps are both a source and an expression of his heroic defiance.

An actual landscape need not be involved in the presentation of the hero. There is the more general conception of the characters of Shakespeare, whom German Romantic critics and even English Neoclassical ones found intimately related to Nature in the abstract. Shakespeare's characters were an important source for the Romantic conception of the hero, and it is interesting to find Alexander Pope writing as early as 1725 that Shakespeare's *"characters* are so much Nature herself, that 'tis a sort of injury to call them by so distant a name as copies of her." [26] Pope's notion of nature is of course rather different from, say, Herder's, but the tendency to associate Shakespearean characters directly with such a term (also evident in Johnson) is a significant preview of later Romantic developments.

There are dangers as well as strengths in this relationship between the heroic figure and his ontological ground, however. Few of the Romantics were as sanguine as Goethe about the essential spirituality of nature, about the essential benevolence of the bond between the human and the natural. At its best Romanticism never wants simply to return to a state of nature, but to recapture something of the vital power of that

25. "Goethe and the Avoidance of Tragedy," in *The Disinherited Mind* (Cleveland, 1959), pp. 56–57. Jung ends his essay "The Origins of the Hero" by quoting from Faust's descent to "the Mothers" in Part Two. The Mothers for Goethe are not the mother figures of modern psychology but the generative matrices of the natural world. Jung's conception of the mother bears some resemblance to Goethe's.

26. "Preface to the Works of Shakespear," *The Works of Alexander Pope,* ed. W. Elwin and W. J. Courthope (London, 1886), 10 : 535.

state at a higher level of awareness.[27] The most antinaturalistic of all the Romantic heroes in Ahab, who would strike the sun if it insulted him, but the idea that the natural world can be a temptation and a diminishment of the hero's human potential can be seen in other Romantic examples as well. The hero must frequently wrest the supernatural powers from their source in order to be able to use them. To put it in Jungian terms, he must at some point overcome the terrible mother in order to become fully human.

Nature is not the only ground against which the hero defines himself in the nineteenth century; there is also the ground of history. Nature and history in fact often act together as a ground for the heroic self, as in a vision of Ahab that Ishmael has as he tries to penetrate to the depth of his hero's motives:

> This is much; yet Ahab's larger, darker, deeper part remains unhinted. But vain to popularize profundities, and all truth is profound. Winding far down from within the very heart of this spiked Hotel de Cluny where we here stand—however grand and wonderful, now quit it;—and take your way, ye nobler, sadder souls, to those vast Roman halls of Thermes; where far beneath the fantastic towers of man's upper earth, his root of grandeur, his whole awful essence sits in bearded state; an antique buried beneath antiquities, and throned on torsoes! So with a broken throne, the great gods mock that captive king; so like a Caryatid, he patient sits, upholding on his frozen brow the piled entablatures of ages.[28]

27. See Geoffrey Hartman, "Romanticism and Anti-Selfconsciousness," pp. 300–01. Harold Bloom puts it more forcefully in "The Internalization of Quest Romance," in *The Ringers in the Tower* (Chicago, 1971), p. 19: "Romantic nature poetry, despite a long critical history of misrepresentation, was an anti-nature poetry, even in Wordsworth, who sought a reciprocity or even a dialogue with nature, but found it only in flashes."

28. *Moby-Dick; or, The Whale*, ed. Charles Feidelson (New York, 1964), p. 249.

There is an imaginative dissolve here, through an ambiguous simile, into a natural and historical ground. The investigation of the self becomes a kind of archeology. Such a transformation is familiar in Byron as well. The Romantic penchant for ruins, in fact, can be seen as an attempt at a *paysage historicisé,* a way of revealing the force of time within a natural landscape.

The ground behind the figure of the Romantic hero is often purely historical, however, and it is Hegel who provides the clearest sense of this relationship:

> Such are all great historical men—whose own particular aims involve those large issues which are the will of the World-Spirit. They may be called Heroes, inasmuch as they have derived their purposes and their vocation, not from the calm, regular course of things, sanctioned by the existing order; but from a concealed fount—one which has not attained to phenomenal, present existence—from that inner Spirit, still hidden beneath the surface, which, impinging on the outer world as on a shell, bursts it in pieces, because it is another kernel than that which belonged to the shell in question.[29]

The hero in this conception is the vessel and agent of an absolute Spirit that is working itself out in history. Napoleon, of course, was the prime candidate for world-historical individual in modern times, and it is interesting to find writers of different nationalities and political views agreeing on Napoleon's heroic status—Hegel, Goethe, Nietzsche, Carlyle, Lermontov, and Kierkegaard, to mention only a few. If the Romantic hero has a political dimension, the political figure of Napoleon has an imaginative dimension as well.[30]

Furthermore, although one can see the potential for a fascist or totalitarian form of government in this Hegelian

29. *The Philosophy of History,* trans. J. Sibree (New York, 1899), p. 30.
30. See esp. *Yale French Studies* 26 (1960–61), an issue devoted to "The Myth of Napoleon."

vision of the hero and his ground, there is also the possibility of a more socialistic reading of it, as Georg Lukács has demonstrated. Despite Hegel's "overrating of the role of the 'world-historical individuals,' " Lukács argues, this heroic figure in the end only gives "consciousness and clear direction to a movement already present in society." [31] Lukács finds Hegel's sense of the hero here closer to the middling, unheroic heroes of Scott than to the extraordinary heroes of the Romantic cult. Lukács emphasizes the historical ground at the expense of the heroic figure, and it is perhaps this possibility in the Hegelian formula that Nietzsche resists so emphatically when he defines the relation of the Superman to history as one of disparity rather than congruence. The source of heroic power is less historical for Nietzsche, more mythical and archaic—in effect, closer to unmediated nature. In discussing the case of Napoleon, Nietzsche is led to remark, "Great men are necessary, the age in which they appear is a matter of chance; the fact that they almost invariably master their age is accounted for simply by the fact that they are stronger, that they are older, that power has been stored longer for them." [32]

Like the metaphysical ground of nature, then, the ground of history can be a threatening one, a ground that if overemphasized can swallow up the hero. The problem is one that Kierkegaard addresses at length in *Fear and Trembling;* like Nietzsche, though for quite different reasons, he rejects the notion of the world-historical individual and the importance of the historical ground. The Romantic hero is frequently jealous of his selfhood, either directly, as Ahab is, or indirectly, as in the case of Kierkegaard's Abraham, who is defended by the narrator Johannes de Silentio.

An interesting consequence of this jealous defense of selfhood is the tendency of the heroic character to free himself from the confines of plot. Aristotle had declared character

31. *The Historical Novel,* trans. Hannah and Stanley Mitchell (Boston, 1963), p. 39.
32. *The Twilight of the Idols,* trans. Anthony Ludovici, *Complete Works,* 16 : 102.

subordinate to plot; for the Romantic hero this subordination puts undue constraint upon his being. As the history of Shakespearean criticism shows, the study of character as an independent entity emerged in the course of the eighteenth century in England; it received a new infusion of energy in *Sturm und Drang* Germany and continued to be a major force up through Bradley's lectures on Shakespearean tragedy. Robert Langbaum has noted the similarity between this approach to Shakespeare through his characters and the dramatic monologue in Victorian poetry, an approach where characters seem to have "a residue of intelligence and will beyond what the plot requires and not accounted for by it, so that they stand somehow above the plot, conscious of themselves inside it." [33] These remarks may be applied to the meditation on the hero as well: there seems to be something in these heroes that is incommensurate with any pattern of action, externally perceived. This does not mean that the hero's acts are unimportant but that a definite causal pattern of action, with a beginning, middle, and end, is something uncongenial to the hero's identity.[34] This is one way of regarding the curious ending of Byron's *Manfred*—as a declaration of the independence of the hero from the plot. Manfred insists that his fate lies in his character, not in the traditional demonic machinery that demands his sacrifice.

33. *The Poetry of Experience* (London, 1957), p. 170. Cf. W. J. Harvey's remarks on the *"DNB"* approach to Shakespeare's characters in the nineteenth century (*Character and the Novel* [London, 1965], pp. 200–05).

34. The difference between the hero's actions and the pattern of actions embodied in the (Aristotelian) plot is best described by Walter Benjamin's distinction between "story," which simply tells what happened, and "information," which tries to explain how and why ("The Storyteller," in *Illuminations*, ed. Hannah Arendt, trans. Harry Zohn [London, 1970]). The distinction is similar to E. M. Forster's distinction between story and plot in *Aspects of the Novel*, but Benjamin associates story with an acceptance of mystery and magic, information with rationally plotted modes of thought, in a way that suggests the difference between the irreducible mystery of the hero and the speculative methods of the narrator in the meditation on the hero.

The relation of the hero to the ground of his actions is thus problematic. Still more problematic is the relation of the hero to his audience, to the socially bound consciousness that tries to comprehend him. There is in this relationship what Nietzsche calls "the pathos of distance." [35] The Romantic hero is set apart from the rest of society. He is a figure from the distant past upon whom a modern intelligence meditates, as in *Fear and Trembling*. Or he is a figure from a foreign land, where the barriers are cultural and geographical, as in the distance between the English editor and the German philosopher in Carlyle's *Sartor Resartus*. Drama and romance have an inherent sense of distance in them—drama in the separation of stage from audience (much more pronounced in nineteenth-century than in Elizabethan theater), romance in its characteristic concern with the supernatural. In the peculiar kind of fiction I am concerned with here—prose fiction conscious of its own prosaic nature—the distance of the heroic from common human experience is maintained more artificially. It is proclaimed by a narrator who insists on his inability to understand the hero even as he seeks this understanding. "I *think* myself *into* the hero," says the narrator of *Fear and Trembling*, referring to the historically determined hero of Hegel, "but into Abraham I cannot think myself; when I reach the height I fall down, for what I encounter there is the paradox." [36]

Again, this dialectical relationship is subject to different emphasis. On the one hand there are those like Kierkegaard who so insist on the hermeneutic distance between hero and narrator and between hero and audience that the hero is truly incomprehensible to the common view. The mystery of Hamlet's motivation in Romantic criticism of Shakespeare is another instance of the triumph of the hero as enigma. On the other hand there are the more confident interpreters of the hero, like Emerson in his essay "Heroism":

35. *Twilight of the Idols*, p. 93.
36. *Fear and Trembling and The Sickness unto Death*, trans. Walter Lowrie (Garden City, N.Y., 1954), p. 44.

All these great and transcendent properties are ours. If we dilate in beholding the Greek energy, the Roman pride, it is that we are already domesticating the same sentiment. Let us find room for this great guest in our small houses. . . . Why should these great words, Athenian, Roman, Asia and England, so tingle in the ear? Where the heart is, there the muses, there the gods sojourn, and not in any geography of fame.

As with so many things about the Romantic hero, the attitude toward Shakespeare's heroic characters provides the blueprint. Samuel Johnson goes as far as to deny the idea of the hero altogether in his desire to bring the character close to the reader's understanding: "*Shakespeare* has no heroes; his scenes are occupied only by men, who act and speak as the reader thinks that he should himself have spoken or acted on the same occasion." Goethe, on the other hand, thought differently: "Shakespeare's characters are on a colossal scale: for which reason we fail to recognize them as our fellows." A. C. Bradley mediates between the two extremes, admitting the common human elements in Shakespeare's tragic characters but insisting that "by an intensification of the life which they share with others, they are raised above them; and the greatest are raised so far that, if we fully realize all that is implied in their words and actions, we become conscious that in real life we have known scarcely anyone resembling them." [37] In the meditations on the hero that concern us here, it is the failure of recognition that is stressed.

One can observe the evolution of this sense of distance between narrator and protagonist most clearly in a series of eighteenth-century English works that are not concerned with

37. *The Selected Writings of Ralph Waldo Emerson,* ed. Brooks Atkinson (New York, 1940), p. 256; Johnson, "Preface to Shakespeare," in *Rasselas, Poems, and Selected Prose,* ed. Bertrand H. Bronson (New York, 1952), p. 243; Goethe in Augustus Ralli, *A History of Shakespearean Criticism* (London, 1932), 1 : 109; Ralli is paraphrasing Goethe's *Stray Thoughts on Shakespeare;* A. C. Bradley, *Shakespearean Tragedy* (Oxford, 1904), p. 20.

the hero at all, but with a more common conception of character. The growing sense of the difficulty of understanding *any* individual within the literary context in Pope, Fielding, and Sterne, provides an analogue and perhaps a source for the later meditation on a specifically heroic character. The first stage comes in Pope's *Moral Essays,* where the obscurity of the other is confronted and triumphantly resolved:

> Judge we by Nature? Habit can efface,
> Int'rest o'ercome, or Policy take place:
> By Actions? those uncertainty divides:
> By Passions? these Dissimulation hides:
> Opinions? they still take a wider range:
> Find, if you can, in what you cannot change.
>   Search then the Ruling Passion: There alone,
> The Wild are constant, and the Cunning known;
> The Fool consistent, and the False sincere;
> Priests, Princes, Women, no dissemblers here.[38]

The peculiarities and obscurities of character are clarified, though not denied, by a single rational principle. The "Ruling Passion" is a means of rationalizing the irrational, according to a dialectical but ultimately fixed notion of human nature. The interpreting intelligence asserts its supremacy.

Fielding extends this Neoclassical principle when he defines his notion of character in *Joseph Andrews,* but he makes it more personal.

> I declare here once for all, I describe not men, but manners; not an individual, but a species. Perhaps it will be answered, Are not the characters then taken from life? To which I answer in the affirmative; nay, I believe I might aver, that I have writ little more than I have seen. The lawyer is not only alive, but hath been so these four thousand years; and I hope G—will indulge his life as many yet to come. He hath not indeed confined himself to one

38. "Moral Essays, Epistle I," *The Poems of Alexander Pope,* ed. John Butt (New Haven, 1963), p. 555 (ll. 168–77).

profession, one religion, or one country; but when the first mean selfish creature appeared on the human stage, who made self the centre of the whole creation, would give himself no pain, incur no danger, advance no money, to assist or preserve his fellow creatures; then was our lawyer born; and whilst such a person as I have described exists on earth, so long shall he remain upon it.[39]

Fielding draws on the Theophrastian tradition of character, revived by La Bruyère; character is a type, but there are many such types, and they are more individualized and more personalized than an abstract ruling passion. Pope frequently attacks historical individuals in his satires, but these individuals are objects of scrutiny only as they come under the classification of a particular ruling passion or ruling vice. Fielding chooses a middle ground for his satire, one which neither names the individual nor subordinates him to an abstract principle. The author is more modest in his claims of understanding his characters.

Sterne in *Tristram Shandy* goes considerably beyond Fielding in insisting on the distance of the knower from the known. Uncle Toby is a type character in many respects, conventionally eccentric, driven by humors, a vestigial form of the Renaissance man of arms. But Sterne insists that to depict Uncle Toby's ruling passion, his hobby horse, is to know less than the whole man:

> If the fixture of *Momus's* glass, in the human breast, according to the proposed emendation of that arch-critick, had taken place,— . . . nothing more would have been wanting, in order to have taken a man's character, but to have taken a chair and gone softly, as you would to a dioptrical bee-hive, and look'd in,—view'd the soul stark naked;—observ'd all her motions,—her machinations; . . . But this advantage is not to be had by the biographer in this planet . . . our minds shine not through the body, but are wrapt up here in a dark covering of

39. *Joseph Andrews,* ed. Maynard Mack (New York, 1948), p. 180.

> uncrystalized flesh and blood; so that if we would come
> to the specifick characters of them, we must go some
> other way to work. . . . In giving you my uncle *Toby*'s
> character, I am determined to draw it by no mechanical
> help whatever; . . . but, in a word, I will draw my Uncle
> *Toby*'s character from his HOBBY-HORSE.[40]

The story of Momus' glass (picked up by Melville in *Pierre*)
shows a concern with the problem of an author's omniscience.
The advantages of such clairvoyance contain liabilities, as the
soul is reduced to a mechanical system. Like Kant, Sterne has
had to deny reason to make room for faith. Character, even as
comic a character as Uncle Toby, becomes a mystery as the
narrative mind recognizes its own distance from the inner
workings of the self of another. The ruling passion is a
serious principle of truth; the hobbyhorse is a comic tool of
approximation.

The sense of distance between a specifically heroic character
and the narrative purview can be seen most dramatically in
Goethe's *Sorrows of Young Werther*. Goethe was influenced by
eighteenth-century English sentimentalism, particularly by
Sterne, but as Peter Thorslev notes, he transformed the man
of feeling from a common man to a hero.[41] *Werther* shows the
Romantic hero in the process of being born, and it is significant that when the hero's suffering reaches a certain level of
intensity the direct presentation of the self through letters is
interrupted and rendered more problematical. The Editor
intrudes under a heading entitled "The Editor to the Reader":

> I wish that we had so many documents by his own hand
> about our friend's memorable last days that I did not
> need to interrupt the sequence of his letters by a con-
> necting narrative.
>   I have felt it my duty to collect accurate information

---

40. *Tristram Shandy*, ed. James Work (New York, 1940), pp. 74–77.
41. *The Byronic Hero*, p. 42. The German *"Leiden,"* connoting "passion" and "suffering" is more suggestive of heroism than the English
"sorrows."

from persons well acquainted with his history. The story is simple; and all accounts agree, except for some unimportant particulars. Only with respect to the character of the persons involved do opinions and judgements vary.

All that is left to do then, is to relate conscientiously the facts which our persistent labor has enabled us to collect, to give the letters found after his death, and to pay attention to even the slightest fragment from his pen, especially since it is so difficult to discover the true and innermost motives of men who are not of the common run.[42]

It is almost a shift to another mode here. Werther has outgrown the limits of the epistolary novel. The Editor, in the beginning simply a device, becomes an important mediating and distancing presence as Werther's "true and innermost motives" become a mystery.

There seem to be several parallel developments of this existential *Verfremdungseffekt* in the Romantic period. Goethe's own development of the Bildungsroman in *Wilhelm Meister,* where the heroic model of Hamlet is held up to the emerging selfhood of the young Wihelm, is one continuation that we shall speak of shortly in another context. In this novel Goethe restricts his authorial comprehension of his character, not so much of Wilhelm's present self as of the future self that he will become. Two other types of novels that similarly deny or limit the author's omniscience are the Gothic novel, with its frequent narrative complexities, and symbolistic fiction, in which the author meditates extensively on a symbolic object.

Goethic novels such as *Frankenstein* and *Melmoth the Wanderer* use an elaborate series of narrative devices to distance the supernatural action from the natural habits of mind of the reader. The narrative structures in both these novels are similar to the narrative forms used by Kierkegaard, Lermontov, Brontë, and Melville. A series of stories told, letters found,

42. *The Sorrows of Young Werther,* trans. Victor Lange (New York, 1949), p. 95.

and manuscripts edited provides an interlocking narrative, one that mediates between a mythical or magical subject and an ironical or skeptical audience. The main difference is that *Frankenstein* and *Melmoth* are less concerned with a single heroic figure than with a series of supernatural events. In *Frankenstein* there are concentric circles of audience: Robert Walton, the polar explorer, writes letters back to his sister in England; Victor Frankenstein, rescued from an ice floe, narrates the story of his life and misadventures to Walton; in the course of Frankenstein's narration the monster tells Frankenstein the story of *his* life and misadventures as they sit together in a lonely hut near Mont Blanc. This is the innermost circle of the narrative. The outer circumference is perhaps Mary Shelley's introduction, where she tells the reader the genesis of the tale, the ghost-story project among the four friends, and her seminal dream vision of the monster gazing at his creator.

In *Frankenstein* the revelations move from inner to outer—a character reveals himself to an audience. In Charles Maturin's *Melmoth the Wanderer* there is some of this self-revelation, but there is more emphasis on the active investigation of the audience into the character—the mind moving in upon its subject from without. The relation of audience to story in *Frankenstein* is one of emotional sympathy (or lack thereof); the relation in *Melmoth* is one of intellectual "curiosity." The construction of *Melmoth* is much looser than that of *Frankenstein,* but the crux of each episode comes when the listener's curiosity has led him into a situation of extreme misery. He or she is then invited to change places with Melmoth, who has sold his soul to the devil. John Melmoth, the last living descendant of the legendary Wanderer, first learns of the Wanderer's existence through a tattered manuscript. His reaction to the discovery is an emblem for the book as a whole:

> The conclusion of this extraordinary manuscript was in such a state, that, in fifteen mouldy and crumbling pages, Melmoth could hardly make out that number of lines. No antiquarian, unfolding with trembling hand the cal-

cined leaves of an Herculaneum transcript, and hoping to discover some lost lines of the Aeneis in Virgil's own autograph, or at least some unutterable abomination of Petronius or Martial, happily elucidatory of the mysteries of the Spintriae, or the orgies of the Phallic worshippers, ever pored with more luckless diligence, or shook a head of more hopeless despondency over his task. He could but just make out what tended rather to excite than assuage that feverish thirst of curiosity which was consuming his inmost soul.[43]

Ultimately, Maturin suggests, the audience is tempted to become the mysterious villain, is tempted, like the narrator, to change places with the hero. Mary Shelley is also concerned with the dangers of an overdeveloped intellectual curiosity, but the narrative form of *Frankenstein* stresses the community of the teller and his audience rather than the individual isolation that the narrator may come to have in common with the outcast figure, stressed in *Melmoth*. In Melville's Ishmael, and in the other narrators of the meditation on the hero, one can see both these attractions at work.

It should be stressed here that the Gothic villains and heroes are ultimately different types of character from the Romantic hero, primarily in their not having gone beyond good and evil, in their characters continuing to be defined by moral categories, however melodramatically intensified these may be. The Romantic hero may be historically related to the Gothic villain—this is a question we shall take up with Heathcliff and *Wuthering Heights*—but it is the common narrative structure for presenting the different types of character that I wish to call attention to here.

It is a similar case with the works of what Charles Feidelson has called "American symbolism": the narrator or author meditates on a seminal mystery, but the mystery resides in a symbolic object rather than in a symbolic human figure.[44] The object or emblem occupies the same privileged space as the hero

43. *Melmoth the Wanderer: A Tale* (Edinburgh, 1820), 1 : 142.
44. *Symbolism and American Literature* (Chicago, 1953).

in the narrator's speculative and skeptical field. *Moby-Dick*
itself is as much concerned with the significance of natural objects—the white whale in particular, whales in general—as it
is with the significance of Ahab as hero. There are smaller
meditations on symbolic objects as well, as in the chapter on
the much-interpreted gold doubloon that Ahab nails to the
mast. It is interesting that the idea of Ahab as hero is the result of Melville's reading of Shakespeare. Broadly speaking,
Moby-Dick brings together the preoccupation with heroic character in Romantic readings of Shakespeare and the preoccupation with "Images, or Shadows of Divine Things" in the
Puritan tradition of Jonathan Edwards.

There is a similar tension between the human form of the
hero and the nonhuman form of the object in Carlyle's *Sartor
Resartus,* a book with which *Moby-Dick* has much in common
and which probably influenced Melville.[45] Carlyle's narrator,
the English editor, would prefer to deal directly with his
heroic subject, Diogenes Teufelsdröckh, but he is forced to approach him through the obscuring medium of Teufelsdröckh's
"Clothes Philosophy," a material mass of documentation. It is
only when the editor can accept the possibility of an object's
revealing a personality, of the "Not-Me" being able to express
the "Me," that he can deal with his heroic subject successfully.
A writer in the symbolistic mode who attaches more importance to the object than to the human form is Hawthorne. In
the fictionalized introduction to *The Scarlet Letter* Hawthorne
writes of the importance of the object or emblem in a way that
is paradigmatic for his narrative art:

> But the object that most drew my attention, in the mys-
> terious package, was a certain affair of fine red cloth,
> much worn and faded. There were traces about it of gold
> embroidery, which, however, was greatly frayed and de-

45. See Leon Howard, *Herman Melville: A Biography* (Berkeley, 1951),
p. 171 and Julie A. Braun, "Melville's Use of Carlyle's *Sartor Resartus*"
(Ph.D. diss., University of California at Los Angeles, 1968). For a more
detailed discussion of the narrative form of *Sartor,* see my article "The
Pattern of Conversion in *Sartor Resartus,*" *ELH* 38 (1971) : 411–31.

faced; so that none, or very little, of the glitter was left.
. . . This rag of scarlet cloth,—for time and wear and a
sacriligious moth had reduced it to little other than a rag,
—on careful examination, assumed the shape of a letter.
It was the capital letter A. . . . My eyes fastened themselves upon the old scarlet letter, and would not be turned
aside. Certainly, there was some deep meaning in it, most
worthy of interpretation, and which, as it were, streamed
forth from the mystic symbol, subtly communicating itself to my sensibilities, but evading the analysis of my
mind.[46]

The piece of cloth arouses Hawthorne's curiosity in a way that
the character of Hester Prynne does not. The scarlet A may
reveal something about her ultimately, as she wears the letter
and makes it express much more than the simple meaning assigned to it by the Puritan moral code, but the locus of the
mystery is more in the letter than in her character. The letter
means something to Dimmesdale as well, and to virtually every
other character in the book.

The relevant aspect of Hawthorne's narrative is not its object but its approach to the object. The mind locates its object
but circles around it instead of trying to seize it directly,
hypothesizing and questioning rather than assenting. This approach is quite similar to the way the narrator approaches the
hero in the works that concern us here. The closest Hawthorne
comes to a meditation on the hero is "Ethan Brand," his
"chapter of an Abortive Romance," as he calls it, which I discuss more fully in the chapter on Melville. At this point I will
merely compare the author's abortive attempt to penetrate the
human mystery directly with the hero's own destructive introspection; both of these end in the reified heart of Ethan Brand,
turned to marble in the lime kiln. The imaginative moral of
the story is that the mind needs to keep a wary distance from
the subject of its scrutiny, or to approach it with a cautious in-

---

46. *The Complete Novels and Selected Tales of Nathaniel Hawthorne,*
ed. Norman Holmes Pearson (New York, 1937), p. 102.

direction. A distinctly unheroic story such as "The Minister's Black Veil," where the author allows the symbolic barrier to remain between his view and the inner recesses of his character, is a more typical and more successful example of Hawthorne's symbolistic mode.

The Romantic hero is thus involved in two external relationships, a relationship to a ground, natural or historical, and a relationship to an audience, personified in the narrative consciousness that meditates upon him. The third relationship, the relation of self to role, is an internal one. There is potentially a paradox here, in that the idea of a hero traditionally presupposes a unified and integral being. Of all the literary designations of selfhood—character, type, role, archetype—the term "hero" is the most substantial. A hero is unique, he has a proper name that he establishes and defends, his identity is fixed by his actions. His fate is personal; it is a *daimon*. "Such men aim at altering the course of things," Ortega y Gasset writes. "They refuse to repeat the gestures that custom, tradition, or biological instincts force them to make. These men we call heroes, because to be a hero means to be one out of many, to be oneself. . . . This will to be oneself is heroism." [47]

Like so many nineteenth-century selves, however, the Romantic hero is at least potentially divided. Identity entails the merging of a self and a role, a uniting of the subjective and objective dimensions of selfhood. This identity is by no means a given for the Romantic hero but is something achieved only with difficulty; his existential substance is by no means secure. There is first the danger of the kind of severance of identity represented in the figure of the double, or doppelgänger, familiar in the Romantic fiction of E. T. A. Hoffmann, Poe, Dostoevsky, and others. [48] There is sometimes the suggestion in

47. *Meditations on Quixote,* trans. Evelyn Rugg and Diego Marin (New York, 1961), p. 149.

48. See Masao Miyoshi, *The Divided Self* (New York, 1969) and Dmitri Chizevsky, "The Theme of the Double in Dostoevsky," *Dostoevsky: A*

the meditation on the hero that the hero may have a double in the narrator—a possibility most fully explored in Kierkegaard's *Repetition*—but the hero, to remain heroic, must generally avoid such an explicit and schematic separation of self. The separation into two may even become a fragmentation into many. This danger is expressed most eloquently by Kierkegaard in *Either / Or:*"Can you think of anything more frightful than that it might end with your nature being resolved into a multiplicity, that you really might become many, become, like those unhappy demoniacs, a legion, and you thus would have lost the inmost and holiest thing of all in a man, the unifying power of personality?" [49]

There are examples in this period of heroes who do dissolve into a multiplicity of roles with no coherent center. The composite figure of Teufelsdröckh in Carlyle's *Sartor Resartus* tends in this direction; he is a patchwork quilt of heroic images. Melville's Confidence-Man is a more extreme case, where the reader has no assurance that the different manifestations of "the Confidence-Man" belong to one character at all. It is even tempting to think of the novels of Dickens from this point of view, with their proliferation of "alternate selves" [50] and the lack of a unifying power in any of the multiple personalities presented. Of course, it would be more accurate to say that panoramic novelists such as Dickens, Balzac, and to some extent Dostoevsky subject the single, extrasocial personality of the Romantic hero to a pluralistic, socializing vision. The extreme of such a fragmentation can be seen in the mock-heroic myth-making of Joyce's *Ulysses* and *Finnegans Wake*. Here we are back to Joseph Campbell's "Hero with A Thousand Faces."

Such fragmentation is avoided, however, in the heroes cov-

Collection of Critical Essays, ed. René Wellek (Englewood Cliffs, N.J., 1962), pp. 112–29.

49. *Either / Or*, Vol. 2, trans. Walter Lowrie, rev. Howard A. Johnson, p. 164.

50. I am indebted to my friend George Fayen of Smith College for this term.

ered in this study. What we find is an inner tension between the uniqueness of the actual self and the typicality of the heroic role. This tension, as I have suggested earlier, is organized along temporal or historical lines. The Romantic hero is *within himself* historical, either aspiring or declining, either in the process of becoming a hero or in the process of outliving a heroic role that is increasingly difficult to maintain. We discussed earlier the hero's special relation to history as a ground outside himself. Here we see that a sense of history is involved in the very concept of the hero. Earlier heroes are relatively fixed in their heroic identity; the Romantic hero usually experiences the evolution of his heroic substance or else its erosion. Either he grows, like Werther, from the common level of humanity to something like heroic stature, or he comes to realize that this heroic stature is somehow archaic, as it seems to me Faust does in Goethe's drama.[51]

In creating the genre of the Bildungsroman in *Wilhelm Meister's Apprenticeship,* Goethe effectively combines both types of Romantic heroism. There is on the one hand the evolving selfhood of Wilhelm, which is tenuous in its heroism but clearly moves toward a heroic ideal. On the other hand is the inherited example of Hamlet, whose play occupies such a central position in the novel. Wilhelm feels that the play, if not the character of its hero, is somewhat dated and needs some revision before it can be staged in the present age. Wil-

---

51. The argument could be made, and perhaps should be, that no hero in literature is entirely free of this conflict. It is certainly evident in Hamlet, who must select the appropriate role from among all those offered him in the play, from the Ghost onward, and fulfill it. It is also true of Don Quixote, who embraces an archaic role only to find it in conflict with contemporary experience (the incongruence is of course stressed here). For a discussion of an inner tension in Achilles, see Adam Parry's "The Language of Achilles," *The Language and Background of Homer,* ed. G. S. Kirk (London, 1964), pp. 48–54; for role conflict in the characters of Shakespeare, see Matthew N. Proser, *The Heroic Image in Five Shakespearean Tragedies* (Princeton, 1965). The Romantic hero is distinguished, however, by the degree to which the conflict is expressed in the medium of temporality.

helm is not Hamlet, any more than Hamlet is Wilhelm. But the ironic view of the one and the mythical view of the other create the profound sense of likeness-in-difference that only Goethe's profoundly organic sense of form can encompass. "For the whole complexity of existence of an actual being, German has the word *Gestalt*," Goethe wrote. "Alive to the static quality of this word of past-participle origin," as Elizabeth Wilkinson comments, Goethe went on to say:

> In using this expression, however, we abstract from what is in constant flux and assume that the collection of parts we call an identity is finished and fixed in its character. But if we consider natural forms, we find that nowhere does anything stable or completed occur. Rather is everything suspended in precarious balance. Wherefore the German language is wont to use, appropriately enough, the word *Bildung* both of the form produced and the process of formation.[52]

Hamlet's identity in the novel is a *Gestalt*, Wilhelm's is a *Bildung*. Although Goethe's emphasis is definitely on the latter, the former is an important foil. The whole genre of the Bildungsroman, in fact, can be seen as an outgrowth of the Romantic meditation on the hero, a genre that emphasizes the emerging substance more than the traditional form but that preserves the old heroic gestalt in the imaginative background.

Both types of hero-in-process are described by Hegel as well as by Goethe. Hegel uses the term "hero," in fact, in two different ways. There is first the hero as "world-historical individual," discussed earlier, who evolves out of the spirit of the age, who looks toward the future and whose futurity is the measure of his greatness. But there is also the hero discussed in *The Philsophy of Fine Art*, a figure whom Hegel sees as antecedent to the social order, upon whom the more modern age looks back with nostalgia:

52. "Goethe's Conception of Form," in E. M. Wilkinson and L. A. Willoughby, *Goethe: Poet and Thinker* (London, 1962), p. 176.

We conclude that the ideal figures of art must be sought in the age of mythos, that is to say, speaking generally, in past times, where we shall find the soil most congenial to their growth. If such material is taken from the age we live in, whose most native form, as we actually find it, is tightly shut off from the imagination . . . then the modifications which the poet can hardly avoid making in it will not readily escape the appearance of a purely artificial and intentional composition.[53]

The present age, according to Hegel's analysis, cannot be made to produce a valid hero for art. The artist must turn to the past, to an earlier heroic age that "has the advantage over later and more civilized times in that the isolated character and personality generally in such an age does not yet find what is substantive either in the sphere of ethical custom, or moral obligation opposed to itself in the necessary embodiment of legal institution, and thereby presents immediately to the poet all that the form of the Ideal requires." [54] When Hegel speaks of the "world-historical individual," he is speaking of the hero in political history, not in the history of art. The modern age may produce its own heroes in this sense, but the hero of political becoming cannot be combined with the hero of artistic retrospection.

These two ways of meditating on a hero recall the two types of poetry that Wordsworth and Coleridge were to produce in *The Lyrical Ballads,* the plan for which Coleridge describes as follows:

It was agreed, that my endeavors should be directed to persons and characters supernatural, or at least romantic; yet so far as to transfer from our inward nature a human interest and a semblance of truth sufficient to procure for these shadows of imagination that willing suspension of disbelief for the moment, which constitutes poetic faith.

53. *The Philosophy of Fine Art,* trans. F. P. B. Osmaston (London, 1920), 1 : 254.
54. Ibid., p. 255.

Mr. Wordsworth, on the other hand, was to propose to himself as his object, to give the charm of novelty to things of every day, and to excite a feeling analogous to the supernatural, by awakening the mind's attention from the lethargy of custom, and directing it to the loveliness and wonders of the world before us. . . .[55]

This passage is important for understanding the mingling of romance and realism in the nineteenth-century novel, where in all but the most militant realists and romancers a mutuality of purpose persists. Everyday life is either elevated into something "analogous" to the supernatural, or the supernatural is translated downward, thus "interesting . . . the affections by the dramatic truth of such emotions," Coleridge says, "as would naturally accompany such situations, supposing them real." [56]

"It is the nature of an hypothesis, when once a man has conceived it, that it assimilates everything to itself as proper nourishment," Tristram Shandy wrote. In trying to define and locate the Romantic hero and the Romantic meditation on the hero in prose, I may so far have seemed to argue the *lucus a non lucendo* or the forest from the absence of the trees. The meditation on the hero is envisioned through most of this study as an ideal structure of the Romantic imagination as well as a concrete fictional form, and its presence is often most interesting where least explicit. In the following chapters I will counterbalance this abstraction in my thesis by focusing more concretely on a few specific texts, leaving aside the question of the centrality or eccentricity of this particular imaginative mode. In a concluding chapter, however, I shall return to some of these larger issues as I describe the survival of the form in more modern works of fiction. The house of fiction has many windows, James said. I am attempting to illuminate a particular darkened wing, a larger part of the architecture than previous ciceroni have recognized.

55. *Biographia Literaria,* ed. J. Shawcross (Oxford, 1907), 2 : 6.
56. Ibid., p. 5

2

Kierkegaard: The Hero and the Poet

There is an increasing recognition that as a philosopher and theologian Kierkegaard is a master of irony and indirection, that there is an aesthetic dimension of his writing that subverts, or at least renders problematical, its apparent claims to truth and faith.[1] It is less recognized that Kierkegaard's subject matter as well as his method of communication were often of a specifically literary nature; in fact, his writings before 1846 show that he was almost as deeply concerned with the literature of Romanticism as he was with Hegelian philosophy and contemporary theology.[2] He was part of a literary

1. The best analysis of the aesthetic dimension from a theological point of view is provided by T. H. Croxall in his *Kierkegaard Studies* (London, 1948) and *Kierkegaard Commentary* (London, 1956). More philosophical interpretations are offered in Josiah Thompson, *The Lonely Labyrinth: Kierkegaard's Pseudonymous Works* (Carbondale, Ill., 1967) and Louis Mackey, *Kierkegaard: A Kind of Poet* (Philadelphia, 1971), the fullest and best study of Kierkegaard's aesthetic imagination to date in English. Thompson's *Kierkegaard: A Collection of Critical Essays* (Garden City, N.Y., 1972) contains valuable essays by Thompson, Mackey, and Stephen Crites; Mackey's essay on *Fear and Trembling* anticipates some of my own insights. The collection unfortunately appeared after my manuscript was essentially complete.

2. The most substantial treatments of Kierkegaard's literary concerns are in Danish but may be glimpsed by the English reader in the following sources: F. J. Billeskov Jansen, "The Literary Art of Kierkegaard," trans. Margaret Grieve in *A Kierkegaard Critique*, ed. Johnson and Thulstrup (New York, 1962), which is a summary of his book; the English summary in Lars Bejerholm's *Meddelelesens Dialektik: Studier i Søren Kierkegaards teorier om sprak, kommunikation, och pseudonymitet*, Publications of the Kierkegaard Society, vol. 2 (Copenhagen, 1962); Aage Henriksen, "Kierkegaard's Reviews of Literature," *Orbis Litterarum* 10

milieu in Copenhagen, a milieu that included Hans Christian Andersen and that was closely attuned to French as well as to German Romantic literature. The three main influences on Kierkegaard's style, according to A. J. Raymond Cook, were the Bible, Hegelian philosophy, and the *Eventyr,* or folktale. Of the latter Kierkegaard had over one hundred volumes in his library.[3]

Kierkegaard's writing is the product of a deeply polemical mind, and he was an outspoken critic of Goethe and other Romantic writers, but in much the same way that he was a critic of Hegel and systematic philosophy. He criticized the opposing views sharply and continually but was also shaped and influenced by them. The relationship is complicated by the fact that some of Kierkegaard's antagonism to both Hegel and Goethe came from his more immediate reaction to J. L. Heiberg, who was the leading exponent of Goethe and Hegel in Copenhagen during the 1830s and 1840s. Henning Fenger speaks of a "Heiberg complex" in Kierkegaard that "undoubtedly drove Kierkegaard further out in his reaction against the idols of his former master." [4]

(1955) : 75–83 (gives a brief summary of his *Kierkegaards Romaner* [Copenhagen, 1954]); and Lee M. Capel's Historical Introduction to his translation of Kierkegaard's *The Concept of Irony* (Bloomington, 1965), which recapitulates parts of Karl Roos's *Kierkegaard og Goethe* (Copenhagen, 1955). Ronald Grimsley's *Sören Kierkegaard and French Literature* (Cardiff, 1966), offers a number of useful comparative essays; also in English is A. J. Raymond Cook's brief but useful notice, "Kierkegaard's Literary Art," *The Listener* 72 (1964) : 713–14 and Henning Fenger's "Kierkegaard—A Literary Approach," *Scandinavica* 3 (1964) : 1–16. Finally, mention should be made of Edith Kern's *Existential Thought and Fictional Technique: Kierkegaard, Sartre, Beckett* (New Haven, 1970), which analyzes in detail the first volume of *Either/Or.* In German there is Martin Thust's older *Sören Kierkegaard Der Dichter des Religiosen* (Munich, 1931); in French, Pierre Mesnard, *Le vrai visage de Kierkegaard* (Paris, 1948) and Jean Starobinski's excellent phenomenological analysis, "Kierkegaard et les masques," *Nouvelle Revue Française* 25 (1965) : 607–22, 809–25.

3. Cook, "Kierkegaard's Literary Art," p. 713.
4. "Kierkegaard—A Literary Approach," p. 10.

This is not to suggest that Kierkegaard's critique of Hegelian philosophy and Romantic art was not profound and
searching, but it is to suggest that he was more involved, more
implicated, in the modes of thought and forms of imagination
that he was attacking than is commonly granted. Kierkegaard's popularity in the twentieth century is in some measure
due to a reaction against the modern evils supposedly bred of
the Romantic movement,[5] and Kierkegaard's independence of
his intellectual environment has been overemphasized. It is
true that he was remarkably clear-sighted in exposing the existential emptiness of the Hegelian "System." But it is also true
that he was still a Hegelian in many of his assumptions—for
instance, in his assumption that the self is to be identified
with an emerging self-consciousness,[6] or in his assumption derived from Hegel's follower Trendelenburg that there were
certain philosophical categories that were not merely forms of
thought but forms of reality. "In his own opinion Kierkegaard
had an infallible knowledge of the categories of 'being,' especially such categories as pertain to spiritual life. No further
argument, however, is given for this professed knowledge of
the categories."[7] Similarly, though Kierkegaard attacked
many of the tenets of Romanticism and many of its major
figures (he called Goethe "the representative of modern char-
acterlessness"[8]), he was inextricably involved in many Romantic assumptions. He criticizes the "aesthetic" life in terms

5. Franklin Roosevelt was introduced to Kierkegaard's writings and
remarked to Francis Perkins, "Kierkegaard explains the Nazis to me as
nothing else ever has" (cited by Lewis A. Lawson in the introduction
to his anthology *Kierkegaard's Presence in Contemporary American Life*
[Metuchen, N.Y., 1970], p. xiv).

6. See James Bogen, "Remarks on the Kierkegaard–Hegel Controversy,"
Synthèse 13 (1961) : 372–89, for some much needed discussion of the points
in common. Lee Capel, Introduction to *Concept of Irony*, p. 37, suggests
that Kierkegaard distinguished between Hegel and the more superficial
Danish Hegelians.

7. Bejerholm, Summary in *Meddelelesens Dialektik*, p. 307.

8. *The Journals of Sören Kierkegaard*, ed. and trans. Alexander Dru
(London, 1938), p. 446 (#1257).

that are easily translatable into other Romantic critiques of a life of simple sensuality and naïveté. "He himself was so full of *Sturm und Drang,* so romantically absorbed in his own genius and the sufferings of his genius, that he never gave up Isaac," Louis Mackey writes of the author of *Fear and Trembling.*

> *Pace* his uncritical biographers, he never really relinquished Regina. He tricked himself out of her by trying to give her freedom, and by presuming to give her her freedom he played God with her. If I had had faith I would have married Regina, he declares in a moment of complete consistency. But he did not have faith and he did not marry her. Because he had to be a genius (aesthetic), he never became a man of faith or a husband.[9]

Such a remark should not be taken as a disparagement of Kierkegaard's genuine achievements in art and philosophy— or religion. But it does provide a necessary corrective to exaggerated claims (his own included) of imaginative autonomy.

A major difficulty in assessing Kierkegaard's relationship to people such as Goethe and Hegel comes from the fact that he is a brilliant parodist: he echoes the terms and methods of his adversaries even as he criticizes their assumptions. There is some disagreement about the nature of *The Concept of Irony,* Kierkegaard's master's thesis: does it represent an early Hegelian phase, or is it a subtle parody of Hegelian views and procedures? *The Sickness unto Death,* Billeskov Jansen observes, is written in a deliberately Hegelian manner.[10] On the Romantic front, Kierkegaard had long planned a major cri-

9. "Kierkegaard's Lyric of Faith: A Look at *Fear and Trembling,*" *Rice Institute Pamphlet* 47 (1960) : 45. Cf. Kiekegaard's own statement: "I am not at all a religious individual, I am a capitally constructed possibility of that; I discover primitively the whole religious catastrophe, but when I would apprehend the religious patterns my philosophic doubt comes in" (quoted by Walter Lowrie in a footnote to his translation of *Stages on Life's Way* [Princeton, 1940], p. 346).

10. See Capel, Introduction to *Concept of Irony,* pp. 7–38; and Jansen, "The Literary Art of Kierkegaard," p. 17.

tique and revision of Goethe's *Faust,* although the project
ended somewhat abortively in a minor Faust parody, "The
Conversation Between the Old and the New Soap Cellar." [11]
The eclectic form of *Either / Or* comes, in Billeskov Jansen's
view, from *Wilhelm Meister's Wanderjahre.* [12] Thus any study
of Kierkegaard, literary or philosophical, must be wary in
dealing with his themes and forms. His writing is the product
of what he himself called "negative thinking," an awareness
of the deceptiveness of all thought and expression. "Negative
thinkers always . . . have one advantage, in that they have
something positive, being aware of the negative element in
existence; the positive have nothing at all, since they are deceived. Precisely because the negative is present in existence,
and present everywhere (for existence is a constant process of
becoming), it is necessary to become aware of its presence
continuously, as the only safeguard against it." [13]

One of the main literary forms that occupied Kierkegaard,
and one in which his predilection for negative thinking found
a particularly apt expression, is the meditation on the hero.
A number of Kierkegaard's aesthetic and philosophical views
are reflected in the way he uses this form. He gives the meditation on the hero a classic definition in *Fear and Trembling:*

> If there were no eternal consciousness in a man, if at the
> foundation of all there lay only a wildly seething power
> which writhing with obscure passions produced every-
> thing that is great and everything that is insignificant, if a
> bottomless void never satiated lay hidden beneath all—

11. See Capel, Introduction to *Concept of Irony,* pp. 20–27. Capel is
drawing on Karl Roos's study in Danish, *Kierkegaard og Goethe* (Copenhagen, 1955).

12. "The Literary Art of Kierkegaard," p. 13. For a more extended
discussion of *Either / Or* as a parody of *Wilhelm Meister,* see Mackey, *A
Kind of Poet,* pp. 273–75.

13. *Concluding Unscientific Postscript,* trans. David Swenson and
Walter Lowrie (Princeton, 1941), p. 75. See Jean Wahl, *Études Kierke-
gaardiennes* (Paris, 1949), wherein the thesis is offered that Kierkegaard
played Hegelian philosophy and Romantic poetry off against one another.

what then would life be but despair? If such were the case, if there were no sacred bond which united mankind, if one generation arose after another like the leafage in the forest, if the one generation replaced the other like the song of birds in the forest, if the human race passed through the world as the ship goes through the sea, like the wind through the desert, a thoughtless and fruitless activity, if an eternal oblivion were always lurking hungrily for its prey and there was no power strong enough to wrest it from its maw—how empty then and comfortless life would be! But therefore it is not thus, but as God created man and woman, so too He fashioned the hero and the poet or orator. The poet cannot do what that other does, he can only admire, love and rejoice in the hero. Yet he too is happy, and not less so, for the hero is as it were his better nature, with which he is in love, rejoicing in the fact that this after all is not himself, that his love can be admiration. He is the genius of recollection, can do nothing except call to mind what has been done, do nothing but admire what has been done; he contributes nothing of his own, but is jealous of the intrusted treasure. . . .[14]

The poet and the hero are clearly differentiated, even though the hero is "as it were" the poet's better nature. They belong together—they have been created by divine fiat, as a

14. *Fear and Trembling and The Sickness unto Death,* trans. Walter Lowrie, rev. Howard A. Johnson (Garden City, N.Y., 1954), pp. 30–31. In all further references to *Fear and Trembling* the page numbers cited parenthetically in the text are from this edition, which is identical to the Princeton Paperback Edition (1968) in text and pagination. Unless otherwise noted, all emphasis is Kierkegaard's. Cf. a late journal entry concerning *Fear and Trembling:* "But one true word was already uttered in it, when attention was directed to the difference between the poet and the hero" (quoted in Lowrie's Introduction, p. 19). Henriksen's *Kierkegaards Romaner* apparently deals with the interaction between hero and narrator in "The Diary of the Seducer," "Guilty / Not Guilty," and *Repetition,* though not in *Fear and Trembling.* See "Kierkegaard's Reviews of Literature," pp. 82–83.

light against the darkness—but they must not be confused with each other. "The poet cannot do what that other does, he can only admire, love and rejoice in the hero." These two imaginative figures, the poet and the hero, were a major concern of Kierkegaard's in his early "aesthetic" writings, either as separate figures or in conjunction with each other.

By himself Kierkegaard's poet is a weak figure, potentially in despair. "Vainly I strive against it," the aesthete A of *Either / Or* writes. "My foot slips. My life is still a poet's existence. What could be more unhappy?" The poet imagines human existence, thinks about it as a possibility, but never is able to appropriate it for himself. In *Concluding Unscientific Postscript* Kierkegaard explains that "the poet can explain (transfigure) the whole of existence, but he cannot explain himself, because he will not become religious and so understand the secret of suffering as the form of the highest life." [15] There is a close parallel between Kierkegaard's idea of the poet and the idea held by Keats: "A Poet is the most unpoetical of any thing in existence; because he has no Identity—he is continually in for—and filling some other body." [16] Kierkegaard's poet (who writes prose rather than verse) is possessed of what Keats calls "negative capability" but is considerably less happy about this condition than Keats was. The negative capability is a liability in Kierkegaard's existential world. This sense of the insubstantiality of the poet leads Kierkegaard to his theory of "indirect communication": through the use of pseudonyms, irony, and humor, the reader is to be directed away from the identity and position of Kierkegaard as author to his, the reader's, own existential condition, where he must appropriate any possible objective truth into his own subjective existence.[17]

15. *Either / Or*, 1 : 35; *Concluding Unscientific Postscript*, pp. 397–98.

16. *The Letters of John Keats, 1814–1821*, ed. Hyder Edward Rollins (Cambridge, Mass., 1958), 1 : 387.

17. For the best account of indirect communication, see Louis Mackey, "Soren Kierkegaard: The Poetry of Inwardness," in *Existential Philosophers: Kierkegaard to Merleau-Ponty*, ed. George Schrader (New York,

Because of his negativity, the poet turns naturally to the hero. "This is the reason my soul always turns back to the Old Testament and to Shakespeare," A writes. "I feel that those who speak there are at least human beings: they hate, they love, they murder their enemies. . . ." [18] The first volume of *Either / Or* is a fragmentary and desultory search for such a positive heroic presence; Don Juan, Antigone (a heroine), Johannes the Seducer, and others are entertained as candidates. Kierkegaard himself was frequently occupied with different heroic figures in his papers and journals. In 1834 he was studying the "Master Thief," an arch-Romantic figure in the tradition of Schiller's Karl Moor. He researched this heroic type in some of its previous literary forms and wrote his own sketches of the character. From 1835 on he was concerned with three different heroes, Don Juan, Faust, and Ahasuerus, the Wandering Jew. He saw them as driven by the daemons of sensuality, doubt, and despair, and he tried to arrange them in some kind of evolutionary triad. He then conceived of a Faust who would embody all three daemons, though the project ended abortively when Kierkegaard found himself anticipated by Martensen's essay and lecture on Faust. [19]

The meditation on the hero was thus a form that Kierkegaard arrived at by considerable study of Romantic heroes and by considerable experimentation of his own. It is a form central to his imagination, at least up through the publication of *Fear and Trembling* and *Repetition* in October 1843. In fact, the literary form can be translated into, though not simply reduced to, the terms of some of his main philosophical concepts. The distinction between the poet and the hero corresponds roughly to the distinction between thought and

1967), pp. 102–04. A more skeptical view of the efficacy of this technique is expressed by Josiah Thompson in "The Master of Irony," *Kierkegaard: A Collection of Critical Essays,* pp. 159–63.

18. *Either / Or,* 1 : 27; also quoted in chapter 1.

19. As noted earlier, I am indebted to Lee Capel's summary of Karl Roos for the information on Kierkegaard's Faust project.

existence, which is such a central opposition in Kierkegaard's philosophical writing. "Existence is cunning," he writes, "and possesses many means of enchantment to catch rash adventurers, and he who is caught, yea he who is caught, out of him is not made exactly what could be called a higher being." [20] One is constantly tempted and deceived into thinking about one's existence instead of living it at is deepest level. There are categories of thought and categories of existence, and Kierkegaard continually insists on the difference between them. The main categories of existence are the aesthetic, the ethical, and the religious; this is a terminology for which he is well known. The differences between these categories are quantitative, but together they represent three "stages on life's way," three phases of an increasing inwardness, an increasing intensity with which the self apprehends its own existence. There are heroes in each of these existential spheres, as we shall see, but the highest form of heroism for Kierkegaard is the religious.[21]

The categories of thought, the province of the poet, are, properly speaking, "immediacy" and "reflection". In fact, "immediacy" for Kierkegaard is a state that can never be attained by thought or consciousness alone; this is one of his major quarrels with Hegel. All thought is *re-flective,* alienated from its object, like the poet in Kierkegaard's description. For Hegel consciousness can be immediate or reflective, but for Kierkegaard "consciousness . . . presupposes reflexion." [22] To oversimplify somewhat, one might say that "immediacy" is a

20. *Stages on Life's Way*, p. 402.
21. Henning Fenger suggests that the idea of the three stages of existence may have emerged from Kierkegaard's earlier studies of the triad of heroes, Don Juan, Faust, and Ahasuerus ("Kierkegaard—A Literary Approach," p. 12).
22. *Johannes Climacus, or, De Omnibus Dubitandum Est,* trans. T. H. Croxall (Stanford, 1958), p. 151. Kierkegaard also held the view that "Language is a function of the 'Reflexion' and thus cannot describe the 'Immediate' as it is" (Bejerholm, Summary in *Meddelelesens Dialektik,* p. 308). Thus all communication is essentially indirect.

category that thought applies to existence, while the category of the "aesthetic" describes a mode of existence that is perilously close to the realm of pure thought. To the poet, the hero seems in a state of prereflective (or postreflective) immediacy. From the point of view of the hero, the poet is an aesthetic self, only marginally existent.[23] Kierkegaard is a complex and by no means systematic philosopher, and such a formulation belies the subtlety, flexibility, and variety of his profoundly dialectical thought. But the central conflict in all his writings, a conflict in which the philosophical categories themselves take part, is the struggle of the self to transcend reflective thought and enter into a newfound immediacy of existence.

Kierkegaard's concern with the poet and the hero came to a head in 1843, his *annus mirabilis* of literary production. Under the pressure of his flight from the engagement with Regina Olsen he published *Either / Or* in February and *Fear and Trembling* and *Repetition* on the same day in October. In *Either/Or* the meditation on the hero is still fragmentary, but in *Fear and Trembling* and *Repetition* it crystallizes into unitary form. In *Fear and Trembling,* Johannes de Silentio meditates on the heroic figure of Abraham, called upon by God to sacrifice Isaac. It is a meditation on an archaic gestalt of the hero, the historically retrospective type of meditation discussed in the previous chapter. In *Repetition* Constantine Constantius plays the narrator to the emerging heroism of an anonymous "young man" who is compelled to sacrifice a girl he loves for religious reasons. *Repetition* is a meditation on the hero in *Bildung*, the temporally prospective mode. The two works thus complement each other dialectically, and it was not accidental that they were published simultaneously. Together they form not an either / or, requiring a choice be-

23. On the relation between the aesthetic and immediacy in Kierkegaard, see Stephen Crites's Introduction to *Crisis in the Life of an Actress and Other Essays on Drama* (New York, 1967), pp. 34–35, and Mackey, *A Kind of Poet,* pp. 3–4.

tween two of the stages on life's way, but an attempt to approach the ultimate stage, the religious, from two different imaginative perspectives.

The young man's heroism in *Repetition* is highly problematical, it is true. The question is complicated by the fact that between the initial writing and the publication events played Kierkegaard false. Regina, whom he had apparently been hoping to regain by a "repetition" of his broken engagement, had in the meantime married Fritz Schlegel. Kierkegaard changed the ending of the book when he learned of this defection. But the problematical nature of the hero in the process of becoming was simply intensified by these events; it is a characteristic of the Bildungsroman that can be seen in both *Werther* and *Wilhelm Meister*. The "hero of our time," to use Lermontov's phrase, is in some sense doomed to heroic incompletion. To what degree of heroism the young man in *Repetition* ultimately rises is a question we will discuss later.

The chronology of composition is unclear. Both books were written mainly in May of 1843 in Berlin. It seems as though a first version of *Repetition* was written before *Fear and Trembling*, but substantial revisions were made in its ending in Copenhagen in July, whereas *Fear and Trembling* was essentially left alone. Thus *Repetition* is the later work of the two if one finds, as I do, the revised ending by and large a philosophical and aesthetic success. For this reason, and because the heroic pattern is somewhat clearer in it, I shall treat *Fear and Trembling* first in my discussion. However, in spite of the exigencies of Kierkegaard's biography, I regard the two books as belonging to the same imaginative moment.

In what sense is Abraham a hero in *Fear and Trembling*? Certainly in the technical sense of being the book's center of attention, but also in the more thematic sense of one who performs actions beyond the ability of most men. In his sacrifice, or attempted sacrifice, of Isaac, Abraham shows an unusual capacity for faith in God, so much so that the Apostle Paul called him "the father of all them that believe" (Rom. 4 : 11).

As a specifically Romantic hero, however, Abraham has a number of unheroic characteristics—even in Kierkegaard's meditation upon him. His strength is purely of the spirit and is virtually unseen. He is an old man by the time Isaac is born; he goes out into the desert to perform the sacrifice, avoiding the eyes of others. Kierkegaard's narrator tries to picture him in modern dress, but finds him virtually indistinguishable from the common man. "As was said, I have not found any such person, but I can well think him. Here he is. Acquaintance made, I am introduced to him. The moment I set eyes on him I instantly push him from me, I myself leap backwards, I clasp my hands and say half aloud, 'Good Lord, is this the man? Is it really he? Why he looks like a tax-collector!' " (49).

In a certain sense, the idea of a hero is foreign to the Old Testament. The idea flourished in Greece and Rome and other cultures with an heroic age and/or epic poetry. Moses Hadas writes, "It is quite probable that the great personages of early Israelite history also once enjoyed something like the status of Greek heroes, but as monotheism with its corollaries of a single authority and a central sanctuary asserted itself, the independent stature of the early heroes would inevitably be diminished." [24] Abraham's relationship to Jehovah is certainly not the relationship of "brilliant Achilles" to brilliant Zeus, where the god responds to the hero's personal request. Nor is it the relationship of the Jungian hero to the "deep wells of being," whether these wells are located in nature, history, or the unconscious.

Indeed, *Fear and Trembling* is a polemic against Hegel and his notion of the hero of political history, the world-historical individual. The initial celebration of the hero and his wor-

24. Moses Hadas and Morton Smith, *Heroes and Gods* (New York, 1965), p. 13. See also John Gunnell, *Political Philosophy and Time* (Middletown, Conn., 1968), pp. 54–71, on the tension between divine or heroic kingship and communal history in the Old Testament, a conflict in which kingship tended to lose out. Byron, of course, had made Cain into a Romantic hero and Vigny did the same for Moses (see p. 66).

shiper the poet was quoted above. Abraham is a hero in this
specific sense. But upon further reflection the poet / narrator
feels the need to distinguish Abraham's example from certain
notions of heroism in political or social spheres. "I *think* myself *into* the hero," Johannes de Silentio now says, "but into
Abraham I cannot think myself; when I reach the height I fall
down, for what I encounter there is the paradox" (44).[25] Johannes continually attacks the Hegelian system of history and
its "Danish shareholders" (25); he is ironical about those
modern thinkers who consider that simply by virtue of their
historical vantage point they have "gone further" than Abraham.

Nevertheless, Abraham is a hero for Kierkegaard, and a
hero in much the same sense that Hegel used the term in *The
Philosophy of Fine Art:* "The ideal figures of art must be
sought for in the age of mythos, that is to say, speaking
generally, in past times, where we shall find the soil most
congenial to their growth." Johannes' panegyric on the relationship of the hero and the poet is apposite to this Hegelian
definition. The religious hero is not to be found in the present
age, but in an earlier age of faith. Also relevant are Hegel's
remarks on the relation of this archaic hero to the sphere of
ethical custom: "The isolated character and personality generally in such an [heroic] age does not as yet find what is substantive either in the sphere of ethical custom, or moral obligation." Although Kierkegaard's hero is *beyond* good and
evil where Hegel's stands *prior* to the emergence of these
moral categories, the formal characteristics of these two versions of the hero are surprisingly similar.[26]

A further indication of Abraham's status as hero, in a Romantic sense, in *Fear and Trembling* can be gained by com-

25. In *The Concept of Irony* Kierkegaard had spoken of Socrates as a
"hero" in the sense of a world-historical individual (p. 233).

26. *The Philosophy of Fine Art,* 1 : 254, 255. Lars Bejerholm observes
that a number of Kierkegaard's anti-Hegelian strictures can be found
in Hegel's own *Aesthetik,* a work which Kierkegaard either chose to ignore
or with which he was not as familiar as the rest of Hegel's writings.

paring Kierkegaard's version of the sacrifice of Isaac with other accounts. There is a considerable body of Jewish commentary on this passage in Genesis, called in Hebrew the *Akedah*. Kierkegaard was almost certainly unaware of this tradition, except for the way it was used in the Epistles of Paul. One of the elements that this tradition stressed and that Paul picked up and used for Christian purposes was the notion of a special merit, the *"Akedah* merit," in Isaac. Abraham was not a hero in isolation; his faith was equaled by the bravery of his son. Paul uses this notion of an *Akedah* merit when he compares Abraham's sacrifice of Isaac to God's sacrifice of Christ. Particularly in Paul's reinterpretation of the sacrifice of Isaac is there little sense in speaking of the merit of the father apart from the merit of the son.[27]

In *Fear and Trembling*, however, Kierkegaard has little use for Isaac. "Then Abraham lifted up the boy, he walked with him by his side, and his talk was full of comfort and exhortation. But Isaac could not understand him. He climbed Mount Moriah, but Isaac understood him not" (27). In another re-creation of the story, Kierkegaard goes as far as to make Isaac lose his faith. Thus in his own reworking of the sacrifice of Isaac, Kierkegaard departs from a tradition of Christian as well as Jewish commentary. He singles out the heroism of Abraham, giving him a status similar to that of a hero of Romantic literature, a status rather different from the one the patriarch enjoys in more orthodox commentary on the biblical passage.[28]

Abraham is thus put in the position of a Romantic hero, even as he is a critique of Romantic heroism in one of its major forms. There is no question of a heroic quest on Abra-

27. For the definitive account of the commentary on the *Akedah* and a discussion of Paul's place in it, see Shalom Spiegel, *The Last Trial,* trans. Judah Goldin (New York, 1967).

28. A journal entry indicates that Kierkegaard was thinking of his own relation to his religiously melancholy father in depicting Isaac's incomprehension, as well as Regina's relation to him. See Johannes Hohlenberg, *Sören Kierkegaard,* trans. T. H. Croxall (New York, 1954), p. 119.

ham's part to participate in the mysteries of the ground of all
being. God calls him and he answers simply, "Here I am." Yet
even in the biblical account there is a strong sense of Abraham
as a figure against a ground, as we defined the hero's relation
to reality in the first chapter. Erich Auerbach, in fact, speaks
of the biblical narrative here as "fraught with background." [29]
That the background is an orthodox God rather than the
heterodox ground of history or nature is a mark of Kierkegaard's quarrel with Hegelian philosophy and Romantic art.
As Kierkegaard puts it, Abraham is in an "absolute relation to
the absolute" (122); there is no mediation between the power
of God's command and the strength of his individual existence. But that the heroic form is itself Romantic and (in one
of two senses) Hegelian is a mark of Kierkegaard's participation in the modes of thought he was opposing. *Fear and
Trembling* is thus a meditation on the hero revised and redeemed.

Once the heroism of Abraham is established in *Fear and
Trembling*, a number of other heroic figures appear. Beginning with a brief allusion to Jeremiah in the "Panegyric
upon Abraham" and continuing through to the much longer
discussion of Faust in Problem III, the narrator of the book
offers a series of lesser heroes for meditation. Structurally it is
not unlike the situation in the *Iliad,* where a series of Greek
warriors attempts to fill Achilles' heroic role while Achilles
holds himself apart. The emphasis in *Fear and Trembling* is
on the radical difference between Abraham's act of faith and
the acts of these lesser figures. The alternate figures are stages
on the way to Abraham, as it were, and in fact they fall into
the two lower "stages on life's way," as Kierkegaard calls them,
the ethical stage and the aesthetic. Abraham, alone on the
heights, is located in the highest stage, the religious. The alternate heroes are invoked for purposes of contrast, but also
because they are more accessible to view. In many ways the
narrator, Johannes de Silentio, finds them more suitable for
meditation than Abraham himself. We come here to the ques-

29. *Mimesis*, trans. Willard Trask (Princeton, 1953), p. 12.

tion of the hero's relationship to his narrator and audience, a question which must be discussed at some length.

In the beginning, after an ironic preface that declares the independence of *Fear and Trembling* from the Hegelian system, Johannes de Silentio begins with a *Stemning,* or prelude.

> Once upon a time there was a man who as a child had heard the beautiful story about how God tempted Abraham, and how he endured temptation, kept the faith, and a second time received again a son contrary to expectation. When the child became older he read the same story with even greater admiration, for life had separated what was united in the pious simplicity of the child. The older he became, the more frequently his mind reverted to that story, his enthusiasm became greater and greater, and yet he was less and less able to understand the story. At last in his interest for that he forgot everything else; his soul had only one wish, to see Abraham, one longing, to have been witness to that event (26).

Two things are noticeable here. The first is the literary mode. The meditation begins as a fairy tale.[30] The relation between the narrator and his hero is one of childlike immediacy; Abraham has cast a kind of spell over Johannes, a spell which persists even as he grows older. The use of the third person is also significant. It is clearly Johannes de Silentio speaking of his own attraction to the biblical story, but as a narrator he seems to have no separate, personal identity of his own. At the end of the prelude Johannes concludes, "Thus and in many like ways that man of whom we are speaking thought concerning this event" (29).

In the middle of the first section the narrative mode changes from that of the fairy tale to that of the Old Testament. The narrator is still impersonal in his presence, but he deals more

30. Emmanuel Hirsch notes the *Märchen*-like quality here, in the notes to his translation, *Furcht und Zittern* (Düsseldorf / Köln, 1962), p. 144. As mentioned above, Kierkegaard was an avid collector of fairy tales.

directly with his subject. The narrative tries to enter into the
minds of the characters and visualizes their interaction: "Abraham prepared everything for the sacrifice, calmly and quietly;
but when he turned and drew the knife, Isaac saw that his left
hand was clenched in despair, that a tremor passed through
his body—but Abraham drew the knife" (29). The characters
are given more of an inner psychology than they have in the
biblical account, but Johannes' attempt is to re-create the
biblical mode. Four times he attempts this re-creation, each
time with a different emphasis. Four times he fails to arrive at
a satisfactory understanding of his hero. A further attempt to
bridge the gap between narrator and hero is made at the end
of each brief Old Testament reconstruction. Here Johannes
offers a parable, in a New Testament manner, about a mother
having to blacken her breasts to wean her child. The parable
attempts to explain the mysteries of faith in everyday terms
But the analogy only breaks down: who in the Old Testament
story is weaning whom? [31] The disproportion between God
trying to wean Abraham of his love for his son and a mother
weaning her child from the breast is simply too great for the
understanding. As Christ said harshly of parables in Matthew
13, those who have faith already can understand them but
those who don't cannot.

   In the beginning, then, the relation of the narrator to his
hero is one of immediacy. The Danish heading *Stemning* has
the connotations of "mood" and "atmosphere." In this "Dia
lectical Lyric," as Kierkegaard subtitles the book, lyricism
precedes the dialectics. And yet a dialectical sense begins to
emerge as the narrator reflects on his hero and gradually be
gins to realize the imaginative distance between his own con
sciousness and the existential act of his subject. The second
section of *Fear and Trembling* is entitled "A Panegyric upon
Abraham." The mode is that of the oration or sermon. Here

   31. There is, of course, the biographical answer that Kierkegaard was
trying to wean Regina from their engagement, but I am interested here
in the imaginative coherence of the text, which is more than a roman
à clef.

the speaker is less intimately bound up with his hero than in the prelude: his relation is public rather than private and his attitude is one of outspoken confidence rather than troubled yearning. Johannes defines the relationship of poet to hero in the passage quoted in the first section of this chapter: "The poet cannot do what that other does, he can only admire, love and rejoice in the hero" (30).

The description of the role of the poet or orator introduces a forceful, well-made oration. Johannes speaks to an imagined congregation: "Thou to whom my speech is addressed, was such the case with thee?" (35). Kierkegaard had given much thought to the sermon as a means of communication,[32] and this section of *Fear and Trembling* is a virtuoso performance in the mode. Even in translation one can observe a style different from the prelude. Sentences are shorter and more emphatic. The argument is arranged in parallel, tripartite form, as in the second paragraph: "But each was great in his own way, and each in proportion to the greatness of that which he *loved*. . . . Everyone shall be remembered, but each became great in proportion to his *expectation*. . . . Everyone shall be remembered, but each was great in proportion to the greatness of that with which he *strove*" (31). The device of repetition, which expressed such hesitation in the prelude, is used here as a tool of eloquence.

Nevertheless, the oration, with its reliance on the spoken word, implies a greater distance between the poet and the hero than the visual immediacy of the prelude, where the narrator longed to "accompany" Abraham and "be present" on Mount Moriah (26). The poet is more sure of himself here but is further removed from the subject of his meditations. This separation or divergence is continued in the section which follows the panegyric, a section with the curious title of 'Preliminary Expectoration." Johannes here treats the oratorical mode more tentatively, using it at one remove. *"If it should fall to my lot to talk of the subject . . . ,"* he begins

32. See Paul L. Holmer, "Kierkegaard and the Sermon," *Journal of Religion* 37 (1957): 1–9.

(42). The locution seems curious for one who has just finished a formal eulogy, unless we see it as part of an imaginative movement away from direct presentation of the hero. Johannes coughs up his former eloquence, gets it off his chest, as it were.[33] He also becomes more critical of his previous designation of Abraham as hero. It is at this point that he makes the distinction between Abraham and the ordinary Romantic hero: "I *think* myself *into* the hero, but into Abraham I cannot think myself" (44). It was just such a thinking of himself into Abraham that he had been trying to accomplish in his meditation up to this point. Now, as Johannes announces at the end of his Expectoration, he will try to *draw* something *out* of Abraham's example: "It is now my intention to draw out from the story of Abraham the dialectical consequences inherent in it, expressing them in the form of *problemata* . . ." (64).[34] In the three longer sections that follow, the meditation adopts a much more philosophical vocabulary: the specific concreteness of Abraham's character will be seen in such general abstractions as "the teleological suspension of the ethical." The meditation on the hero becomes more speculative than poetic and the dialectics emerge from the lyrical matrix.

In more philosophical terms, the relationship between Johannes and Abraham has moved from a state of relative immediacy to a state of increasing reflection. Kierkegaard adopted the term "immediacy" from Hegel but refused to accept its Hegelian opposite, "mediation." Mediation for Hegel was the ongoing process wherein mind reconciles oppositions between itself and its objects, eventually coming to realize itself as absolute. In Kierkegaard's view, however, one

33. The term "expectoration" occurs in the original. Kierkegaard also uses it in *Either / Or* (2 : 156). The Latin *expectorare* has the figurative meaning "to expel, to banish from the mind."

34. Robert Payne's translation of *Fear and Trembling* (Oxford, 1939), p. 74, puts it more concretely: "To draw out of the story of Abraham the dialectic that lies concealed within it."

cannot overcome the divisions between subject and object within mind alone. For him, the opposite of immediacy can only be reflection, the endless process in which thought regards its objects from an increasing distance. Kierkegaard rejects the fundamental principle of Hegel that mind is finally absolute, that thought can be identified in the end with Being. Such a principle ignores the whole intermediate realm of existence, within which even the philosopher must live. Kierkegaard does not deny that reflection entails a necessary departure from immediacy. He follows Hegel in conceiving of the "phenomenology" of the human spirit as the development of self-consciousness. But he does deny Hegel's "one lunatic postulate," as he calls it, that human thought can be identified with absolute being: it is this postulate that allows Hegelian philosophy to ignore the irreducible existence of a hero like Abraham and to flatter itself that it has "gone further" than Abraham's act of faith.[35]

Fear and Trembling thus dramatizes the impossibility of thought fully comprehending and transcending existence, the impossibility of the poet identifying himself with the hero and going beyond him. "Johannes *de silentio* is therefore not himself . . . an existing individual," Kierkegaard wrote later; "he is a reflective consciousness who . . . repeatedly runs himself into a collision with the understanding." [36] The meditation on the hero discovers a growing disproportion between the concrete person of Abraham and the abstracting intelligence of the narrator. To fill this widening gap and to maintain a foothold in the lyrical and the literary, Kierkegaard introduces a series of contrasting heroic figures, figures deduced or "educed," as Johannes says (121), from Abraham's

---

35. *Concluding Unscientific Postscript,* p. 279. Hegel himself had written of Abraham, interestingly enough, that "it was through God alone that Abraham came into a mediate relationship with the world, the only kind of link with the world possible for him" (*Early Theological Writings,* cited by Bogen, p. 387).

36. *Concluding Unscientific Postscript,* p. 234.

heroic example. Even though the meditation becomes more philosophical in its language, it continues to focus on the heroic figure.

The deductive nature of the meditation can be seen in the title of the first of the three "problems" that occupy the rest of the book: "Is there such a thing as the teleological suspension of the ethical?" The question is rather a rhetorical one; as soon as it is posed we realize that this must be a description of Abraham's case, one of the "dialectical consequences inherent in it." What we are offered is not a deeper understanding of Abraham's inner self but a broader view of Abraham in relation to a whole realm of other human concerns. We learn that there is a realm of experience called "the ethical" that has been suspended in Abraham's case. The mode of the meditation here is distinctly speculative and Hegelian; Kierkegaard is imitating the Hegelian manner even as he attacks Hegelian conclusions. The reasons for this parody of philosophical discourse, or the imaginative significance of it, are twofold. On the one hand, it dramatizes a further distancing of the narrator from his hero. Johannes, in his language of abstraction, is further away from the concrete example of Abraham than ever. On the other hand, it is a mode of discourse peculiarly suited to the alternate type of hero who is introduced into the meditation at this point—"the tragic hero."

Kierkegaard's presentation of the tragic hero in *Fear and Trembling* is curiously unsympathetic. This hero is seen as someone who is forced to break an ethical law, but only does so in the name of a higher ethical law. In fact, the conception of tragedy alluded to here is not Kierkegaard's own but Hegel's, where the tragic is defined as a conflict between different ethical demands made upon the individual.[37] Kierkegaard

---

37. For Kierkegaard's own views on tragedy see Pierre Mesnard, "Is the Category of the 'Tragic' Absent from the Life and Thought of Kierkegaard?" trans. Margaret Grieve, in Johnson and Thulstrup, *Kierkegaard Critique*, pp. 102–15. For Hegel's views, see *The Philosophy of Fine Art*, 4 : 293–345 and A. C. Bradley, "Hegel's Theory of Tragedy," *Oxford Lectures on Poetry* (London, 1909), pp. 69–92.

caricatures Hegel's views, to be sure, rather than presenting
them fairly. The inward suffering of the tragic hero is virtually ignored; his agon is seen in external, legalistic terms,
where a higher law overrules a lower one. "The tragic hero
still remains within the ethical. He lets one expression of the
ethical find its *telos* in a higher expression of the ethical; the
ethical relation between father and son, or daughter and
father, he reduces to a sentiment which has its dialectic in relation to the idea of morality" (69). The tragic hero does not,
like Abraham, have to obey God's command *and* continue to
love and have hope for Isaac. He may sacrifice the private
morality of the family to the public morality of the community or state.

The ethical sphere is thus dramatized here as curiously cold
and abstract, the realm of a universal humanity, where divine
transcendence and human individuality are both out of place.
"So the whole existence of the human race is rounded off
completely like a sphere," Johannes observes, "and the ethical
is at once its limit and its content. God becomes an invisible
vanishing point, a powerless thought, His power being only in
the ethical which is the content of existence" (78). The concrete identity of the individual is a similar vanishing point as
all human inwardness obeys the ethical injunction to make
itself public. "The tragic hero" is conceived as an abstract,
ideal, and generic figure. Even when a specific example from
literature or history is offered, the hero's name is not revealed
until the last minute, as in the formal portrait of Brutus, who
had to order the execution of his sons.

> When a son is forgetful of his duty, when the state en-
> trusts the father with the sword of justice, when the laws
> require punishment at the hand of the father, then will
> the father heroically forget that the guilty one is his son,
> he will magnanimously conceal his pain, but there will
> not be a single one among the people, not even the son,
> who will not admire the father, and whenever the law of
> Rome is interpreted, it will be remembered that many

interpreted it more learnedly, but none so gloriously as Brutus (68–69).

In the ethical sphere the name and identity of the hero are almost an afterthought.[38]

Problems I and II are concerned with this ethical sphere and the contrasts it presents with the religious example of Abraham. Problem III moves one step further down "the stages on life's way," to the sphere of the aesthetic. The narrator is thus still further from the concrete existence of his hero, since the aesthetic in Kierkegaard's scheme is at two removes from the religious, but Johannes has also moved to a realm where the heroic name and identity regain their earlier importance. Problem III eschews the abstract formulations of Problems I and II and asks more concretely, "Was Abraham ethically defensible in keeping silent about his purpose before Sarah, before Eleazar, before Isaac?" Again, the question is largely rhetorical, but it leads Johannes into a more specific kind of character analysis. Alternate heroes are again introduced: a bridegroom mentioned by Aristotle in the *Poetics,* the merman from the legend "Agnes and the Merman," Sarah from the Book of Tobit (whom Johannes changes to a man to suit his purposes), and the archetypal Romantic hero, Faust. Johannes "[calls] before the curtain [these] several poetic personages" (97),[39] and he treats them as if he were playwright, stage manager, and drama critic. He isolates them from their previous literary context and places them in new situations to bring out new elements in their personalities. In the first chap-

38. Kierkegaard is perhaps imitating a technique of Hegel's here, particularly notable in *The Phenomenology of Mind,* where Hegel describes a general situation in the abstract (e.g. *Sittlichkeit*) as though it were a general condition of human consciousness but is in part alluding to a specific historical or literary example (e.g. Sophocles' *Antigone*). See Walter Kaufmann, *Hegel: Reinterpretation, Texts, and Commentary* (Garden City, N.Y., 1965), pp. 141–49.

39. Lowrie's translation here improves on the Danish, which does not use this theatrical metaphor, although the image is certainly an appropriate one.

ter we noted the connection between the meditation on the hero and Romantic criticism of earlier dramatists such as Shakespeare. Kierkegaard carries to an extreme the Romantic focus on dramatic character, character independent of plot.

The problem Kierkegaard is concerned with in Problem III is to discover a kind of hero who does not simply sacrifice his individual identity to the demands of some universal ideal. Ethically, Abraham ought to have been open about his intended sacrifice of Isaac. Religiously, this revelation was impossible. Kierkegaard moves the discussion into the sphere of the aesthetic in order to discover an analogous situation in which a hero has remained silent about his heroic conflict, even though for a nonreligious reason. The four aesthetic heroes whom Johannes adduces are in situations similar to Abraham's: they all must sacrifice someone they love, yet they cannot reveal their reasons for doing so. The tragic hero in the two previous sections had also to perform such a sacrifice, but he had been required to make his reasons known. Johannes's surname, "de Silentio," expresses his generic concern with heroes who have kept silent about their heroics. In one sense—in terms of penetrating the existential substance of the hero—Johannes is further away from Abraham than ever when he descends to the aesthetic sphere. However, in the sense of describing the spiritual structure or form of the heroism, he is closer to a formal comprehension of Abraham's heroic act of faith.

One may observe here a peculiarity of Kierkegaard's notion of the three stages of existence: the aesthetic and religious stages, in their common opposition to the ethical, tend to resemble one another. Commentators on Kierkegaard have noted this tendency, some more critically than others. Pierre Mesnard speaks of Kierkegaard's "continual temptation to project back onto the aesthetic plane a religious dream incapable of realization in the absolute form he chose to impose upon it." Georg Lukács sees the ethical stage as an unsuccessful attempt on Kierkegaard's part to separate the aesthetic from the religious, the first and last stages nevertheless con-

tinually collapsing into one another.[40] Kierkegaard himself
describes the parallelism of faith and art, through his narrator, in terms of a previous and a subsequent immediacy:
"For faith is not the first immediacy but a subsequent immediacy. The first immediacy is the aesthetical, and about this
the Hegelian philosophy may be in the right. But faith is
not the aesthetical—or else faith has never existed because it
has always existed" (92).

I am not concerned here to pass on the philosophical validity
of this separation of similars, though it seems to me that
Kierkegaard is well aware of the weaknesses described by
Mesnard and Lukács. What I am interested in is the fact that
the retreat to the aesthetic sphere revives Johannes de Silentio's
meditation on the hero. He discusses his four understudies to
Abraham with enthusiasm and confidence, even with over-
bearing. He manipulates the circumstances in which the heroes
are involved in order to increase the spiritual conflict within
them. He arranges the plots to make their suffering more intense. "For as Gregory of Rimini was called *tortor infantium*
because he espoused the view of the damnation of infants, so
I might be tempted to call myself *tortor heroum;* for I am
very inventive when it is a question of putting heroes to the
torture" (119). The balance of power between narrator and
hero has shifted considerably from the prelude.

The meditations on the four aesthetic heroes in Problem III
are perhaps the most interesting in *Fear and Trembling,* if
only because the inner workings of these heroes are most in
evidence. I shall consider only one of these submeditations,
and I shall do so as a way of returning the discussion to Abraham himself. The figure I shall discuss, the merman, is
significant in the way he further reveals the relationship of the
narrator to the hero, which we have been discussing at some

40. Mesnard, "The Category of the 'Tragic,'" p. 114. See Lucien Gold-
mann's discussion of Lukács on Kierkegaard in *Kierkegaard Vivant,*
Colloque organisé par l'Unesco, 1964 (Paris, 1966), pp. 125–66. Lukács's
latest views on Kierkegaard are in *Die Zerstörung der Vernunft* (Berlin,
1955), pp. 198–243.

length. He is also significant in revealing something about the hero's relationship to himself, the third of the hero's dialectical relations outlined in the previous chapter. The merman, in other words, sheds light on Abraham's relation to his audience and also on Abraham's identity as hero.

"I will follow . . . with a sketch which involves the demoniacal," Johannes begins. "The legend of *Agnes and the Merman* will serve my purpose. The merman is a seducer who shoots up from his hiding-place in the abyss, with wild lust grasps and breaks the innocent flower which stood in all its grace on the seashore and pensively inclined its head to listen to the howling of the ocean. This is what the poets hitherto have meant by it" (103).[41] The merman is introduced not as an individual but as a type, an instance of "the demoniacal"; he has his being under a certain idea. Johannes is not content with this primitive, poetic version of the demoniacal, however. It is too immediate, too much a matter of unconscious desire. With the imaginative freedom allowed in the aesthetic sphere, he proposes a revision of the merman's character, a revision that will move him somewhat closer to Abraham's condition. "Let us make an alteration," he says. In this rewriting of the legend the merman seizes Agnes but "he is not able to resist the power of innocence, his native element is unfaithful to him, he cannot seduce Agnes. He leads her back again, he explains to her that he only wanted to show her how beautiful the sea is when it is calm, and Agnes believes him" (104). The merman then falls into despair.

What Johannes is doing in his meditation is bringing out a potential for spiritually conscious heroism in the merman's character. Johannes complicates the possibilities for action on the merman's part by raising his hero's consciousness, raising

41. "The poets" include Hans Christian Andersen, whose version of the story Kierkegaard recites, (Hirsch, *Furcht und Zittern*, p. 154). Kierkegaard was highly critical of Andersen's inconsistent sentimentality. Matthew Arnold's version of this legend, "The Forsaken Merman," makes the merman a victim of the girl's orthodoxy, which only shows the malleability of a folktale.

it from an easy sensual immediacy to a more consciously tormented reflection. The meditation on his character is a kind of
miniature Bildungsroman: "We will now bestow upon the
merman a human consciousness and suppose that the fact of
his being a merman indicates a human pre-existence in the
consequences of which his life is entangled" (105).

The fairy-tale character is thus remolded to bring him closer
to the religious heroism of Abraham. Even in the remoteness
of the aesthetic sphere, the religious paradigm begins to
emerge. "There is nothing to prevent him from becoming a
hero," Johannes observes of his built-up character, "for the
step he now takes is one of reconciliation" (105). And yet further difficulties emerge. The merman is faced with a conflict
about reconciliation: should he repent privately and keep his
past hidden or should he repent openly and hope to regain
Agnes on the ethical level? Johannes has the merman choose
the first of these alternatives because the merman has now
stumbled on a still higher category of human consciousness,
the category of sin. In considering repentance the merman arrives at a religious intuition; sin is not something that can be
pardoned by another person, on an ethical level, but can only
be absolved religiously by God.

Johannes has thus worked the merman up to a level of primitive religiosity. The meditation here is a kind of phenomenology, in the Hegelian sense, of the demonic element in the
merman's character, since the demoniacal is traced dialectically
from its unconscious, sensuous immediacy to increasing higher
levels of conscious reflection. Johannes reminds us at this point
that there is still a wide gulf between the merman and Abraham, however, and that this gulf consists precisely in the degree to which each is able to reconcile the two conflicting
claims upon his selfhood. The merman cannot reconcile the
religious claims imposed on him by his new awareness of sin
with the more human claims imposed by his desire to love,
honor, and presumably marry Agnes. He remains a divided
self. This does not "explain" Abraham, as Johannes reminds
us, since Abraham was not a sinful man. But it does provide
a negative analogy with what Abraham as hero was able to do.

He was able to unite two claims upon him that were in absolute conflict with each other. It is here that we encounter the question of the identity of the hero as hero, the hero's relation to himself.

From the beginning, in fact, the undivided selfhood of Abraham has been a given, although this identity has constituted a paradox. On the one hand, Abraham intends complete obedience to God's command that he sacrifice Isaac. On this count there can be no doubt. But neither can Abraham be undecided or resigned about his love for Isaac. He must continue to love Isaac fully and to believe in this love that Isaac will survive.

> Abraham believed, and believed for this life. Yea, if his faith had been only for a future life, he surely would have cast everything away in order to hasten out of this world to which he did not belong. But Abraham's faith was not of this sort, if there be such a faith; for really this is not faith but the furthest possibility of faith which has a presentiment of its object at the extremest limit of the horizon, yet is separated from it by a yawning abyss within which despair carries on its game. But Abraham believed precisely for this life (34–35).

"It is about the temporal, the finite, [that] everything turns in this case," Johannes later explains (60). The paradox is not that God should command Abraham to sacrifice Isaac and that Abraham should obey, although this is not easy to comprehend itself. The paradox is rather that Abraham is also able to maintain a hold on his temporal, finite existence, by believing in the future life of Isaac as well as the present necessity for his sacrifice. The logical "either / or" becomes an existential "both / and." In the end the hero's relationship to God is less problematical than his relationship to human life, and it is on this second phase of the "double movement of faith" that *Fear and Trembling* focuses. The problem is to live in the world after one has seen beyond it. It is not so much the existence of God that is problematical in Kierkegaard as the existence of a fully integrated human self.

God commands, making Abraham aware of an eternal imperative that contradicts all temporal ideals of duty, love, and justice. Abraham internalizes this command, apparently, without rejecting the temporal ideals it contradicts; he seems to do so to such an extent that he embodies within himself both an eternal and a temporal consciousness. Abraham is thus a paradox, his faith is faith "by virtue of the absurd" (46). The paradox is more than a logical contradiction. "Paradox is not a concession but a category," Kierkegaard wrote, "an ontological description expressing the relationship between a personally existent spirit and eternal truth." [42] In terms of Kierkegaard's own religious development, Abraham's paradoxical union of opposites, temporal and eternal, points toward the more absolute paradox of the Christian incarnation, in which the divine literally assumes a human form. Although Kierkegaard never puts it this way, Abraham is a kind of *figura* for Christ, an Old Testament prefiguration of the New.[43] The same may be said of the related concept of the absurd: "In its absolute form this contradiction is contained only in the declaration of the incarnation of God. All other forms of the absurd are only lower analogies in relation to the absurd on the highest level (*sensu eminentiori*)." [44]

The paradox of Abraham represents a stage in Kierkegaard's

42. Quoted by Hermann Diem, *Kierkegaard's Dialectic of Existence,* trans. Harold Knight (Edinburgh and London, 1959), p. 50.

43. The figural nature of *Fear and Trembling* is discussed in a somewhat different way by Mackey, *A Kind of Poet,* pp. 222–23. There are of course important differences between the Old Testament example and the New. "It is not easy to have both the Old Testament and the New Testament, for the O.T. contains altogether different categories. What, indeed, would the N.T. say about a faith which believes that it is going to be well off in the world, in temporality, instead of giving this up in order to grasp the eternal" (*Sören Kierkegaard's Journals and Papers,* ed. and trans. Howard and Edna Hong [Bloomington, Ind., 1967], 1 : 84). See also Diem, *Kierkegaard's Dialectic,* p. 60, for the idea that the paradox is "redoubled" with the advent of Christ: whereas Abraham must struggle with God *and* time, the Christian must struggle with God already *in* time.

44. Commentary by Gregor Malantshuk in *Journals and Papers,* 1 : 497–98.

own *imitatio Christi*. It is an imaginatively projected ideal in the all-important task "of becoming a Christian," as a later persona puts it.[45] To what extent Kierkegaard succeeded in fulfilling this task within his own existence is difficult to judge, and it is beyond the scope of this study to deal with the depths of Kierkegaard's personal religious commitment. Regina was soon to disappoint the specific hope he held at the time of writing *Fear and Trembling*—the hope that in spite of his religiously motivated sacrifice of her he could also have her as his wife. What I am more concerned in showing is that Abraham's identity as hero, his paradoxical resolution of the claims of divinity and the claims of humanity, is a resolution of the identity problem of the earlier Romantic hero.

The Romantic hero, as I argued in the first chapter, is a potentially divided self; his identity is a conflict between his heroic essence and a more personal, more present existence. The conflict is expressed by Faust in his famous *"zwei Seele"* speech:

> Two souls abide, alas, within my breast
> And each one seeks for riddance from the other.
> The one clings with a dogged love and lust
> With clutching parts unto this present world,
> The other surges fiercely from the dust
> Unto sublime ancestral fields.[46]

In order to be a hero of or for "our time," the Romantic hero must achieve some resolution of his divinely sanctioned heroic gestalt, awe-inspiring but alien, and his more personal *Bildung*, the human form and process of formation with which his audience can identify. Usually the narrator aids him in this task; by meditating on his hero, the narrator can mediate between the hero of the past and his audience of the present.

45. *Concluding Unscientific Postscript*, p. 7.
46. *Faust, Part One and Part Two*, trans. Charles E. Passage (Indianapolis, 1965), p. 42. Passage emphasizes the temporality in "this present world" which Goethe leaves implicit: "Die eine hält, in derber Liebeslust / Sich an die welt. . . ."

The meditation on the hero in *Fear and Trembling* seems to be of this historically retrospective type. Yet Johannes signally fails to make Abraham more immediate to us. On the contrary, as we have seen, his meditation dramatizes a growing conceptual distance between Abraham's identity and our modern view. But Abraham is not seen as a figure of the remote historical past; he still participates in the present. In fact, it is not the narrator who makes Abraham present, Kierkegaard shows, but the hero himself. By virtue of his own act of faith Abraham belongs to our time and to temporality in general.

The Romantic hero, I suggested in the first chapter, finds himself divided along historical lines, either declining from an earlier heroic essence or generating a new heroic existence from the present age. Abraham resolves his identity along lines that are historical not in any external sense, but only in the internal context of personality. The whole attack launched against Hegelian notions of history in *Fear and Trembling* is a rejection of the idea that the hero of the past is frozen in place in the historical system, that he is automatically outmoded and transcended by the present. In place of this speculative conception of history, Kierkegaard offers an existentially inward definition. Where Hegel's philosophy of history shows the progress of the Absolute through social and political history, Kierkegaard's dialectical lyric shows the progress—the moment—of the absolute in the history of the individual.

Thus it is not a question of the present age generously reviving an ancient figure for modern appreciation and understanding. The power to revive Abraham does not lie in the poet who celebrates him but in the hero himself. Abraham is a hero of our time, Johannes shows, by virtue of his commitment to his own temporality. Abraham's "double movement of faith" effects among other things a resolution of his past self (his love for Isaac) with his present self (the command to sacrifice Isaac) in a way that makes this past a genuine hope for the future. He has achieved what Kierkegaard calls in his other volume a "repetition," the faith that makes the memory of something lost in the past into the experience of something to be gained in the future.[47]

The meditation on the hero in *Fear and Trembling* becomes a means of defending the hero, a means of defending his religiously immediate existence against the false appropriations of reflective thought. The meditation is a *via negativa,* in that it negates its own powers of comprehension. "Abraham I cannot understand" (48), Johannes continually confesses, and his confession is a mark of Abraham's triumph. Abraham's heroic identity is resolved and integral; there is nothing in him that betrays "the infinite in its heterogeneity with the finite," no "cranny through which the infinite is peeping" (49–50). The hero of religious faith, we are shown, has the balance and wholeness of self that all the heroes in the lower spheres are struggling for and unable to attain.

In presenting Abraham's heroism as such a fait accompli, however, *Fear and Trembling* demands of the reader a kind of vicarious faith of his own. Part of the authority of Abraham as hero rests on his being a figure from the Old Testament, which, the higher criticism notwithstanding, gives him a decided edge over the heroes of, say, Shakespeare or Goethe in the legitimacy of his spiritual example. But the problem *Fear and Trembling* raises for the reader is not so much that it demands a belief in the Old Testament but that it demands a belief in the way in which the Old Testament figure is able to enter into the fully temporal, commonplace aspects of human existence. When Johannes de Silentio imagines his "knight of faith" in modern dress, he can only picture a tax collector. To

47. The personal historical element is not simply something Kierkegaard imposes on Abraham out of Romantic preconceptions, however. As Auerbach notes, there is a strong sense of historical development in the Old Testament figures: "This element of development gives the Old Testament stories a historical character, even when the subject is purely legendary and traditional" (*Mimesis,* p. 18). On "The Historicity and Temporality of Consciousness" in Kierkegaard see Adi Shmueli's *Kierkegaard and Consciousness,* trans. Naomi Handelman (Princeton, 1971), pp. 176–89.

appreciate the shift in emphasis one need only compare
Kierkegaard's Abraham with Vigny's Moses, another biblical
patriarch converted into a Romantic hero. Vigny's Moses is a
hero of godlike proportions; he meets God face to face on
Mount Pisgah and recites an epic catalogue of his heroic ac-
complishments. The only humanizing trait that Vigny gives
him is his desire for burial and rest, as he is barred from the
Promised Land: "Alas, I am, Lord, powerful and alone, / Let
me fall asleep with the sleep of the earth." [48]

On the other hand, there is the Abraham of Kafka, ironically adapted from Kierkegaard and pushed to the commonly
human extreme. Kafka's several versions of Abraham's sacrifice
of Isaac involve either a hero who is smugly accomplished and
stands only to gain by the sacrifice, or a hero who is radically
unsure of his heroic gestalt:

> But take another Abraham. One who wanted to perform
> the sacrifice altogether in the right way and had a correct
> sense in general of the whole affair, but could not believe
> that he was the one meant, he, an ugly old man, and the
> dirty youngster that was his child. True faith is not lack-
> ing to him, he has this faith; he would make the sacrifice
> in the right spirit if only he could believe he was the one
> meant. He is afraid that after starting out as Abraham
> with his son he would change on the way into Don
> Quixote.[49]

Kafka's Abraham is not simply a parody—he is still a potential
hero of faith in a way that only Kafka can make us accept—
but he is a hero whose immersion in the finite and the temporal is so complete that he has become unrecognizable even

48. *"Hélas, je suis, Seigneur, puissant et solitaire, / Laissez-moi m'endor-
mir du sommeil de la terre,"* Poèmes (Paris, 1837), p. 11.
49. "Abraham," trans. Clement Greenberg, in *Parables and Paradoxes,*
ed. Nahum Glatzer (New York, 1961), p. 43. On Kafka's interest in Kierkegaard see Jean Wahl, "Kierkegaard and Kafka," in *The Kafka Problem,*
ed. Angel Flores (New York, 1946), pp. 262–75, and Brian F. M. Edwards,
"Kafka and Kierkegaard: A Reassessment," *German Life and Letters* 20
(1967) : 218–25.

to himself. Although Kierkegaard's Abraham is by no means so insecure in his spiritual authority, this problematic nature of the hero's immersion in a world of time that Kafka is exploiting is certainly present in *Fear and Trembling*. It is perhaps because of this potential invisibility of the heroic in Abraham that Kierkegaard published it together with a complementary meditation on the hero, *Repetition*.

Repetition, as I suggested earlier, is essentially the obverse of *Fear and Trembling* in its imaginative structure. Like *Fear and Trembling*, it takes the form of the meditation on the hero: a skeptical "poetic" narrator, Constantine Constantius, meditates on the single figure of an anonymous "young man." Constantine is a more intrusive, more active narrator than Johannes de Silentio. He enters into the plot, tries to manipulate his hero, even tries to realize the hero's program in his own person, but he is ultimately an "observer," as he himself puts it. The "young man" is much less a hero then Abraham—it is questionable whether he actually achieves the heroic act of "repetition" that his narrator projects for him—but he is clearly aspiring to be a hero of faith. He attempts to sacrifice, for religious reasons, it turns out, a girl he is in love with, just as Abraham attempted to sacrifice Isaac. Another Old Testament "hero" is introduced in the young man's letters that Constantine publishes; the young man chooses Job as the model for his aspiring faith.

What we have in *Repetition* is a meditation on an emerging hero, the hero in *Bildung* with Job as the heroic gestalt. Like the figure of Hamlet in *Wilhelm Meister,* Job functions as an ideal form toward which the young man develops and against which he is finally judged. That the young hero never actually becomes a Job in his own person, never attains the status of the Old Testament figure, does not negate the validity of the ideal. The story is one of progress toward the goal rather than a realization of it. The hero is anonymous throughout, never acquiring the distinction of identity that a name implies.

Repetition, in fact, can be described as the abstracted es-

sense of a Bildungsroman, where plot and setting are reduced to a minimum and the question of character development becomes the exclusive concern. Development, as in
Fear and Trembling, is not a gradual, drawn-out process but
the affair of a critical moment. "If I were to pursue in detail
the moods of the young man as I learned to know them, not
to speak of including in a poetical manner a multitude of irrelevant matters—salons, wearing apparel, beautiful scenery,
relatives and friends—this story might be drawn out to yard
lengths. That, however, I have no inclination to do," Constantine declares. "I eat lettuce, it is true, but I eat only the
heart; the leaves, in my opinion, are fit for swine." [50]

The contrasts between *Repetition* and *Fear and Trembling*
are many. Where *Fear and Trembling* is a dialectical lyric, the
dialectics being drawn out of a lyrical apprehension at the
start, *Repetition* is "An Essay in Experimental Psychology," a
dialectical exercise where a lyricism gradually emerges from
the philosophical concepts. Whereas *Fear and Trembling* presents the character of Abraham first and derives philosophical
categories from his concrete example, *Repetition* begins with
the category of its title and adduces the young man as a kind
of test case; the category is explored at some length before the
hero is even introduced. Kierkegaard seems to have been influenced by a technique he noted in *Wilhelm Meister,* about
which he wrote, "By the end of the novel the view of the
world the poet has advanced but which previously existed
. . . outside of Wilhelm, now is embodied and living within
him." [51] In *Fear and Trembling,* one would have to say, the
view of the world is disembodied from Abraham.

Larger contrasts between the two books can be seen in the
different cultural traditions that they invoke. *Fear and Trembling* draws its sustenance from Hebraic tradition; it is written
itself in an Hebraic mode. *Repetition,* on the other hand, is

<hr>

50. *Repetition,* trans. Walter Lowrie, Harper Torchbook edition (New
York, 1964), pp. 43–44. In all further references to *Repetition* page numbers cited parenthetically in text are from this edition.
51. *Journals and Papers,* 2 : 158.

essentially Hellenistic. It approaches truth philosophically, through speculation and dialectic, rather than through prophecy and revelation. Constantine Constantius presents his conception of repetition as a revised version of Platonic recollection. The book's epigraph ("On wild trees the flowers are fragrant; on cultivated trees, the fruits") is from *Stories of Heroes* by Philostratus the Elder, a third-century dialogue that reviews and reinterprets the heroes of the *Iliad*. Constantine is scornful of the Hebraism of his young hero: "Here he thinks he has found what he sought, and in this little circle of Job and the wife along with three friends the truth, as he thinks, seems more glorious and joyful and true than in a Greek symposium" (90).

In fact, both Constantine and the young man turn up later in Kierkegaard's writing in an actual Greek symposium, modeled on Plato's dialogue of that name. The first section of *Stages on Life's Way* (1845) uses the symposium to express the aesthetic stage of existence. Five characters, including Constantine, offer speeches on the nature of love. All the speeches deal with the existential experience of love *ab extra,* from the detached perspective of the aesthete. It is only in the ethical and religious stages that the speakers become more personally and existentially involved. What *Fear and Trembling* did, it will be recalled, was to move from the religious stage to the aesthetic. *Repetition* moves in the opposite direction, beginning with the aesthetic and trying to approach the religious from this vantage point. The aesthetic consciousness of the narrator in *Repetition* tries to proceed inductively from itself toward the religious existence of the hero. At a critical point in this process the original narrative mode is transcended: the speculations of Constantine Constantius give way to the letters of the young man. These letters come to Constantine from an existential beyond, the nature of which, he confesses, remains a mystery to him.

Repetition finally contrasts with *Fear and Trembling* in the objects of its attack. Like all of Kierkegaard's "aesthetic" writings, *Repetition* is a parody and a critique as much as a posi-

tive statement. In *Fear and Trembling* the primary targets
were Hegel and speculative philosophy; here they are Goethe
and Romantic art. These differences are not absolute—references to Goethe and Hegel appear in both volumes—but
Repetition devotes itself more to the poetic and novelistic
abuses of existence than to the philosophical.

We have already noted some connections with Goethe's
Wilhelm Meister, as in Constantine's remark that the outer
layers of the Bildungs-experience are unfit for human con-
sumption. Kierkegaard sees the social focus of the novel as at
best a distraction from its spiritual purpose. *Repetition* also
echoes *Werther* in its partially epistolary form and more
explicitly in the earlier version of the manuscript that Kierkegaard changed when he learned Regina had married. Originally the young man is said to have shot himself.[52] It is also
probable that the concern with Job here is intended as a reply to Goethe's *Faust,* where the "Prologue in Heaven" invokes the Book of Job as a paradigm for Faust's temptation.
Kierkegaard is, in effect, correcting the liberties that Goethe's
Romantic rendering had taken with the biblical text.

The critique of Romanticism extends further than to
Goethe, however. One of the central motifs of Romantic poetry
is the place revisited, where an observer returns to a spot
visited in the past and seeks, through past memories and present perception, to overcome the divisions of temporal selfhood. This Romantic motif is invoked and parodied when
Constantine Constantius attempts to return to Berlin and to
recapture a moment of aesthetic rapture he had experienced
there in the past. The sense of connection that Wordsworth
achieves by revisiting Tintern Abbey, to take a familiar example, fails to emerge for Constantine in Berlin. For Wordsworth on the banks of the Wye five years after his initial visit,
the "beauteous forms" stored in the memory are reconfirmed
and solidified by present perception. The poem moves from
the isolated state of present consciousness toward the past, and

52. Mackey, *A Kind of Poet,* p. 276, makes some of these same points,
drawing, he says, on Karl Roos.

also looks, through the invocation of the poet's sister, to future perceptions of the same scene that will outlive the poet himself.

> Once again
> Do I behold these steep and lofty cliffs,
> That on a wild secluded scene impress
> Thoughts of more deep seclusion; and connect
> The landscape with the quiet of the sky.[53]

The poet's mind receives the impressions, perceives the connections, but transmits them back to the landscape: cliffs impress thoughts on a *scene* and connect landscape with sky. The process presents a spatial emblem of the way a natural past, present, and future achieve relatedness through the poetic consciousness.

What Constantine discovers in revisiting Berlin is the failure of any such temporal reunification. He returns to his old lodging and finds the rooms the same, but his host, formerly a bachelor, is now married. He goes to the theater to recapture an evening of lyrical immediacy; the same play is being performed, but he is only bored. He tries again the next night, but is forced to conclude, "The only thing repeated was the impossibility of repetition" (75). Constantine of course visits a theater rather than a landscape—he is closer to Proust than to Wordsworth in his search for a *temps perdu* in this— but in an extended invocation in the midst of his theatrical experience Constantine shows that his quest for aesthetic immediacy has its roots in Romantic nature poetry.

> My nursery maid never to be forgotten, thou fugitive nymph which hadst thy dwelling in the brook which ran past my father's farmstead and didst ever take a helpful part in the child's play, although thou wast only looking after thyself! Thou faithful comforter who throughout

53. "Lines Composed a Few Miles Above Tintern Abbey . . . ," *The Poetical Works of Wordsworth*, ed. Thomas Hutchinson, rev. E. de Selincourt (Oxford, 1950), p. 163 (ll. 4–8). Kierkegaard almost certainly did not know of Wordsworth or this poem.

the years hast preserved thy innocent purity, hast ever re
mained young, whereas I have become old; thou quie
nymph to whom again I had recourse when I was weary o
men, weary of myself, so that I needed an eternity t
repose; when I was sorrowful, so that I needed an eternit
to forget. Thou didst not deny to me that which mer
would deny me by making eternity just as busy and even
more terrible than time. There I lay by thy side and
vanished from before my own eyes into the prodigious ex
panse of heaven above my head, and forgot myself in thy
lulling murmur. . . . Thus it was that I lay back in my
loge, caste aside like the clothing of a bather, flung beside
the stream of laughter and merriment and jubilatior
which foamed past me incessantly (70–71).

The moral that Constantine draws from his project is tha
repetition is an empty concept: "I discovered that there is nc
such thing as repetition." But Kierkegaard suggests something
different—not that such a *redintegratio in statum pristinum*
(as Constantine calls it) is impossible, but that Constantine is
not enough of a self to bring it about in his own person. Notice
how in the quote above Constantine forgets himself in the
murmur of the stream, vanishes into the heavens. Constantine
is ultimately a narrator, a poet. He needs a hero, who will
carry into the realm of actuality and action what for the poet
remains in the realm of possibility and thought. Constantine's
attempt at repetition fails because, as Johannes de Silentic
puts it, "The poet cannot do what that other does, he can
only love, admire and rejoice in the hero."

What exactly is this "repetition" that both the narrator and
the hero are trying to achieve? The term is introduced by
Constantine in an a priori Hegelian fashion; it is a category
in search of a definition. Constantine contrasts "repetition"
with "recollection": "Repetition and recollection are the same
movement, only in opposite directions; for what is recollected
has been, is repeated backwards, whereas repetition properly
so called is recollected forwards. Therefore repetition, if it is

possible, makes a man happy, whereas recollection makes him unhappy . . . " (33). Recollection perceives the past as a reflective distance; it involves a sense of loss. Repetition experiences the past as a new and immediate future, in which what seemed to be lost is regained.[54] The idea of repetition is thus a paradox, and in fact it is another form of the paradox of faith described in *Fear and Trembling*, that "double movement" of the spirit where the awareness of something eternally denied is joined to the sense of that same thing temporally realized. In both paradoxes, "it is about the temporal, the finite [that] everything turns" (*FT*, 60). The past has an eternal mode of being for Constantine (as for Plato), but only in the active faith of repetition can this eternity enter into the reality of the present. The Danish word for repetition, *Gentaglse(n)*, T. H. Croxall says, has the root meaning of "taking again" or "taking anew"; it suggests a dynamic act rather than a static reoccurrence.[55]

As with *Fear and Trembling*, the possibility of resuming the broken engagement with Regina is Kierkegaard's stimulus to explore the paradox, but a more general interpretation of human existence is entailed. "If God himself had not willed repetition, the world would never have come into existence," Constantine claims. The creation itself brought eternal purpose into temporal being. For man, "Repetition is the reality, and it is the seriousness of life" (35). One is reminded of

54. Cf. Heidegger, *Being and Time*, trans. John Macquarrie and Edward Robinson (New York, 1962), p. 437: "The authentic repetition of a possibility of existence that has been—the possibility that Dasein may choose its hero—is grounded existentially in anticipatory resoluteness; for it is in resoluteness that one first chooses the choice which makes one free for the struggle of loyally following in the footsteps of that which can be repeated. But when one has, by repetition, handed down to oneself a possibility that has been, the Dasein that has-been-there is not disclosed in order to be actualized over again. The repeating of that which is possible does not bring again . . . something that is 'past,' nor does it bind the 'Present' back to that which has already been 'outstripped.' "

55. Croxall, *Kierkegaard Commentary*, p. 128.

Coleridge's definition of the imagination as "a repetition in the finite mind of the eternal act of creation in the infinite I AM." [56] Where Coleridge says "mind," however, Kierkegaard would say "existence," concerned as he is to distinguish these realms from one another.

We are left with the question of the connection between Constantine's own attempt at repetition and his desire to promote and celebrate a repetition achieved by his hero. The persona of the narrator dominates the first part of this two-part book, and one is forced to examine Constantine's methods and motivation. On the one hand we have Constantine's plan for the young man whom he has befriended: he is to break off his unhappy love affair by a series of deceptions, then test whether the relationship might be resumed in spite of the prohibitions against it. "If the young man had believed in repetition, of what might he not have been capable? What inwardness he might have attained!" (49). On the other hand, we have Constantine's ultimately futile attempt to achieve repetition by himself. The problem is in deciding which comes first chronologically. It is difficult to tell from Constantine's account. The trip to Berlin seems to be a reaction to the disappearance of the young man and the apparent failure of Constantine's vicarious heroic project; but it is also possible that the trip to Berlin is an initial approach to repetition that has failed before the young man appears on the scene. The order of these two events is further complicated when Constantine alludes to a third crucial event in his aesthetic life. At the end of the first part of the book he describes an experience of mystic elation (reminiscent, in fact, of the "serene and blessed mood" Wordsworth describes in "Tintern Abbey," when "We see into the life of things"), an experience that lasted for several hours and abruptly disappeared.

> The whole of existence seemed to be as it were in love with me, and everything vibrated in preordained *rapport* with my being. In me all was ominous, and everything was

56. *Biographia Literaria,* ed. J. Shawcross (Oxford, 1907), 1 : 202.

enigmatically transfigured in my microcosmic bliss, which was able to transform into its own likeness all things, even the observations which were most disagreeable and tiresome, even disgusting sights and the most fatal collisions. When precisely at one o'clock I was at the highest peak, where I surmised the ultimate attainment, something suddenly began to chafe one of my eyes, whether it was an eye-lash, a mote, a speck of dust, I do not know; but this I know, that in the selfsame instant I toppled down almost into the abyss of despair . . . (79).

There are thus three moments of aesthetic crisis for Constantine, but they bear no discernible temporal relation to one another. The description of the third moment only complicates the problem of relating the other two. Constantine's narrative simply refuses to take the shape of a plot in which he himself is involved, and this lack of direction in his story is significant. It dramatizes the limits of his poetic being, the being of a man who looks at existence from the outside. Each event repeats the other two in a sense, but only in an analogical way. Each event exists in an indefinite past, which is really only a narrative present. The past is recollected, but never in a way that it can enter into the existential present, as a repeated or resumed reality. Constantine is unable to enter into the world of time; he remains imprisoned in the false eternity of a purely poetic consciousness. Like his repetitive name, Constantine Constantius, he is ultimately a parody of repetition as a category of human existence.[57]

There are suggestive resonances in the relationship of Constantine and the young man that go beyond the philosophical thrust of the narrative, however. The young hero emerges figuratively as a version of the narrator's early self, a recollected self from the past which he is trying to realize again in the

57. In a long letter written after the publication of *Repetition*, Kierkegaard explained (still through the persona of Constantine), "The young man's problem is *whether repetition is possible*. It was as a parody of him that I made the journey to Berlin to see whether repetition was possible" (quoted by Lowrie, "Editor's Introduction," p. 14).

present. One is reminded of the relationship in *The Ambassadors*, where the aging Strether meditates on the ambiguous *Bildung* of Chad Newsome. Strether discovers at the end that his young hero has failed him, that his own imaginative perceptions have generously attributed to Chad a value the young man would never realize. Like Wordsworth, James redeems the aesthetic consciousness; the vulgar world of action, of "doing," rarely lives up to the expectations of those who truly and discriminatingly "see." But James shows that such seeing is usually only achieved by the sacrifice of an active existence, and it is just this sacrifice of the existential to the aesthetic that Kierkegaard cannot accept. When the paradox of repetition fails to realize itself existentially, when the young man fails to bring Constantine's own past into the present, no aesthetic consolation remains. Whereas James's fictional relationships are basically interpersonal transactions between the self and others, Kierkegaard's are essentially intrapersonal relations of the self with itself and with its double.

In "Repetition," the second part of this complexly repetitive book, Constantine Constantius recedes from the foreground as a narrative presence. The young man is reintroduced through a series of letters, which he writes to Constantine after his earlier disappearance. Constantine gives us the letters and allows the young man to dramatize his own heroic emergence. The hope for repetition is revived. But if the young man can be taken as a figure of Constantine's own youth, the repetition this figure is striving for is something Constantine cannot comprehend. "A religious movement I am unable to make, it is contrary to my nature." However, he admits, "I am not inclined for this reason to deny the reality of such a thing, or deny that one can learn a great deal from a young man. If he succeeds, he will have no admirer more zealous than I" (90–91).

To what extent does the young man succeed in making such a religious movement; to what extent does he become a hero of faith? His spiritual dilemma is similar to Abraham's, though less clearly presented. It is also a representation of Kierkegaard's own spiritual crisis. The young man loves a girl and is loved in return but discovers that there is a prohibition against his marrying her or continuing the relationship. The prohibition is not an explicit command from God but a predisposition toward melancholy, *Tungsind,* a brooding introspection of religious intensity,[58] which is in complete conflict with the openness demanded by the ideals of married love. If the young man refused to listen to his religious daemon he would be less than heroic; if he simply sacrificed the girl, he would be a "knight of infinite resignation," a hero of otherworldliness, but not a knight of faith, one who holds to the temporal and the finite notwithstanding.

Constantine's scenario was for the young man to pretend to the girl that he was really a shallow spirit and unworthy of love, so that she would reject him. Only then would it be possible for a resumption of the affair, the repetition, to take place. But the young man has failed to carry out this program: "Thus to be a hero, not in the eyes of the world, but within oneself, to have no plea to present before a human tribunal, but living immured within one's own personality to be one's own witness, one's own judge, one's own prosecutor, to be in oneself the one and only" (94). The young man acknowledges the validity of this definition of heroism. (The definition fits Abraham very well.) "Unfortunately, however, I was not the artist capable of sustaining this role, nor had I the endurance for it" (94). He must search for a mode of heroism that is more truly his own.

What he must search for, in fact, is a ground for his heroic existence and a heroic role or precedent to give shape to his unformed strivings. Neither of these things are provided by Constantine's abstract aesthetic. The ground for such heroism, Kierkegaard makes clear, can only be provided by a radically transcendent God. The young man's letters dramatize his struggles to achieve the "religious movement" that Constantine is unable to make. But this ground is only dimly perceived, intuited through the psychological categories of his predisposition toward melancholy and introspection. It is the search for

58. Croxall, *Kierkegaard Commentary,* p. 130.

a role, a heroic gestalt, that occupies most of the young man's
reports on his spiritual progress. Here the figure of Job becomes important.

"Job! Job! Job! Job!" he writes in the letter dated September 19. "Didst thou indeed utter nothing but these beautiful
words, 'The Lord gave, the Lord hath taken away, blessed be
the name of the Lord?' Didst thou say nothing more? . .
What went on in thy soul?" (101). "If I had not Job!" he
writes again on November 15. "It is impossible to describe and
to *nuancer* what significance he has for me, and how manifold
his significance is" (109). His letters become a meditation on
the hero within the meditation on the hero, an existentially intensified "repetition" of the book as a whole. Job is not a
consummate a religious hero as Abraham, but for this very
reason he provides a heroic model that is more susceptible to
the young man's imitation. "Job is not a hero of faith, he
gives birth with prodigious pains to the category of 'trial'—
precisely because he is so developed he does not possess this
category in childlike immediacy" (116).[59] The young man seeks
to understand his own trial in the light of Job's, not only in its
negative aspects, but also in its possibly positive results: "The
Lord gave Job twice as much as he had before." But the most
important attribute of Job is that he refuses to accept his sufferings as a sign of his unrighteousness, he refuses to resign
himself to his fate until he is answered directly by God himself, out of the whirlwind. The second-to-last letter from the
young man shows him waiting for such a response from God:
"I am expecting a thunderstorm . . . and repetition" (119).

It is at this point that the reality of Regina seems to have
intruded on the book's imaginative form. Originally, the young
man was to have killed himself, his heroism reverting to the
aesthetic condition of Werther instead of attaining the religious condition of Job; this was apparently the plan. But
when Kierkegaard learned that Regina had married Fritz

59. I have emended Lowrie's translation on Croxall's suggestion, sub-
stituting "childlike" for "childish." Abraham is a hero of faith who
does possess his faith in childlike immediacy.

Schlegel and that repetition of their engagement was impossible for more mundane reasons, he tore out the last ten pages of the manuscript and substituted another ending. Regina's behavior apparently made the original tragic ending too ludicrous, as deeply involved as the book was in Kierkegaard's relationship to her. The revised ending shows the young man achieving repetition, but in a much redefined sense. He loses the girl, he loses his relation to the temporal and the finite. What he regains is himself: "I am again myself, here I have the repetition, I understand everything, and existence seems to me more beautiful than ever. It came as a thunderstorm after all, though I owe its occurrence to her magnanimity" (125). As Johannes Hohlenberg suggests, the revised ending is ironic rather than tragic.[60] There is considerable bitterness in the reference to the girl's "magnanimity." It is true that this notion of a spiritual rebirth is more orthodox in Christian tradition, but it is undeniable that the young man has suddenly changed the terms of the repetition he was trying to achieve. "And what is a repetition of earthly goods which are of no consequence to the spirit—what are they in comparison with such a repetition [i.e., regaining onself]? Only his children Job did not receive again double, because a human life is not a thing that can be duplicated. In that case only spiritual repetition is possible, although in the temporal life is it never so perfect as in eternity, which is the true repetition" (126). In reaction to his disappointment the young man turns his back on the world of time—on the world where children can be miraculously sacrificed and regained.

Must we then conclude that this ending is inconsistent with the design of the book as a whole? It seems to me that we need not, since the emergence of the young man's heroism was problematic to begin with. Even in the original ending, he was to fail; the attempt at a religious movement was to collapse back into the aesthetic sphere with the young man's suicide. Though this is a more intense and demonic gesture than the present ending allows, the regaining of oneself rather than the

60. *Sören Kierkegaard*, pp. 124–25.

girl has a similar reductive effect. The sense of collapse is carried even further by a letter Kierkegaard appends to the two parts of *Repetition,* a letter from Constantine Constantius addressed to "the book's real reader." [61] Here Constantius collapses the fictional form of the book as a whole: he reveals that the young man is his own imaginative creation. "The young man *whom I have brought into being* is a poet" (134). What began as a meditation on the hero ends up as a portrait of the artist as a young man.

In the beginning of the chapter it was noted that "the poet" for Kierkegaard was a typically negative figure, a narrative persona who observes the struggles of others but has no concrete identity or existence of his own. But it was also noted in the analysis of *Fear and Trembling* that the aesthetic sphere bears a curious resemblance to the religious and in fact often seems to approximate the religious in its formal outlines, even though not in its spiritual content. At the end of *Repetition* the discovery that the young man is a poet and an imaginative creation does not negate his religious potential or his aspiring heroism as much as we might expect. The religious movement has been collapsed back into the aesthetic realm, but the aesthetic is also identified and partially redeemed. Kierkegaard's categories have a "dialectical elasticity," as Constantine puts it, that is a source of both logical confusion and imaginative vitality.

The poet, we now learn, is best seen as an anticipation of the religious individual. He is an exception to the demands of the human universal. "He represents the transition to the more properly aristocratic exceptions, namely, the religious exceptions" (134). With the word "transition" the distance between the poetic consciousness and the religious existence suddenly shrinks. Kierkegaard puts it this way in an early entry in his *Papirer:* "It is an extraordinarily sad feeling that grips you when you see the poetic making its appearance

61. "To N——— N———, Esq. / this book's real reader." N——— N——— stands for Nicholas Notabene, another of Kierkegaard's psuedonyms. The book is thus no longer addressed to Regina.

through an individual in the course of his development. For the poetic is indeed the divine woof in the purely human existence: it is the fibres through which the divine sustains existence. . . . The poetic existence is the unconscious sacrifice, the divine *molimina*—it is first in the religious that the sacrifice becomes conscious, the disproportion abolished." [62] In the young man's case, the sacrifice or suffering is still unconscious at the end of the book. "In his earlier letters," Constantine observes, "the movement came much closer to a really religious conclusion; but the instant the temporary suspension is lifted he gets himself again, now however as a poet, and the religious sinks down to the bottom, that is, it remains as an unutterable substratum" (136).

Kierkegaard came to see his whole career as author, in fact, as a movement from "the poet" to the religious writer. "So the aesthetic production is certainly a deceit," he wrote later in *The Point of View for My Work As an Author,* "yet in another sense it is a necessary elimination. The religious is present from the very first instant and has a decisive predominance, but for a while it waits patiently to give the poet leave to talk himself out." [63] As those two modes of being come to seem less incontrovertibly opposed to Kierkegaard, as the possibility emerges of an integral movement from one "stage on life's way" to another instead of a moment of critical choice between them, the form of the meditation on the hero loses its centrality in Kierkegaard's writing. The hero and the poet are no longer so categorically opposed to one another.

In the year following the appearance of *Repetition* and *Fear and Trembling,* Kierkegaard's aesthetic writings, still pseudonymous, take a distinctly more philosophical turn. *The Concept of Dread* and *Philosophical Fragments* are no longer centrally concerned with the problems of personal identity expressed in the figure of the Romantic hero. In *Stages on Life's*

62. Quoted by Grimsley, "Kierkegaard, Vigny, and 'the Poet,'" in rawing, he says, on **Karl Roos.**
63. *The Point of View for My Work As an Author,* trans. Walter Lowrie, Harper Torchbook edition (New York, 1962), pp. 73–74.

Way, published in 1845, Kierkegaard returns to romantic
themes and literary forms, and in the section of this book entitled "Guilty / Not Guilty" he uses a narrative form not unlike that of *Repetition.* A Frater Taciturnus plays the narrator
to the heroic sufferings of another anonymous young man
given the title of Quidam. But although Frater Taciturnus,
like Constantine Constantius, has "invented" his hero, Quidam
is much more his own narrator than the young man of *Repetition* was capable of being. "Guilty / Not Guilty" effects a
synthesis of the opposing figures of poet and hero to a much
greater degree. Quidam's diary at the time of his romantic
crisis is combined with his diary exactly one year later. The
hero is thus able to reflect upon *himself* to a considerable
extent, and the meditation on the hero *ab extra* becomes a
secondary form.

What the figure of the Romantic hero dramatized for
Kierkegaard was a concrete existence and identity that he felt
himself, as writer and "poet," to lack. In a curious reversal o
more common literary notions of mask and role, the figure o
the hero, even when admittedly invented by a poetic mind, i
more real, more authentic, than the consciousness that invent:
him. Kierkegaard is the opposite of Sartre in this respect, a
Jean Starobinski has so brilliantly argued.[64] For Sartre, al
literary masks, heroic ones especially, are inauthentic and in
human. For Kierkegaard, the mask dramatizes the possibilit
of a more authentic, more inward existence. Whereas Sartre
sees the "I" behind the words as the ultimate existential truth
Kierkegaard feels that this "I" is lacking in substance and
validity. "I stand in an altogether poetic relationship to my
work," he writes, "and I am therefore myself a pseudonym." [6]
For Kierkegaard, to assume a persona is not to diminish one'
individuality but to increase it: "Antiquity's *persona—per*

64. "Kierkegaard et les masques," pp. 607–10.
65. Quoted by Croxall, *Kierkegaard Commentary,* p. 7. See also th
journal passage cited by Starobinski, "Kierkegaard et les masques," p. 61:
where Kierkegaard feels his personality as the reflection or the doubl
of others.

sonare—to intensify the voice of the individual while it is still the voice of the individual," Kierkegaard writes.[66] The same holds true when a narrator discovers or invents a hero: a 'unifying power of personality" is posited that resists the erosions of self-conscious thought. Thus Constantine Constantius can say at the end of *Repetition,*

> My dear reader, thou wilt understand that the young man is the focus of interest, whereas I am a transitory figure, like a midwife in relation to the child she has brought to birth. And such in fact is my position, for I have as it were brought him to birth, and therefore as the older person I do the talking. My personality is a presupposition psychologically necessary to force him out, while my personality will never be able to get to the point he has reached, for the primitive power by which he advanced is a new and different factor (137).

In all his writing Kierkegaard remains intensely aware of the negativity of thought and language, highly critical of those premature and self-deluding attempts at seizing existence in its immediate state. But in his own development as author, one can observe the voice of the poet becoming more sure of itself, the aesthetic becoming more sure of the religious substratum beneath it. As Kierkegaard's personality becomes more integrated, the figure of the hero, that intrapersonal "other," becomes less important in his imagination. Like the young man of *Repetition,* Kierkegaard did lose Regina and was unable to effect the heroic integration of temporal and eternal impulses which he had, following the Romantic conceptions of the hero, projected for himself. But like the young man also, he did gain a stronger, more concrete selfhood and a better sense of his aesthetic and religious nature at this time. In fact, Kierkegaard spoke of the writing of *Repetition* and the events surrounding it as the decisive conversion of his life, even though he experienced other spiritual crises before and after.[67]

66. *Journals and Papers,* 1 : 278.
67. See Croxall, *Kierkegaard Studies,* p. 157.

The meditation on the hero provided the imaginative form in which this conversion was dramatized, if not finally resolved. As he put it in *Fear and Trembling,* it is only the religious that redeems the aesthetic out of its conflict with the ethical, but one can also say that it is the aesthetic, in the form of the meditation on the hero, that gave the author access to his own religious nature.

3

Brontë and Lermontov: The Hero In and Out of Time

Wuthering Heights has always been regarded as something of a *lusus naturae* in the history of the English novel. While there are anticipations of it in the novels of Sir Walter Scott (*The Black Dwarf* is a demonstrable source) and reverberations from it in D. H. Lawrence, Emily Brontë's novel seems to stand apart from the traditions and conventions of English prose fiction.[1] The only figure close to Heathcliff in his preeminence and passion is Lovelace, but Richardson's character is a villain and an aristocrat, of which Heathcliff is neither. Like the villains of Gothic novels, Lovelace is defined by clear moral categories. Like other Romantic heroes, Heathcliff has gone beyond such conventional good and evil. *Wuthering Heights* is similarly hard to place in the context of Emily Brontë's own development, if only because so little of her development is known. She took part in the family creation of Angria, the literary game run by the older Charlotte and Branwell; then during the ten years prior to the writing of *Wuthering Heights* she and her younger sister Anne collaborated on the saga of Gondal, in prose and poetry, of which only the poetry survives.[2] While the Gondal saga was full of

1. Winifred Gerin in her recent biography, *Emily Brontë* (Oxford, 1971), pp. 213–14, notes that except for Scott Emily's reading was quite apart from the major English novelists of the nineteenth century. The relevance of *The Black Dwarf* was established by Florence Dry, *The Sources of* Wuthering Heights (Cambridge, 1937).

2. Fannie Ratchford attempts to piece together this epic in *Gondal's Queen: A Novel in Verse by Emily Jane Brontë* (Austin, 1955). Her

conventional heroic figures—lovers, soldiers, and monarchs—
there is little resemblance to the intensity and focus of
Wuthering Heights.

Yet if the sources of the novel in Brontë's developing literary imagination are obscure, the narrative structure of the
finished work is not. It is formally a meditation on the hero;
more specifically, it is a joint recounting by two narrators of
the life and death of a single heroic figure, who for the first
half of the narrative shares the stage with a heroine. The
other characters function as foils, impediments, or alternatives to the central heroic conflict. Heathcliff is not a hero of
religious faith but a hero of romantic love. His daemon is his
possessive passion for Catherine.

To move from Kierkegaard to Emily Brontë is to move
from one extreme of Romanticism to the other, from the
deeply "sentimental," to use Schiller's term, to the intensely
"naïve." Whereas Kierkegaard subjects Romantic themes and
forms to a highly reflective irony, Brontë assimilates them
into a world of personal myth. There is very little of the
literary self-consciousness of *Repetition* and *Fear and Trembling* in *Wuthering Heights.* There are moments of reflexivity,
as when Lockwood fancies himself a King Lear in his cursing,
or when Heathcliff speaks scornfully of Isabella's "picturing in
me a hero of romance and expecting unlimited indulgence
from my chivalrous devotion," [3] but these ironic moments are
only occasional foils for the fundamentally unironic presentation of heroic passion. There is little of Kierkegaard's "negative thinker" in Brontë. Kierkegaard subjects the hero to a
searching philosophical critique; Brontë invests him with an
emotional intensity—an intensity that is sometimes objected
to as being in excess of its vehicle.

This is not to say that *Wuthering Heights* and Heathcliff

---

argument that all Emily's poems were part of the Gondal saga is not
substantiated.

3. *Wuthering Heights,* ed. V. S. Pritchett (Cambridge, Mass., 1956), pp.
14, 128. In all further references to the novel page numbers cited
parenthetically in text are from this edition.

are purely natural and spontaneous creations, owing nothing to literary tradition. This becomes clear once one looks beyond the mainstream of the nineteenth-century novel. As a number of studies of Emily Brontë's sources have shown, there is a good deal of earlier literature being absorbed into *Wuthering Heights*—Shakespearean drama, *Paradise Lost*, Byron, and a number of minor Gothic romances. It is of some interest that these sources are mainly native. Although she had been exposed to French and German literature in her year at the Pension Héger in Belgium, the traces of this foreign influence are slight in comparison.[4] Much more important for the plot of *Wuthering Heights*, along with Scott's *The Black Dwarf*, were an anonymous Gothic romance published in *Blackwoods*, "The Bridegroom of Barma" and a local story of a family near Law Hill whose adopted son's acts of usurpation are strikingly similar to those of Heathcliff's.[5] Of as much interest as the sources themselves is the way in which Brontë uses them. Given enough time and learning, one could write a minor *Road to Xanadu* on the eclectic assimilation by which Brontë's literary memory works. Rather than undertaking the wholesale revival and radical revision to which Kierkegaard subjects his sources, Brontë uses a piecemeal approach in which the original is frequently disguised, perhaps unrecognized by the author herself, and at the same time more organically rooted in the substratum. Since our concern here is with the heroic character of Heathcliff rather than with the various aspects of the plot, I shall give a few examples of the way Brontë unselfconsciously invokes literary support for her hero. Heathcliff is like many other Romantic heroes in re-

4. E. T. A. Hoffmann's story "The Entail" ("Das Majorat") is advanced as an important source by some critics; e.g. Augustin-Lewis Wells, *Les soeurs Brontë et l'etranger* (Paris, 1937), pp. 149–57; Ruth M. Mac Kay, "Irish Heaths and German Cliffs: A Study of the Foreign Sources of *Wuthering Heights,*" *Brigham Young University Studies* 7 (1965) : 28–39. But the most that Brontë could have derived here, aside from some typical Gothic effects used elsewhere, is the device of the narrator's dream as he spends his first night at the castle.

5. Gerin, *Emily Brontë,* pp. 76–80.

viving earlier, more authoritative examples of heroism, largely from outside the conventions of the novel. The only difference is that in him the revival is less explicit.

There is first the influence on Heathcliff of the Gothic villain, the mysterious figure of evil whose fatal effect is most often felt by the beautiful women he seduces and by the good families whose inheritance he usurps. Besides the villain of *The Black Dwarf*, the figure of the devil in James Hogg's *Confessions of a Justified Sinner* seems a possible prototype.[6] But again, it is important to observe the transvaluation of Gothic values that Brontë brings about. As Lowry Nelson puts it, the universe of *Wuthering Heights* "is almost frighteningly without either God or devil; the God of conventional fiction, even a tyrant God, has effectually disappeared, just as the devil of earlier gothic diabolism has disappeared as the archfiend." [7] The same might be said of the social ethics or morals in the novel, as the continuing critical debate over the relative vice and virtue in Heathcliff will attest; they have disappeared as discernible or controlling values.

More important than the Gothic villains as prototypes for Heathcliff, and more truly foreign to the genre of the novel, are the tragic heroes of Shakespeare. The passing allusion to King Lear, mentioned earlier, is largely ironic. However, Catherine's mad scene in chapter 12 echoes Ophelia's madness in *Hamlet:* " 'That's a turkey's,' she murmured to herself; 'and this is a wild duck's; and this is a pigeon's. Ah, they put pigeon's feathers in the pillows—no wonder I couldn't die' " (104). Later Heathcliff echoes Hamlet himself: "If he loved with all the powers of his puny being, he couldn't love as much in eighty years, as I could in a day" (127). As Lew Girdler notes, Heathcliff is not simply a Hamlet figure. He is

6. Ibid., p. 217. I am indebted to Gerin for this source, although I would make less of it.

7. "Night Thoughts on the Gothic Novel," *Yale Review* 52 (1962) : 253. One might say of the Gothic villain, however, as Peter Brooks does of the melodramatic mode in general, that the moral values involved are exaggerated precisely because they are no longer felt to be secure; see "The Melodramatic Imagination," *Partisan Review* 39 (1972) : 209–11.

rather a composite of Shakespeare's tragic heroes—Romeo in his early love for Catherine, Hamlet in his loss of her and in his need for revenge, Richard III in his evil usurpation, Macbeth in his hallucinations, Lear in his isolated rage.[8] As we shall see when we come to *Moby-Dick,* this polymorphous revival of Shakespeare is not unique to *Wuthering Heights;* Brontë is simply more subtle and more sparing in her evocations than Melville.

The presence of Milton's Satan, the archetypal hero of English Romantics such as Blake and Shelley, is also felt in Heathcliff, though less intensely. Catherine makes the identification explicit: "It is as bad as offering Satan a lost soul— Your bliss lies, like his, in inflicting misery . . ." (96). She herself has a Miltonic dream about being cast down from heaven onto Wuthering Heights, and Heathcliff's earlier description of them both looking in on the Linton children in their beautiful, splendid drawing room recalls, in a vague but suggestive way, the passage in Book IV of *Paradise Lost* where Satan looks in on Adam and Eve in Eden. Milton was Mr. Brontë's favorite poet, and he is supposed to have known *Paradise Lost* by heart.[9] The children themselves were prob-

8. Cf. Catherine's mad scene with *Hamlet,* IV, v, 175–78: "There's fennel for you, and columbines; there's rue for you; and here's some for me; we may call it herb of grace o' Sundays; oh, you must wear your rue with a difference." The parallel is also noted by Arnold P. Drew, "Emily Brontë and *Hamlet," Notes & Queries,* n.s. 1 (1954): 81–82, and Lew Girdler, "*Wuthering Heights* and Shakespeare," *Huntington Library Quarterly* 19 (1955–56): 389–90. Cf. Heathcliff's lines with *Hamlet,* V, i, 257–59: "I loved Ophelia; forty thousand brothers / Could not, with all their quantity of love, / Make up my sum." I am indebted to Girdler for this parallel. As V. S. Pritchett suggests in his Introduction to *Wuthering Heights* (p. x) Nelly Dean recalls the Nurse in *Romeo and Juliet.*

9. Gerin, *Emily Brontë,* p. 47. Edgar and Isabella are a parodic Adam and Eve, of course, just as Heathcliff is a Romantically transvalued Satan. Brontë evokes earlier works less by specific verbal echo than by pose and gesture; even in the allusion to Ophelia's speech, where verbal parallels are identifiable, it is the gesture of plucking (flowers, feathers) that carries the burden of the similitude. For an interesting discussion of the "valorization of gesture" in Romantic prose fiction, see Brooks, "The Melodramatic Imagination," pp. 207–09.

ably more versed in Byron, however, and we find here a similar case of an atmosphere that transcends the specificity of
allusion. Heathcliff is a composite of Byronic gestures and
emotions.

Charlotte Brontë signals the debt to Byron when she says
of Heathcliff in her Editor's Preface, "These solitary traits of
humanity omitted, we should say he was child neither of
Lascar or gypsy, but a man's shape animated by demon life—
a Ghoul—an Afreet" (xxviii). Apparently unconsciously, she
is remembering "The Giaour":

> Go—and with Gouls and Afrits rave;
> Till these in horror shrink away
> From Spectre more accursed than they!

What is paramount in Byron's heroes that is generally lacking
in Shakespeare's tragic heroes and Milton's Satan is the
primary interest in romantic love. Heathcliff's heroism is in-
separable from his love for Catherine. Like Heathcliff in the
novel, the Giaour has a vision of his dead lover's ghost, and
his meditations on her grave may have suggested one of
Heathcliff's more macabre schemes for uniting himself with
his beloved:

> She sleeps beneath the wandering wave—
> Ah! had she but an earthly grave,
> This breaking heart and throbbing head
> Should seek and share her narrow bed.[10]

Another poem of Byron's entitled "The Dream" shows a remarkable similarity in plot outline with *Wuthering Heights.*
The dreamer sees two young people, in love as brother and
sister. The girl loves another as well, the boy flees and travels
in exotic lands, then returns. The girl, now older, is wed to
someone she does not love; the boy also marries someone he
does not love. The girl goes mad, the boy is left alone in

10. *The Works of Lord Byron,* ed. E. H. Coleridge (London, 1904),
3 : 123 (ll. 784–86) and 136 (ll. 1123–26). The reunion in the lady's grave
does occur in *The Bridegroom of Barna,* however.

"Hatred and Contention," though eventually he reaches some understanding with "the quick Spirit of the Universe." [11]

What is interesting about this poem is that it is thoroughly autobiographical, dealing with Byron's love for Mary Chaworth and his lack of love for his wife. Emily Brontë, in fact, though probably unintentionally, supplements the plot of this poem by adapting an incident in Moore's *Life of Byron* also involving Mary Chaworth. When Heathcliff overhears Catherine telling Nelly it would degrade her to marry him, missing, of course, her subsequent declaration, he reenacts a situation in which the infatuated Byron overheard Mary saying to her maid, "Do you think I could care for that lame boy?" Byron was deeply hurt, according to Moore, and ran out into the night.[12] Given the interest in Byron, it is also not difficult to see the relations between Heathcliff and Catherine as a purer version of the relationship of Byron and Augusta, as known at the time, or as dramatized in *Manfred,* another Byronic work echoed in *Wuthering Heights.*[13]

In other words, Brontë's use of Byron confirms a cardinal point about Byron's literary reputation, namely, that his life was fully as influential as his works. Although Heathcliff comes trailing clouds of Shakespearean and Miltonic glory, he grows up in the hothouse of Byronic legend. What distinguishes him as a hero from his Byronic predecessors, and from Emily's earlier attempts at Byronic heroes in her Gondal poems, is his emotional presentness. Byron's Giaour and Corsair and even Manfred are interesting because of their distance. The essence

11. *Works,* 4 : 40, 41 (ll. 189, 196). This correspondence was discovered by Anne Lapraik Livermore, "Byron and Emily Brontë," *Quarterly Review* 300 (1962) : 337–44.

12. Gerin, *Emily Brontë,* p. 45.

13. Livermore, "Byron and Emily Brontë," p. 338: "It becomes possible to perceive that probably *Wuthering Heights* was planned as an intertwining of *The Dream* with the facts as then known of Byron's ambiguous love for his half-sister, his marriage to Anne Isabella, and her flight from him." Helen Brown's "The Influence of Byron on Emily Brontë," *Modern Language Review* 34 (1939) : 374–81, deals mainly with Byron's influence on the poetry.

of their heroism is their obscurity: "Behold—but who hath seen, or e're shall see, / Man as himself, the secret spirit free" ("The Corsair," ll. 247–48); "You could not penetrate his soul, but found, / Despite your wonder, to your own he wound" ("Lara," ll. 377–78). Healthcliff's mysterious origins and his three-year rise to eminence are relatively unimportant to his status as hero. Past deeds of glory or of secret sin do not interest us so much as the forceful and assertive presence, what J. Hillis Miller has called the "permanent and unceasing attitude of aggression." [14] There is a force and a substance in Heathcliff that reveals the passivity and hollowness of Byron's heroes by contrast.

Such a comparison is not intended to dismiss the Byronic hero as a sham, but to distinguish his existential nature from Heathcliff's. Byron's heroes are simply more alienated than Heathcliff, more divorced from any immediacy, or, to recall the terms of our previous discussions of the hero, more isolated from any ground of being. A poem of Brontë's written some eight years before *Wuthering Heights*, "The soft unclouded blue of air," expresses this Byronic dilemma explicitly. The speaker reposes in the ground of nature and immortality recalled from early childhood:

> The soft unclouded blue of air;
> The earth as golden-green and fair
> And bright as Eden's used to be:
> That air and earth have rested me.
>
> Laid on the grass I lapsed away;
> Sank back to childhood's day:
> All harsh thoughts perished, memory mild
> Subdued both grief and passion wild.

Beside her, however, sits an anonymous Byronic "iron man." The speaker wonders if this imposing figure retains any connection with the immediacy of nature or childhood:

14. *The Disappearance of God* (Cambridge, Mass., 1963), p. 167.

But did the sunshine even now
That bathed his stern and swarthy brow,
Oh, did it wake—I long to know—
One whisper, one sweet dream in him,
One lingering joy that, years ago,
Had faded—lost in distance dim?

That iron man was born like me,
And he was once an ardent boy:
He must have felt, in infancy,
The glory of a summer sky.[15]

In spite of her desire to connect this hero with the ground she herself feels a part of, the speaker ends with a confession of her failure to do so.

In the light of this earlier effort to give the Romantic hero some support in a mythical realm of nature, Brontë's achievement in *Wuthering Heights* becomes more clear. Heathcliff is an "iron man" successfully provided with a childhood and an intense communion with the landscape. There has been considerable disagreement among critics of *Wuthering Heights* as to the specifically human nature of Heathcliff. Dorothy Van Ghent suspected that "Heathcliff might *really* be a demon," participating, as she saw him, in "the raw, inhuman reality of anonymous natural energies." [16] Other critics emphasize the sympathetic psychological presentation of Heathcliff as a per-

15. *The Complete Poems of Emily Jane Brontë*, ed. C. W. Hatfield (New York, 1941), pp. 104–06. The speaker of the poem is probably a Gondal character.

16. *The English Novel: Form and Function* (New York, 1953), pp. 154–157. See also Philip Drew, "Charlotte Brontë as a Critic of *Wuthering Heights*," *Nineteenth-Century Fiction* 18 (1964): 365–81, who suspects Heathcliff of being a bona fide ghoul or afreet. Thomas Moser uses a more psychological idiom: "Over a century ago Emily Brontë dramatized what Freud subsequently called the id. She discovered and symbolized in Heathcliff . . . that part of us we know so little about. . . ." ("What is the Matter with Emily Jane? Conflicting Impulses in *Wuthering Heights*," in *The Victorian Novel*, ed. Ian Watt (Oxford, 1971), p. 183.

son who suffers and reacts to rejection and abuse.[17] The only one to perceive the complex and shifting relation of self and ground is J. Hillis Miller, and his description of their interdependence is worth quoting at length:

> For Emily Brontë no human being is self-sufficient, and all suffering derives ultimately from isolation. A person is most himself when he participates most completely in the life of something outside himself. The self outside the self is the substance of a man's being in both the literal and the etymological senses of the word. It is the ultimate stuff of the self, and it is also that which "stands beneath" the self as its foundation and its support. A man's real being is outside himself. . . . The poems and the novel suggest three possible entities with which the self may be fused: nature, God, and another human being.[18]

I would, however, qualify Miller's analysis in two ways. First I would make it more specific: it is only the heroic individual (Heathcliff and to a lesser extent Catherine) who has this outside substance available. It is only the exceptional self that is capable of such participation, it being clearly beyond any other character in the novel. Second, I would rule out the possibility of God as an entity with which the self can fuse. God has not simply disappeared for Brontë in *Wuthering Heights,* He has been replaced by the other two ontological entities that Miller invokes, nature and the object of romantic love.[19]

17. See, e.g., John Hagan, "The Control of Sympathy in *Wuthering Heights,*" *Nineteenth-Century Fiction* 21 (1967) : 305–23. Other studies that stress the humanity, moral and psychological, of the hero are W. A. Craik's excellent chapter on *Wuthering Heights* in her *The Brontë Novels* (London, 1968), and F. H. Langman, "*Wuthering Heights,*" *Essays in Criticism* 15 (1965) : 294–312.

18. *The Disappearance of God,* p. 172.

19. Miller in fact has trouble establishing the relevance of a Christian God to his analysis. He brings Him in by taking seriously the caricature of Methodism in Joseph, and by making too explicit and orthodox a very implicit and displaced Calvinism in Brontë's writing.

The plentitude of nature and the immediacy of love—together these substances provide the ground for Heathcliff's and Catherine's heroics. Kierkegaard would reject such a naïve resolution of the metaphysical dilemma, but Brontë is neither philosophically nor theologically inclined and adopts the natural super-naturalism of Romantic tradition quite uncritically.

The relationship of Heathcliff to the literary archetypes of the hero (Gothic, Shakespearean, Miltonic, Byronic) in fact resembles the relationship of the heroic figure in the novel to this metaphysical ground. In both cases there is a lack of full differentiation, a tendency of the individual to draw energy and sustenance from a powerful source without achieving full autonomy. Thus Heathcliff echoes Hamlet in the same way that he evokes the moors: as an echo that cannot easily be distinguished from the original sound. The relationship to sources, literary and metaphysical, is almost symbiotic, which is both a strength in the hero and a limitation. As we have seen with Kierkegaard, and as we shall with Lermontov, there are other meditations on the hero where immediate relatedness is notably lacking, where autonomy is fully achieved, but at the expense of strength.

The most heightened invocations of the natural ground in which hero and heroine participate come at the moments of greatest crisis in their relationship. It is when Catherine tells Nelly she is unable to marry Heathcliff and prefers Edgar Linton as a husband that she bursts out with her famous analogy and identification: "My love for Heathcliff resembles the eternal rocks beneath—a source of little visible delight, but necessary. Nelly, I *am* Heathcliff . . ." (70). This moment marks the initial sundering of their romantic identity with one another. There is the equally famous reunion *d' outre-tombe,* where Heathcliff conjures up Catherine's ghost and dies to join it. Lockwood's wondering "how anyone could ever imagine unquiet slumbers, for the sleepers in that quiet earth" (287) misses the point, as usual with him, in that it assumes that their ghosts must be tormented still to walk the moors. Their spirits become *genii loci,* ghosts with a local habitation, rather than Byronic exiles doomed to wander the earth.

This is not to say that Brontë is a literal believer in the popular superstitions of the highlands that she evokes. Her supernaturalism is not a simple animistic belief but the more complex assent that Coleridge called "poetic faith": "My endeavors should be directed to persons and characters supernatural, or at least romantic; yet so as to transfer from our inward nature a human interest and a semblance of truth sufficient to procure for these shadows of imagination that willing suspension of disbelief for the moment, which constitutes poetic faith." [20] Brontë, it seems to me, is dramatizing the supernatural in much this way—as an outward supernaturalism given substance by an inward human interest of a more natural kind. It is not that the supernatural elements can simply be reduced to a more basic human psychology, but that such a psychology is used as an imaginative support.

The central crisis in the love of the hero and heroine makes clear the nature of this supporting psychological interest in *Wuthering Heights:* it is an intense evocation of childhood. Between their initial separation and final reunion Heathcliff and Catherine attempt a reconciliation in the social realm and fail. Catherine is psychically torn between the claims of Linton and the claims of Heathcliff. In the course of the heroine's mental breakdown Nelly Dean observes that "our fiery Catherine was no better than a wailing child" (106). Catherine goes on to validate this rather crude perception:

> Nelly, I'll tell you what I thought, and what has kept recurring and recurring till I feared for my reason—I thought as I lay there, with my head against that table leg, and my eyes dimly discerning the grey square of the window, that I was enclosed in the oak-panelled bed at home; and my heart ached with some great grief which, just waking, I could not recollect—I pondered, and

20. *Biographia Literaria,* ed. J. Shawcross (Oxford, 1907), 2 : 6.

worried myself to discover what it could be; and most
strangely, the whole last seven years of my life grew a
blank! I did not recall that they had been at all. I was a
child; my father was just buried, and my misery arose
from the separation that Hindley had ordered between
me, and Heathcliff—I was laid alone, for the first time,
and, rousing from a dismal doze after a night of weeping
—I lifted my hand to push the panels aside, it struck the
table top! I swept it along the carpet, and then, memory
burst in—my late anguish was swallowed in a paroxysm of
despair—I cannot say why I felt so wildly wretched—it
must have been temporary derangement for there is
scarcely cause—But, supposing at twelve years old, I had
been wrenched from the Heights, and every early association, and my all in all, as Heathcliff was at that time,
had been converted, at a stroke into Mrs. Linton, the lady
of Thrushcroft Grange, and the wife of a stranger; and
exile, and outcast, thenceforth, from what had been my
world—You may fancy a glimpse of the abyss where I
grovelled (106–07)!

Many commentators have noted the regressive qualities in the
love of Catherine and Heathcliff, which are simply made explicit at this point. The present crisis in the Grange is inter-
woven with the past crisis at the Heights in a way that makes
it quite difficult to distinguish them in Catherine's speech. The
intimations of timelessness in the love of Catherine and
Heathcliff are grounded in the nature of the moors, but they
are also strongly supported by these recollections of early
childhood. Brontë is often interpreted in a Freudian context,
but given the general chastity of the relationship of her hero
and heroine, she seems closer to Wordsworth.[21] This concern
with nature as experienced by the mind of the young child

21. See Thomas Vogler's introduction to his *Twentieth-Century Interpretations of* Wuthering Heights (Englewood Cliffs N.J., 1968), p. 10 for a
perceptive comparison of Brontë with Wordsworth and Blake on the
treatment of visionary childhood.

can be seen in the poem quoted above: "He must have felt, in infancy, / The glory of a summer sky."

In fact, it is primarily in association with the emotions of early childhood that nature makes its presence felt in the novel. If one compares Brontë with Hardy, another novelist of the English landscape, one is reminded of how little specific, concrete nature detail is given in *Wuthering Heights*. The winds and the moors provide a general atmospheric background, but very little visual imagery. An exception is the mention of various birds and their nests—for example, Nelly notices a pair of ousels building a nest as she approaches Heathcliff to tell him of Catherine's death—but the symbolism of childhood is obvious: Heathcliff is the cuckoo raised in the nest of another. We are reminded here of Mr. Earnshaw's initial indiscretion with the stray child, even as we are given a natural image for his human childhood. A similar fusion of landscape and early recollection occurs in the description of Heathcliff entering the Grange to take the younger Catherine up to the Heights: "It was the same room into which he had been ushered, as a guest, eighteen years before: the same moon shone through the window; and the same autumn landscape lay outside. . . . Heathcliff advanced to the hearth. Time had little altered his person either. There was the same man . . . " (242). Brontë weaves together the different levels of "sameness" by the repetition of the adjective; the initial memory spreads out quickly to embrace the landscape and the earlier self.

What is remarkable in Brontë's evocation of childhood as the basis of her hero's identity is that it rarely makes one feel that Heathcliff is merely childish. The child is the father of the man, but the man is not therefore to be taken less seriously. What *Wuthering Heights* anticipates, in a curious way, is the interpretation of the literary hero given half a century later by Otto Rank in *The Myth of the Birth of the Hero*. Not only does Heathcliff have the requisite mysterious birth and orphanhood described by Rank (unlike all other Romantic heroes treated in this study), but he is also a figure of revolt against an oppressive family structure. "The true hero of the romance, is therefore, the ego, which finds itself in the hero, through its first heroic act, i.e., the revolt against the father." Brontë differs from Rank, however, in the way she uses this psychological insight—as a means of investing the hero with a renewed emotional intensity, instead of as a means of demythologizing the myth.[22]

There is something of the willfulness of the child in the self-assertions of Catherine and Heathcliff. On the one hand their relationship is a romantic identification of lover with loved one; on the other hand it is a partnership in resistance and rebellion against adult authority—an adult authority falsely assumed by Hindley, the older brother. Thus in her mad scene Catherine recalls the traumatic separation from Heathcliff that had been ordered by Hindley. To use a more technical vocabulary, Brontë seems to be dramatizing a particular stage of childhood, the stage described by Erik Erikson as "Early Childhood and the Will to Be Oneself." "This whole stage," Erikson writes, "becomes a *battle for autonomy*. . . . It becomes decisive for the ratio between loving good will and hateful self-insistence, between co-operation and willfulness, between self-expression and compulsive self-restraint or meek compliance." [23] The struggle is clearer in Catherine than in Heathcliff, perhaps, but Erikson's terms describe quite well the emotional content of many of the acts and expressions of both.

From this psychoanalytic perspective, Heathcliff can be seen

22. Quote is from *The Myth of the Birth of the Hero,* trans. Robbins and Jelliffe (New York, 1952), p. 81. Cf. ibid., p. 82: "Myths are, therefore, created by adults, by means of retrograde childhood fantasies, the hero being credited with the myth-maker's personal infantile history."

23. *Identity, Youth and Crisis* (New York, 1968), pp. 108–09. It is tempting to use Erikson further to describe Heathcliff's retentive kind of revenge ("Avarice is growing with him a besetting sin," Catherine says, though this is never really shown [87]). Heathcliff's usurpation of the property and his sudden relinquishing of it are recalled by Erikson's emphasis on "the ability—and doubly felt inability" at this stage "to coordinate a number of highly conflicting action patterns characterized by the tendencies of 'holding on' and 'letting go' " (p. 107). A final intriguing point of similarity between Brontë and Erikson is the emphasis on the social institution of the law as a safeguard for the individual's autonomy at this stage.

as a figure from a "family romance"—as Rank, following Freud, called it—who has been placed within a realistic family history. He is literally a stray child discovered in Liverpool, but in terms of the family chronicle that constitutes so much of *Wuthering Heights,* he is the stranger, the outsider, eventually the usurper. Herein lies his essential difference from Catherine: unlike her he has no legitimate social role within the family—his three years abroad count for nothing when he returns. The focus of the novel is on his asocial, antisocial being rather than on Catherine's social conflict. "If Catherine is the impetus of the story, Heathcliff is its structure," W. A. Craik observes. "Lockwood asks Ellen for his history; he gets exactly and completely what he asked for. Every detail Emily Brontë reveals is present because it is relevant to one or other of Heathcliff's two ruling forces—love and the urge to revenge —whether it is recognized at the time or is merely seen to be so in retrospect." [24] *Wuthering Heights* thus cannot be seen ultimately as a novel of psychosocial or family conflict, however sensitively it probes some of these issues. In its imaginative structure the book belongs to the genre of the meditation on the hero, and it is to the terms of my first chapter that I should like to return here.

Wuthering Heights is a meditation on a hero who exists outside the continuum of social history. We have seen how his heroic action, gesture, and diction incorporate traces of earlier literary heroes, but Heathcliff is not so much a hero of an earlier age as one who belongs, through nature and childhood, to a mythical permanence. In spite of all obvious differences, he is like Kierkegaard's Abraham in this one respect: he is a hero of timelessness trying to enter a world of time. It is important that we first meet Heathcliff as a fully developed figure in Lockwood's introduction to *Wuthering Heights.* Even though we are presented with the story of his childhood by Nelly Dean, we are given little sense of the development of his character after he is introduced into the Earnshaw family. From the first he shows the autonomy, defiance, and general

24. Craik, *The Brontë Novels,* p. 22.

inscrutability that characterize him throughout the novel. It is true, as a number of critics have argued, that his later acts of brutality are shown to grow out of his mistreatment at the hands of various members of the household,[25] but it is significant that Brontë characteristically presents the causal sequence in reverse. For example, we learn of Heathcliff's brutal attack on Hindley from Isabella in chapter 17. Yet the underlying reason for Heathcliff's rage—that he has been trying frantically to communicate with Catherine, corpse and ghost, when he finds the door barred—is only revealed in chapter 29. The genesis of the heroic rage is less important than the expression of it, and we never see the hero in the process of becoming.

Like Abraham, Heathcliff is a hero in the eyes of eternity, but as in Abraham's case also, this eternity is unable to turn its back on time. Kierkegaard would find Heathcliff a hero of the aesthetic, the lower immediacy, rather than of the higher immediacy like Abraham. Yet neither can fully resign himself to living out of the temporal world. Abraham cannot simply accept God's command because he must retain his love for Isaac, in order to realize the paradox of faith. "It is about the temporal, the finite, everything turns in this case." Heathcliff is certainly no Knight of Faith, but neither can he be a Knight of Infinite Resignation. Heathcliff is unable to remain an outsider, ultimately because of his love for Catherine, but also because he has been brought into the family early on. He actively tries to enter into the realm of history, which for Brontë is the genealogical history of the Earnshaws and the Lintons. He was perhaps brought to Wuthering Heights to take the place of a dead son—we never know what moved Mr. Earnshaw to bring him home in the first place—but he is only given that son's first name, not the surname. The name Heathcliff suggests the breadth and height of the natural landscape, but in the social system of family naming it is only half an identity. It is not that Heathcliff actively worked to become

---

25. See Hagan, "The Control of Sympathy"; Craik, *The Brontë Novels;* and Edgar Shannon, "Lockwood's Dreams and the Exegesis of *Wuthering Heights," Nineteenth-Century Fiction* 14 (1959) : 95–109.

Mr. Earnshaw's favorite (although he does become this) or that his desire to marry Catherine is a conscious wish to attain social respectability. But because of the situation he is placed in at the start and is unwilling or unable to resist, he is forced to seek a way of relating to the sequence of generations into which he has been thrust. His love for Catherine is the precipitating crisis. In and of himself, Heathcliff is not a divided self, but as he finds his substance in Catherine ("How can I live without my soul?" he asks on learning of her death), he experiences the alienation that is characteristic of the Romantic hero.

Wuthering Heights is often seen as a novel of the conflict between nature and society, but it seems to me that the conflict can be defined more accurately in terms of temporality. The basic clash is between the values of permanence and the values of change, and though permanence is more commonly associated with natural things, nature can change and social institutions can seem permanent. Thus in her famous declaration of divided loyalties, Catherine identifies her affection for Edgar Linton with a natural image subject to mutability: "My love for Linton is like the foliage in the woods. Time will change it, I'm aware, as winter changes the trees—my love for Heathcliff resembles the eternal rocks beneath . . ." (70). Linton, like Heathcliff, is eventually buried in the quiet earth beside Catherine, but long before his death, Nelly tells us, "Time brought him resignation," a natural healing to which Heathcliff is not privy.[26]

Conversely, in Heathcliff's scheme of revenge, we see a man closely allied with nature skillfully employing the means of society, as Arnold Kettle was the first to point out: "What Heathcliff does is to use against his enemies with complete ruthlessness their own weapons . . . of money and arranged marriages. He gets power over them by the classic methods of

26. Two useful discussions of the temporality of the novel are Robert F. Gleckner's "Time in *Wuthering Heights*," *Criticism* 1 (1959) : 328–38; and Thomas A. Vogler, "Story and History in *Wuthering Heights*," *Twentieth-Century Interpretations*, pp. 78–99.

the ruling class, expropriation and property deals." [27] What Kettle's Marxist analysis ignores, however, is the degree to which Heathcliff is trying to participate in the social milieu of the landlords; he is hardly a proletarian Robin Hood. For a while, at least, Heathcliff is actively trying to enter into the social realm by grafting his scion, young Linton, onto the family tree and by becoming himself the master of the property. At this stage in his career Heathcliff resembles most closely the villain of the Gothic novel, whose villainy often consists in interfering with a legitimate inheritance. "I want the triumph of seeing *my* descendant fairly lord of their estates; my child hiring their children, to till their fathers' land for wages," Heathcliff tells Nelly (177). Though these dynastic ambitions are a product of his desire for revenge, they involve him quite deeply in the realm of society. Yet in Heathcliff's hands the mechanisms of social transference and change become a means of establishing the permanence and finality of his revenge: "I get levers and mattocks to demolish the two houses . . ." (274).

The mythical permanence of the hero is therefore not sufficient unto itself. It needs, for a variety of reasons, to integrate itself with the ongoing processes of social history. If Heathcliff and Catherine could simply *be* one another out on the moors as children, they would be happy, but their inevitable growth brings inevitable socialization. Only in death can they get back out of time, and although this is the ultimate point they reach, it cannot be seized directly. As Blake puts it, eternity is in love with the productions of time. It is not really that Heathcliff wants to get into the stream of history and change, but that he must, because he has mortgaged part of his mythical identity to history by loving Catherine. Even after her death he wants Catherine back, and his revenge is an attempt ultimately to subdue the temporal to the eternal. However, the pursuit of this ultimate goal involves at least a temporary participation in temporality.

The need for myth to enter into history seems to me to lie

27. *An Introduction to the English Novel* (London, 1951), 1 : 149–50.

behind a number of the scenes and motifs in the novel, indeed
behind what Bachelard would call its "poetics of space." The
motif I am referring to has to do with the attempt of a force
to get into a room or house from out of doors, a motif of
breaking and entering which has often been noticed in this
novel and variously interpreted.[28] The most striking instance
of this motif is the incident in Lockwood's much-interpreted
dream during his first night at the Heights, when he brutalizes
the ghost of the child Catherine Earnshaw trying to get in
through the window. While it is possible to read this dream
in the light of Lockwood's rejection of the young woman at
Bath, or in the light of the brutal treatment he has received as
a guest at the house, the forced entry and resistance to it become such a pervasive motif in the novel that they transcend
the particularity of Lockwood's character and experience. In
fact, what the ending of the novel suggests, with Heathcliff's
pursuit of Catherine's ghost and his own death before the
same open window, is that Lockwood's dream has been a negative response to a vision that really belongs to Heathcliff.
Whereas Lockwood bars the way, Heathcliff has actively solic-
ited the ghost to come in.

To say that the entry of the ghost into the house is an entry
of myth into time may seem like special pleading here. But
notice how pervasively the houses in the novel are identified
with history. Immediately before entering the Heights for the
first time Lockwood notices the date over the door: 1500. Some
structures are subject to decay, like the chapel; others, like the
Grange, are subject to improvement. But all are involved in
the movement from one generation to another. It is also significant that Brontë sets her novel some two generations earlier
than the time at which she is writing. The house is the focus
of the genealogy that is given piecemeal throughout the narrative.

The initial act of extralegal entry is, of course, Heathcliff's

28. See Van Ghent, *The English Novel;* Moser, "What's the Matter
with Emily Jane?" and the more sophisticated Ronald E. Fine, "Lockwood's Dreams and the Key to *Wuthering Heights," Nineteenth-Century
Fiction* 24 (1969) : 16–30.

arrival at the Heights wrapped in Mr. Earnshaw's greatcoat. "Mrs. Earnshaw was ready to fling it out of doors," we are told (30), but her husband imposes his will on the family and the child remains. There is then the scene where Heathcliff and Catherine look in through the windows of the Linton Grange and are treated harshly as intruders. Both are taken into the house after the dogs attack them, but Heathcliff is thrown out for cursing. Heathcliff is then driven to leave the Heights when he overhears Catherine say it would degrade her to marry him. After three years he attempts another series of entries into the Grange, which become more and more violent. He is able to enter the Heights now, and eventually gains possession of it, but with Catherine's death this becomes a hollow victory. He is master of the property but is still unable to belong to its history.

Chapter 29 is particularly rich in variations on this theme, and the association of the house with the values of temporality is clear. Nelly and the younger Catherine are seated in the library when Heathcliff's approach is announced by a servant, who asks if he should "bar the door in his face" (242). Heathcliff successfully intrudes, however. There follows the passage quoted earlier: "It was the same room into which he had been ushered, as a guest, eighteen years before: the same moon shone through the window; and the same autumn landscape lay outside." But the interior of the room has significantly changed, for the portraits of Catherine and Edgar hang on the wall. Heathcliff is permanent and unchanging ("Time had little altered his person. . . . There was the same man"), but Catherine has been transformed by time—into the artificial image of the portrait, and into the natural image of her daughter. Both these time-bound images Heathcliff has come to claim as his own. As he talks to Nelly, however, he reveals his more avid pursuit of Catherine's ghost, a manifestation of her eternal presence. It is here that he tells about an earlier scene of forced entry:

> Having reached the Heights, I rushed eagerly to the door. It was fastened; and, I remember, that accursed Earnshaw

and my wife opposed my entrance. I remember stopping to kick the breath out of him, and then hurrying upstairs to my room, and hers—I looked around impatiently—I felt her by me—I could *almost* see her, and yet I *could not!* I ought to have sweat blood then from the anguish of my yearning, from the fervour of my supplications to have but one glimpse (245–246)!

At this point Heathcliff seems to sense the futility of his attempt to break into the family as a revenge for his earlier exclusion. "When I sat in the house with Hareton, it seemed that on going out I should meet her; when I walked on the moors I should meet her coming in. When I went from home, I hastened to return, she *must* be somewhere at the Heights, I was certain" (246). The house no longer contains her spirit, either to love or to take revenge on. In a curious reversal of their positions, Heathcliff is now inside the house, soliciting her to come in and haunt him. Catherine's ghost does not come of its own accord, apparently: Heathcliff must will it to reenter his own temporal existence. Only then, in the logic of the book's double time scheme, can he leave this existence behind. Having entered the world of time on a false basis, the hero must work his way back out, into the communion of the supernatural. The open window Nelly discovers in the room where she finds Heathcliff dead recalls the open window that led to Catherine's death earlier. It is the emblem of a final retreat from the world of time.

Thus Heathcliff never does become "a hero of our time." Just as his blood passes through the genealogy of the Earnshaws and the Lintons without leaving a trace, his entry into the continuum of history never really takes place. He is a hero who tries to force his way into a world of past, present, and future, but his actions, like the narrative itself, only come full circle. In one sense it is Heathcliff's triumph, but in another sense his identity never gains the temporal fullness of humanity. As a figure he gradually reverts back to the ground from which his heroism emerged; this is the way I interpret the softening of his vengeful resolve when he begins to see Catherine's image in every cloud and tree. The culmination of this reversion comes when he is literally buried beneath the quiet earth. Thus as a hero Heathcliff remains archaic and primitive, eternally out of date; *Wuthering Heights* is thus what we have called a retrospective meditation on the hero as gestalt: a figure from the heroic past is considered from the perspective of the unheroic present. The figure of Hareton Earnshaw, however, presents the complementary mode of the hero in development. The revenger's tragedy is succeeded, chronologically, by a miniature Bildungsroman.

Whether the marriage of Hareton and Catherine Linton is an adequate resolution of the conflicts in the novel is open to question. My own feeling is that the marriage works on a thematic level, but that it lacks the imaginative intensity of the love between Heathcliff and the older Catherine. The resolution works thematically because it shows a merging of the natural self and the social context in an organic continuity of time. Hareton is the successor to Heathcliff in his intractableness and unsociability, in his exclusion from social life. Through the natural influence and cultural tutelage of the younger Catherine he is reclaimed for the family, reintegrated into the genealogy of the novel after being dispossessed by Heathcliff. Brontë presents the shift as analogous to the change in Shakespeare's plays from the tragedies to the later romances. There are reminders of *The Tempest* in the relationship of Hareton and Catherine—for example, the "discovery" of them at their lessons, recalling Prospero's revelation of Ferdinand and Miranda playing chess. Hareton appears initially as Caliban but becomes a Ferdinand as upon his nature nurture *is* made to stick.

What is interesting for our discussion of the meditation on the hero is the way Brontë uses the Bildungs-motif as a kind of coda to her meditation on the heroic gestalt of Heathcliff. Although Heathcliff finally abandons his assault on the world of time, his surrogate Hareton is educated into the progression of family history. It is clear, however, that the price that is paid for this resolution is the sacrifice of the heroic substance. Hareton is a Heathcliff only in speech and dress. Vestiges of the willfulness of the older pair remain—Hareton is educated by slaps on the cheek—and, in teaching him to read, Catherine is righting one of the wrongs committed against Heathcliff in the beginning, which was to deny him access to books. But there is no sense that Hareton is thereby developing a potential heroism within himself. The shift in modes provides a thematic resolution of the conflict between permanence and change, but the emotionally charged myth of the hero is replaced by a more stereotyped romance. The story of Hareton runs the story of the adult Heathcliff in reverse, but it fails to be a true mediation between the mythical permanence of the hero himself and the historical progression of "our time." We are left with the problem, in the words of Robert Frost, of what to make of a diminished thing.

The attempt to complement the meditation on a hero of the past with a heroic Bildungsroman was something that we noted in Kierkegaard, of course. *Repetition* complements *Fear and Trembling* in this manner, and within *Fear and Trembling* itself the sketch of the merman complements the meditations on Abraham. I would add another example here of the complementarity of the two modes in Mary Shelley's *Frankenstein*, which is closer to *Wuthering Heights* than are Kierkegaard's two novels and which may even be regarded as an influence.[29]

Frankenstein, in fact, is a Bildungsroman that turns into a revenger's tragedy, the reverse of the sequence we have noted in *Wuthering Heights*. The Bildungs-motif is present in each of the concentric circles of the narrative. Robert Walton briefly sketches his early education in his first letter to his sister, reminding her of the reading in their uncle's library

29. Although positive evidence is lacking, Gerin thinks that some of Mary Shelley's novels were familiar to Emily Brontë, either through publication or review in *Blackwoods*, which the Brontë children read extensively in back numbers. *Frankenstein* was reviewed, with generous plot summary, in *Blackwoods* of March 1818.

that led him to a conquest of the North Pole. Victor Frankenstein narrates at greater length to Walton the story of his
early reading in Cornelius Agrippa, his father's disparagement
of such "sad trash," and his rebellious continuation of his
studies. From here he proceeds to the university and the
fatal specialization of his apprenticeship. Finally, in a more
fantastic turn of events than anything the horror movies have
envisioned, the monster sits his creator down in a hut on Mont
Blanc and narrates the story of *his* education—first his struggles with the rudiments of perception, then his acquisition of
language, and finally his formal education: *Paradise Lost,*
Plutarch's *Lives,* and *The Sorrows of Young Werther.*

But this series of Bildungsromans leads to a tragic conclusion. Like Heathcliff, the monster tries to break into the world
of human society, and also like Heathcliff, he is driven out. He
becomes Milton's Satan rather than Milton's Adam (with
whom he previously compared himself), just as Frankenstein
is transformed from the "Modern Prometheus" of the subtitle
to the tyrannical Jupiter of *Prometheus Unbound.* (When it
comes to Romantic myth-making Mary Shelley is more sophisticated and more explicit than Emily Brontë.) Neither the
monster nor Victor Frankenstein becomes a specifically heroic
figure in the sense in which we have defined the hero here,
but they become locked in a master–slave relationship that
leads to an accelerating tragedy of revenge.

Thus whereas *Wuthering Heights* offers the novel of apprenticeship as a means of resolving the tragically heroic conflict
Heathcliff has experienced from the start, *Frankenstein* derives
the revenger's tragedy from a novel of education gone awry.
The only consolation at the end of Mary Shelley's novel is that
Walton, the would-be conqueror of one of nature's secrets, is
persuaded to turn back from his quest by Frankenstein's example. Walton is perhaps to be compared with Hareton in
Wuthering Heights, as a surrogate survivor, but Mary Shelley
devotes a good deal less time to Walton's recovery than Brontë
does to Hareton's. Unlike the monster and Frankenstein, on
the other hand, Heathcliff and Catherine seem to achieve a

positive reconciliation in death. One could hardly imagine any
thing *but* unquiet slumbers for the former pair.

A further similarity between *Frankenstein* and *Wutherin*
Heights, again with significant differences, has to do with th
narrative structure of the two novels. The tale within the tal
within the tale of *Frankenstein* finds a rather precise parallel i
the interlocking narratives of Lockwood, Nelly Dean, and, fo
a brief space, Isabella—a "Chinese puzzle box" of narrators, a
Kierkegaard would call it.[30] The major difference here, as
indicated in chapter 1, is that Mary Shelley's narrators ar
telling their own stories, not meditating on a hero. I have re
served for last a discussion of the narrators of *Wutherin*
Heights and the relation of the hero to his audience, largel
because the narrators in this novel seem to me much mor
caught up in the existence of the heroic figures than the narra
tors of Kierkegaard or, as we shall see, of Lermontov or Mel
ville. As a hero Heathcliff is a figure who has some difficult
emerging from his ground; at the end of the novel he literall
sinks back into it. In a similar way, Lockwood and Nelly ar
narrators who never fully separate themselves from the her
and heroine they are meditating upon. Since this view run
counter to the views of many commentators on *Wutherin*
Heights—the topic of the narrators has been a popular one—
shall have to explain myself at some length.

Most discussions of Lockwood and Nelly Dean are con
cerned with establishing some kind of moral judgment o
them in comparison to the hero and heroine: Nelly is see
either as the "villain" of the book (in the way she is always in
terfering in the action), or as a shrewd and sane ethical norn
against which the failings of Heathcliff and Catherine have t
be measured.[31] These conflicting claims can be balance
against one another, as in John Mathison's argument tha

30. *Either / Or,* 1 : 9.

31. James Hafley, "The Villain of *Wuthering Heights,*" *Nineteenth*
Century Fiction 13 (1958) : 199–215, and John Fraser, "The Name of Ac
tion: Nelly Dean and *Wuthering Heights,*" *Nineteenth-Century Fiction*
20 (1965) : 223–36, respectively.

'Nelly is an admirable woman whose point of view . . . the reader must reject." [32] Similar judgments, pro, con, or mixed, are offered on the character of Lockwood. He is "epicoene," as Dorothy Van Ghent sees him, more sinned against than sinning, or like Nelly, a sympathetic guide with some obvious limitations. Such moral judgments are not at all irrelevant to our experience of the novel, but they do not give adequate consideration to the different imaginative level on which, as narrators, Lockwood and Nelly exist. Although Nelly has participated in the story she tells, and this is a question we shall consider shortly, both she and Lockwood are essentially observers of the actions of others, mediating, however complexly, between the strangeness of the hero and heroine and the familiarity of the hypothetical reader's view of human nature. Thomas Vogler is the only critic I am aware of who sees that their modes of perception are fundamentally different from one another. Constrasting the narrators with Heathcliff and Catherine he suggests "the possibility that the novel is about the problem of contrasted vision itself, perhaps even about the impossibility of adopting decisively one or the other mode of vision." [33]

Oddly enough, this is a view I shall want to advance myself in discussing the relation of narrator and hero, Ishmael and Ahab, in *Moby-Dick.* In *Wuthering Heights,* however, it seems to me to go too far in giving the narrators an imaginative autonomy from the hero and heroine. Nelly and Lockwood do not see the world in a radically different way from Catherine and Heathcliff. Although the narrators are tamer, they are quite implicated in the heroic struggle.

A comparison with Kierkegaard may help here. The poet or narrator, says Kierkegaard, cannot do what the hero does. "He

32. "Nelly Dean and the Power of *Wuthering Heights,*" *Nineteenth-Century Fiction* 11 (1956): 106–29. Mathison's synthesis was made before the thesis and antithesis of Hafley and Fraser.

33. "Introduction," *Twentieth-Century Interpretations,* p. 12. Vogler's essay in this volume, "Story and History in *Wuthering Heights,*" gives sophisticated and wide-ranging support to his suggestion.

is the genius of recollection, can do nothing except call to mind
what has been done; he contributes nothing of his own, but is
jealous of the intrusted treasure" (FT, p. 30). Is it true that
Nelly Dean cannot do what Catherine does, or that Lockwood
contributes nothing of his own to his story of Heathcliff? One
is inclined to say "yes" until one thinks of the capacity for
"doing" that both these superficially passive narrators seem to
have. As an observer and reporter Nelly is intimately involved
in the action of the plot. It is she who conceals from Catherine
that Heathcliff has overheard part of her confession of divided
love, it is she who urges Heathcliff "to frame high notions of
[his] birth" (48). She is in many ways a literal *tortor heroum*,
to use Kierkegaard's figurative phrase from *Fear and Trembling,* though to brand her as "the villain" as James Hafley
does is to ignore how pervasive this kind of behavior is among
other characters in the novel. Nor is Lockwood immune from
such participation in the willfulness and violence of the story,
as his dream of rubbing the wrists of the ghost child on the
broken windowpane shows. Even his rejection of the young
lady at Bath, which is often interpreted as a sign of his emotional inadequacy, shows a duality of warmth and coldness
which is not unlike that of his hero.

That Lockwood and Nelly share the narrative function in
Wuthering Heights is a reflection of the fact that Heathcliff
shares the stage as hero with Catherine. In fact, Lockwood is
presented as a version of Heathcliff, partly parodic but partly
also a restatement of the heroic theme in a minor key. Lockwood begins to empathize with Heathcliff upon meeting him,
and though most of his speculations are wide of the mark,
Brontë does not simply expose him by her irony but allows him
to restrain himself: "No, I'm running on too fast—I bestow my
own attributes over liberally on him. Mr. Heathcliff may have
entirely dissimilar reasons for keeping his hand out of the way,
when he meets a would-be acquaintance, to those which ac-
tuate me" (3). In his waking experience Lockwood makes several blundering misinterpretations, but in his dream he experiences a vision curiously close to the vision which, we learn at

the end of the novel, Heathcliff himself has been pursuing. Indeed, Edgar Shannon has argued convincingly that Lockwood's two dreams dramatize in capsule form the sequence of isolation, suffering, and desire for revenge that forms the psychological basis of Heathcliff's character.[34] There is certainly a good deal of superciliousness in Lockwood's behavior and conversation, but on a more intuitive level he is not as antithetical to Heathcliff as one might suppose.

A further parallel between the male narrator and the hero is in their similar positions as outsiders. The correspondence between Heathcliff's position and Lockwood's is obvious at the beginning of the novel, when Lockwood tries to gain access to a house where he is quite unwelcome, but it is also emphasized at the end of the book, when Lockwood describes himself in a way that seems unselfconsciously reminiscent of Heathcliff. Lockwood has just overheard and seen the affectionate instruction of Hareton by Catherine: "They came to the door, and from their conversation, I judged they were about to issue out and have a walk on the moors. I supposed I should be condemned in Hareton Earnshaw's heart, if not by his mouth, to the lowest pit of the infernal regions if I showed my unfortunate person in the neighborhood then, and feeling very mean and malignant, I skulked around to seek refuge in the kitchen" (261). Varying the *Paradise Lost* pattern, Adam and Eve move out into nature and Satan is left in the house.

Nelly is Lockwood's opposite, and similar to Catherine in this respect. Like Catherine, she is the insider in family affairs, privy to the secrets of all, including Heathcliff. If Lockwood resembles Heathcliff in his icy reserve, Nelly resembles Catherine in her willfulness and self-assertion. Again, there is much in her character to distinguish her from her mistress, but Brontë is not out to sharpen our powers of judgment and discrimination as she presents the struggles of Catherine and Nelly, each for her own way. "To hear you, people might think *you* were the mistress!" Catherine cries out at her at one point (95). The trouble with Nelly as a narrator is that she is an

34. "Lockwood's Dreams," pp. 16–30.

agent as well as an observer. Her response to Heathcliff is fre
quently hostile, but she is also capable of sympathizing with
him and encouraging him in his rebellion. "Nelly, make me
decent, I'm going to be good," Heathcliff confides in her, only
to get this support: "You could knock him [Edgar Linton
down in a twinkling; don't you feel that you could?" (47)
"Were I in your place," Nelly tells him, "I would frame high
notions of my birth" (48). While she deplores Heathcliff's
pride, she encourages him in it; while she opposes his schemes
she is often instrumental in furthering them, as when she car
ries the letter from Heathcliff to Catherine in chapter 14. But
in her minor encouragements and betrayals she is not unlike
Catherine, whose similarly ambivalent treatment of Heathcliff
is so instrumental in his fate.

   The function or effect of such a reduplication of the traits of
hero and heroine in the persons of the narrators is to implicate
the narrative observers in the heroic actions they are wit
nessing. Although Lockwood and Nelly are to some extent foils
for Heathcliff and Catherine, ironic reflections of their mythi
cal substance, the difference is not so much of kind as of degree.
Rather than the ironic discrimination that Kierkegaard works
so carefully to effect, it is an imaginative fusion at which
Brontë seems to aim. There is first of all little attempt to
dramatize the potential difference between Lockwood's percep
tions and Nelly's, even though they remain clearly distinct as
characters. "She is, on the whole, a very fair narrator and I
don't think I could improve her style," Lockwood says at one
point (132). Secondly, both narrators, the outside observer and
the inside informer, participate in the tale in a way that allows
for little reflection on the part of the reader. One of the effects
of Nelly's "prying," as Heathcliff calls it (247), or "carrying
tales" (132), as she calls it herself, is to create a moral am
biguity in the realm of the narrator that helps divert our atten
tion from the moral ambiguity in the realm of the hero. Nelly
acts as something of a moral insulator in the way she presents
her majority of the narrative.

   Nevertheless, since this participation of the narrators in their heroes is based on an active assertion of the will, a will antagonistic to the plans and wishes of others, the narrators of *Wuthering Heights* do, in the final analysis, retain an important degree of autonomy in their meditations. If they were more accepting or devout in their hero worship they would be less effective in keeping Heathcliff and Catherine at the imaginative distance necessary for the hero to maintain *his* autonomy. I would like to insist here on the importance of this distance in the meditative form. If the hero is presented too unquestioningly, too much at heroic face value, he becomes a dogmatic assertion rather than an imaginative possibility. Carlyle's *On Heroes, Hero-Worship, and the Heroic in History,* with its flat, unironic celebration of an unchanging heroic substance, is a case in point. Other instances of the hero threatened by a loss of imaginative otherness can be found in Byron, where the dramatization of various heroic figures is always on the verge of collapsing into thinly veiled autobiography. In a letter to Hobhouse prefacing the Fourth Canto of *Childe Harold's Pilgrimage,* Byron gracefully admits defeat:

> With regard to the conduct of the last canto, there will be found less of the pilgrim than in any of the preceding, and that little slightly, if at all, separated from the author speaking in his own person. The fact is, that I had become weary of drawing a line which everyone seemed determined not to perceive: . . . it was in vain that I asserted, and imagined that I had drawn, a distinction between the author and the pilgrim; and the very anxiety to preserve this difference, and disappointment at finding it unavailing, so far crushed my efforts in the composition, that I decided to abandon it altogether—and have done so.[35]

One could hardly envision such a collapse of the narrative distinction in *Wuthering Heights;* it is only another heroically privileged being who can say "I *am* Heathcliff." The narrators of *Wuthering Heights* thus preserve the willful autonomy of the heroic presence by a willful antagonism of their own.

35. *Works,* 2 : 323.

A secondary way in which the narrators preserve the heroism of Catherine and Heathcliff is in diverting attention from the so-called structure of the novel. In an essay written in 1926 called "The Structure of *Wuthering Heights*," C. P. Sanger noted the surprisingly symmetrical genealogies of the Earnshaws and the Lintons, which are mirror images of one another and which merge geometrically in the marriage of Hareton Earnshaw and Catherine Linton.[36] But such a structure is only perceived upon a careful reflection and analysis of the book, as is the exact chronology of events that Sanger also reconstructs. What the accounts of Lockwood and Nelly do is to subsume this structure of plot—who marries whom, who does what next —to a structure of narrative, a structure that focuses attention on the heroic figures. We learned in chapter 1 that the Romantic hero was often conceived of as too large to be contained by a conventional plot, as were the tragic heroes of Shakespeare in Romantic criticism of his plays. It is significant that Brontë carefully constructs the realistic basis for her story that Sanger has discovered, but it is also significant that she deliberately conceals the realistic groundwork by means of the narrative form of the meditation on the hero.[37]

In the chapter on Kierkegaard we noted the psychological implications of this peculiar narrative form for the author's developing sense of selfhood. For Kierkegaard, the form dramatized a strong existential self virtually inaccessible to its own speculative intelligence. The psychological dimensions of Emily Brontë's use of the meditation on the hero are harder to discern, but no less interesting. Her sister Charlotte was able to present a Romantic hero in a more traditional novelistic mode: Jane Eyre tells her own story in the first person, a story in which Rochester is an important character but by no means such an exclusive focus as Heathcliff in *Wuthering Heights*. A

36. Reprinted in *Twentieth-Century Interpretations*, pp. 15–27.

37. A similar effect was apparently achieved in the Gondal saga, where there was a clearly worked out history and sequence of events in prose alluded to only obscurely in the poems. The poems are chiefly dramatic monologues.

major psychological difference between the two sisters which may explain this difference between the two Brontë novels lies in Emily's obsessive concern with privacy. Charlotte unintentionally but traumatically invaded this privacy on two occasions in her own quest for public recognition. The first crisis came when she discovered by accident the notebook containing Emily's Gondal poems and urged her to publish them, the second when Charlotte revealed Emily's identity as "Ellis Bell" to her publishers. Emily took the protection of her pseudonym much more seriously than either of her sisters.[38]

A possible link between the psychological makeup of the author and the dynamics of the literary form can be forged from Northrop Frye's speculation on the relation of the Byronic hero to Byron: "If we ask how a witty, sociable, extroverted poet came to create such a character, we can see that it must have arisen as what psychologists call a projection of his inner self, that inner self that was so mysterious and inscrutable even to its owner." [39] Brontë was Byron's psychological opposite in this respect, deeply introverted in her withdrawal from public view, even from the view of her family. If Heathcliff is a more vital Byronic hero than Byron's own characters, the reason may lie in this, that the hero for Brontë represents an innermost self that is intimately known but carefully hidden from the eyes of others. In this light the failure of the narrators of *Wuthering Heights* to comprehend their hero and heroine, even as they share some of the latters' traits, takes on a biographical significance.

The absence of evidence about Emily's view of herself makes it difficult to determine the significance of *Wuthering Heights* in her ongoing imaginative development, but it is hard to ignore certain parallels between her life and art. As noted earlier, the writing of *Wuthering Heights,* following the joint publication of the Brontë sisters' *Poems*, represented a dramatic emergence of Emily as author. She moved out of the

---

38. On these two incidents and Emily's reactions, see Gerin, *Emily Brontë* pp. 231–34, 281–83.

39. "Lord Byron," *Fables of Identity* (New York, 1963), p. 177.

shared privacy of the Gondal romances, poems and prose into a much more public world. The Gondal world was private; it was also essentially mythic. As J. Hillis Miller puts it, "There is no assertion that the stories have been invented. Rather Emily and Anne speak of their writing as the recording of events which have a prior and objective existence. . . . In one sense the Gondal saga was a sequence of temporally related events like history. In another sense it was a simultaneous existence of all its events in a perpetual present outside of time." [40] In *Wuthering Heights,* as our discussion has emphasized, there is a strong impulse on the part of the mythical hero to enter into history, a history that involves both the experience of passing time and the socialization of a recalcitrant private selfhood. It would seem that the novel enacts a similar impulse on the part of the author herself, a desire to move beyond her accustomed role as family romancer and into a future role as novelist in the company of her sisters.

What happened to Emily after the publication of *Wuthering Heights* is less clear. There is inconclusive evidence that she began a second novel and clearer indications thaat she wrote more Gondal poetry.[41] But she survived the publication of her novel by only one year. The death of Branwell in September of 1848 plunged her into a psychological withdrawal and a physical decline, which ended in her death on December 18. That there was some connection between Branwell and the figure of Heathcliff is evident, and it seems that Emily increasingly resented Charlotte's attempts to exclude Branwell from the literary ventures of the family.[42] One can only wonder whether in

40. *The Disappearance of God,* pp. 160–61.

41. See "Emily Brontë's Second Novel," *Transactions of the Brontë Society* 15 (1966) : 28–33. Certainly a twenty-five-line revision of a long narrative poem was written; the whole piece may have been written after *Wuthering Heights* (Ratchford, *Gondal's Queen,* pp. 32, 183).

42. Gerin, *Emily Brontë,* p. 234. My own guess is that Heathcliff reflects Emily's strong sympathy for her brother, the hero's orphanhood being a sign of the brother's exclusion from family affairs by Charlotte, while Hindley, from whose affection Heathcliff wins Catherine initially, reflects the disgust which Branwell's dissipation inspired even in Emily herself.

the increasingly autistic privacy of her imagination Emily felt that her only satisfaction lay in joining her brother in a world out of time and family conflict, that her life might well follow the pattern of her art.

*   *   *   *

Mikhail Lermontov's dates, 1814–1841, are close to those of Brontë's; his life was very different. There was nothing of the recluse about him. He was a soldier decorated for bravery, a political exile, and a well-known poet hailed as successor to Pushkin. Lermontov lived in the midst of the social, political, and literary milieu of the emerging Russian intelligentsia, personally hated by the Czar (for his poem on the death of Pushkin) and personally admired by the great Russian critic Belinsky. His reading was wide in French, German, and English literature as well as in Russian. He was influenced by Pushkin, Schiller, and to some extent Goethe, but the greatest impact on his own writing was made by Byron. It is his preoccupation with Byron that gives him something in common with Brontë and provides some historical basis for a comparison of *A Hero of Our Time* with *Wuthering Heights*.[43]

In his early career as a poet Lermontov simply borrowed whole passages from Byron, whom he had read in translation, and incorporated them into his own numerous narrative poems. He also absorbed Byron through the romantic poems of Pushkin, who had gone through a Byronic phase of his own in the 1820s.[44] By the age of sixteen Lermontov had learned enough English to read Byron in the original and Moore's *Life of Byron* with great interest. Like Brontë, he found the man as interesting as the poetry. Unlike Pushkin, he felt a strong sense of personal identification with the English poet. In 1830 he wrote a poem, "To ——— (On reading Moore's

43. There are two critical biographies of Lermontov in English; Janko Lavrin, *Lermontov* (New York, 1959) and John Mersereau, *Mikhail Lermontov* (Carbondale, Ill., 1962).

44. John Bayley's *Pushkin: A Comparative Commentary* (Cambridge, 1971), pp. 71–106, gives a masterful treatment of Pushkin's debt to Byron and his transformations of the Byronic example.

Life of Byron)," which makes the identification embarrassingly clear:

> Young as I am, song blazes in my heart;
> On Byron's lyric wings I long to soar;
> Our souls are one, and all our woes a part
> Each unto each—would that our paths were more.[45]

As Lermontov developed as a poet he became less derivative; in 1832 he wrote a poem declaring his independence, "No, I'm not Byron":

> No, I'm not Byron: set apart
> Like him, by Fate (though I'm unknown yet),
> Like him, I am an exile—homeless;
> But in me beats a Russian heart.[46]

The identification of course still shows through. As Janko Lavrin puts it, "His early acquaintance with Byron's poetry was, beyond any doubt, a great event in his life. Yet Byron only intensified (and perhaps clarified) some of those innate 'Byronic' features which were latent in Lermontov before he had ever heard the name of Byron." Eventually Lermontov was able to transcend the Byronic model without simply rejecting it, as Pushkin was also able to do in, for example, *Eugene Onegin*.[47]

Not only was Lermontov attracted to the same poet as Emily Brontë, he was also attracted to some of the same poems. His play *The Strange One* has an epigraph from "The Dream," and the narrative poem *The Boyar Arsha* has epigraphs from

45. *Michael Lermontov, Biography and Translation,* trans. C. E. L'Ami and Alexander Welikotny (Winnipeg, 1967), p. 130. This is one of three recent anthologies of Lermontov's writing in English; the others are Guy Daniels, ed. and trans., *A Lermontov Reader* (New York, 1965) and Eugent M. Kayden, trans., *The Demon and Other Poems* (Yellow Springs, Ohio, 1965).

46. Daniels, *Lermontov Reader,* p. 75.

47. "Some Notes on Lermontov's Romanticism," *Slavonic and East European Review* 36 (1957–58) : 69. Bayley discusses Byron's impact on Pushkin and Pushkin's greater dissociation from the Byronic hero.

"The Giaour." [48] In Lermontov's first attempted novel one finds another surprising coincidence; this novel, like *Wuthering Heights*, draws extensively on Scott's *The Black Dwarf*. Beneath these coincidences lies a common fascination with a Romantic hero's proximity to the Gothic villain.

Before writing *A Hero of Our Time* Lermontov began two novels that he never completed; his apprenticeship in prose fiction is of more concern to our study than his poems and plays. *Vadim,* the first attempted novel, apparently failed because he could not cope with the moral ambiguity of his hero. This, at least, is the opinion of John Mersereau: "The novel differs from the usual specimens of the historical romance in that there is a lack of consistency in the depiction of the central character, who at first is presumably the hero [he attempts to regain a family property illegally seized] but who ultimately becomes the villain [he falls in love with his sister and tries to kill her lover]." [49] The similarities between this character and Heathcliff are remarkable, and it was just a synthesis of good and evil traits, one might note, that Brontë did manage to achieve in her hero.

A second uncompleted novel deals with a more contemporary figure, in a social rather than in a historical mode; the society tale was a popular genre in Russian prose at the time. *The Princess Ligovskaya* is a story about Grigory Pechorin, the character who later appears as the hero in *A Hero of Our Time,* but it presents him in a more pathetic than heroic role. He meets a woman he has been in love with, now married for rank and money to someone else. He suffers in the memory of what he has lost although he himself has been partly to blame. There is some pathos, some revenge, and a good deal of social satire. Lermontov may have abandoned the novel for external reasons (his arrest in 1837 interrupted the writing of it at chapter 9), but there were perhaps internal reasons as well. Mersereau notes a problem that is relevant to

48. I am indebted to John Mersereau for this information, as well as for the information about *Vadim,* which is untranslated.

49. *Mikhail Lermontov,* p. 38.

the form of the meditation on the hero, the form that
Lermontov finally achieved in *A Hero of Our Time:* "The narrative perspective of *The Princess Ligovskaya* is especially
confused. At times the narration is omniscient, at times the
author adopts the posture of being a witness to that which he
describes. Now certain facts are available to him, now other
facts of the same nature are not." [50]

A Hero of Our Time, published in 1840, was Lermontov's
first and only completed novel, as he was killed in a duel the
following year. The novel is a series of linked stories that
center on the figure of Pechorin. The narrative point of view
is carefully controlled. In the first two stories Pechorin is
meditated upon by two narrators, the anonymous author
traveling in the Caucasus and the army officer, Maxim
Maximich, who fancies himself Pechorin's friend. In the re-
maining three stories Pechorin himself takes over as narrator
through a journal that he leaves behind, which the first narrator presents to the public.[51] The form the book takes is
that of the meditation on the hero, and the Byronic emphasis
on the hero in love relationships makes the work formally com-
parable to *Wuthering Heights.* There is a further similarity
in the use of a remote setting. The heroic otherness of
Heathcliff is supported by the alien moors and crags of
Yorkshire; the heroism of Pechorin by the spectacular mountains of the Caucasus, a Romantic frontier for nineteenth-
century Russia. The beauty and wildness of the landscape in
both novels provides the hero with an appropriate setting.

A Hero of Our Time begins with the story "Bela," in which
we are introduced to the first narrator en route: "I was travelling post from Tiflis," he begins.[52] Even before we have

50. Ibid., p. 61. *The Princess Ligovskaya* is available in Guy Daniels,
Lermontov Reader.

51. John Bayley considers that Lermontov learned this narrative technique from Pushkin's *Tales of Belkin,* which has a similar plurality of
narrators (*Pushkin,* p. 388). The device of the journal left behind seems
to be adapted from Benjamin Constant's *Adolphe.*

52. *A Hero of Our Time,* trans. Vladimir and Dimitri Nabokov (Garden
City, N.Y., 1958), p. 3. In all further references to this novel, page numbers cited parenthetically in text are from this edition. There are two

identified him as an author, he comments ironically on his role: "All the luggage in my small springless carriage consisted of one valise stuffed half-full of notes on my travels in Georgia. The greater part of them, luckily for you, has been lost; while the valise with its other contents, luckily for me, remains safe" (3). The narrator thus undercuts his interest in the exotic even as he tells of his pursuit of it. In the course of a difficult ascent of a mountain, the narrator encounters Maxim Maximich, a Russian officer, and his interest is aroused: " 'You've surely had a lot of adventures,' I said, prompted by curiosity. . . . I was dying to get some kind of yarn out of him—a desire peculiar to all people who travel and take notes" (8–9). Again we see the mixture of ironic self-deprecation and fascination with the adventurous life around him. The author imagines the officer's life: "Around you there is a wild people, provoking one's curiosity, there is danger every day, extraordinary incidents happen" (9). The author is clearly barking up the wrong tree with Maxim, however, who is a cautious and ordinary soul. But Maxim has a story of someone more heroic than he, namely Pechorin. "You know," Maxim says, "there really exist certain people to whom it is assigned, at their birth, to have all sorts of extraordinary things happen to them." " 'Extraordinary things?' I exclaimed with an air of curiosity, while I poured him some more tea" (11).

What Lermontov is dramatizing in his narrator, and mocking as he does so, is a predisposition to hero worship, the desire of the romantically inclined to find a Byronic hero and hear of his exploits. Maxim, in fact, provides the first narrator with a rip-roaring Byronic tale, with a stolen horse, an abducted Circassian maiden, a native bandit who seeks revenge, and the maiden's bloody death. In the middle of the story Maxim pauses to say that Pechorin and Bela were happy: " 'How dull!' I exclaimed involuntarily. Indeed, I had expected a tragic denouement, and, all of a sudden, my hopes had been deceived so unexpectedly" (27). The first narrator is

---

other recent translations, one by Philip Longworth, in the Signet Classic series (New York, 1964), and one by Paul Foote, a Penguin Classic (Baltimore, 1966).

subsequently reassured; the lovers' happiness is short-lived. This narrator himself then turns around and plays in a similar way on the expectations of the reader, in a teasing manner reminiscent of *Tristram Shandy:* "But perhaps you would like to know the ending of Bela's story? In the first place, it is not a novella I am writing, but travelling notes; consequently, I cannot make the junior captain tell the story before he actually began telling it. Therefore, wait a while, or, if you wish, turn several pages" (31–32).

Rather than an intimate understanding of the hero himself, we are given an ironic analysis of the hero worship that would embrace him. Lermontov's irony puts him closer to Kierkegaard than to Brontë in many respects. Yet it is not so much irony at the expense of the hero or the idea of a hero here as irony at the expense of those who would live vicariously in the hero as a relief from the boredom of their own lives. What is doubly ironic is that Pechorin himself is plagued by the same sense of boredom. He loses interest in Bela after he has secured her love, and even after her agonizing death he can only laugh bitterly. But in Pechorin we find the boredom of the narrator raised to a higher power; it is fatal to others—literally, in Bela's case—as much as it is a burden to him.

In "Maxim Maximich," the second story, we move closer to the actual character of Pechorin, beyond the exaggerated Byronic gestalt that the first story has imposed on him. As the first narrator and Maxim continue their journey, they learn that Pechorin is nearby. Maxim is overjoyed at being able to produce the hero of his earlier tale and to confirm the friendship he has been boasting of, but upon their reunion Pechorin treats Maxim with casual disdain. Pechorin's rejection of the warmth of his former friend is a comic version of the effect of this *homme fatale* that was given melodramatically in "Bela." The first narrator is unmoved by Maxim's disappointment, however, and continues his technique of giving with one hand and taking away with the other. Having seen the hero, the narrator launches into a formal portrait. He generously attributes heroic qualities to Pechorin on the basis of slight evidence. "He was of medium height; a slim waist and broad shoulders testified to a sturdy constitution which was suited to bear all the hardships of a roving life and the changes of climate, and was undefeated either by the dissolution of city life or by the tempests of the soul. . . . " But the generosity of imagination is abruptly withdrawn: "However, these are but my private notes based on my own observations, and by no means do I expect you to believe in them blindly" (56). There is a double irony here, in that Pechorin has been described in a string of clichés.

The first two stories, then, subject the idea of a hero to an ironic critique, purging through the narrative irony the Byronic stereotypes of the hero from the reader's mind. But this deconstruction of an outmoded heroic image is followed by a reconstruction of the Romantic hero as "a hero of our time." Pechorin leaves his journal behind with Maxim Maximich, who in his pique leaves it to the first narrator. This narrator alludes to the Bildungsroman in his Introduction to Pechorin's journal: "The history of a human soul, be it even the meanest soul, can hardly be less curious or less instructive than the history of an entire nation . . . " (63). What happens from this point on in the novel is the gradual emergence of Pechorin as a hero of a new, contemporary kind. The demythologizing is followed by a remythologizing in a new key. Thus the narrator ends his introduction by questioning the basically ironic mode of the hero's presentation to this point: "Perhaps some readers will want to know my opinion of Pechorin's character. My answer is the title of this book. 'But what wicked irony!' they will say. I wonder" (64).

The first story from Pechorin's journal does not overcome the ironic burden of the meditation on the hero thus far, however. In "Taman," Pechorin presents himself as an inexperienced young man who becomes involved unwittingly in a band of smugglers. The blind boy he meets turns out not to be blind, the old deaf women proves not to be deaf, and the beautiful young girl he can only perceive in literary categories —"a regular water nymph," an "undine"—though he is aware

of the bookishness of his perceptions. "I imagined I had discovered Goethe's Mignon—that extravagant product of his
German imagination" (74). In spite of his sense of irony, however, which is perhaps a function of the retrospective view of
his earlier self, Pechorin is deceived by the girl. He is lured
into her boat and almost pushed overboard. Although he over-
powers the girl and escapes, his actions are hardly heroic. He
overhears the girl talking to Yanko, her corsair lover whom
she has been meeting in secret, and watches them both sail off
together. "What business did fate have to land me into the
peaceful midst of *honest smugglers?*" he thinks ruefully (79).[53]

The only heroic quality of Pechorin's at this point is the
"fatal" nature of his involvement with others. He has acci-
dentally broken up a ring of "honest smugglers" and caused
pain to all concerned. As with his rejection of Bela, which led
to her melodramatic death, and with his rejection of Maxim
Maximich's friendship, which led to the tearful disappointment of that benevolent hero-worshiper, Pechorin enters into
a situation of harmony and immediacy and imposes his dis-
ruptive, reflective distance upon it. At this point in the
presentation of the hero, the "fated" nature of what he does
seems little more than accidental bumbling. But the self-
portrait of the hero as a young man is succeeded by a record
of his maturity in the next and longest story in the book, "The
Princess Mary."

The point of view in "The Princess Mary" is more immediate than it was in "Taman," where Pechorin looked back on
the whole adventure from an emotional and temporal distance. Here we have a series of journal entries noted down
with the day's date. There is thus less ironic separation be-

53. There is an excellent discussion of the irony of this story, in much
greater detail, in R. A. Peace's "The Role of 'Taman' in Lermontov's
Geroy nashego vremeni," *Slavonic and East European Review* 45 (1967):
12–29. Although Peace focuses on this one story, he suggests an overall
interpretation that is in line with my own. Andreas Guski analyzes the
way Lermontov's irony transforms the pathos of the Byronic hero into
the will to power of other Romantic hero types (*M. Ju. Lermontovs
Konzeption des literarischen Helden* [Munich, 1970]).

tween the narrative perspective and the heroic presence, although Pechorin continues to comment on his own actions with a certain wry detachment. What is markedly different in this story is that the hero is provided with an alter ego, Grushnitski, a former acquaintance of Pechorin's. Grushnitski, like him, is a soldier and, as Pechorin engineers the situation, Pechorin's rival in love for Princess Mary. "His object," Pechorin notes, "is to become the hero of a novel" (85). Grushnitski, ludicrous in his posturing and conceit, is in fact the Byronic stereotype that we have been misled into taking Pechorin for earlier. "At this point the ladies moved away from the well and came level with us. Grushnitski had time to assume a dramatic attitude with the help of his crutch, and loudly answered me in French: *'Mon cher, je hais les hommes pour ne pas les mépriser, car autrement la vie serait une farce trop dégoutante'* " (87). Pechorin mocks him in reply: " *'Mon cher,'* I answered, trying to copy his manner, *'je méprise les femmes pour ne pas les aimer, car autrement la vie serait un melodrame trop ridicule'* " (88). Even more damaging to Grushnitski's would-be heroism is the fact that he repeats in all seriousness the very phrases that Pechorin has previously disposed of as clichés. "So often has he tried to convince others that he is a being not made for this world and doomed to suffer in secret," Pechorin says, "that he has almost succeeded in convincing himself of it. That is why he wears, so proudly, that thick soldier's coat of his" (85). A page later we hear Grushnitski: "And what do they care whether or not there is a mind under a numbered regimental cap and a heart under a thick army coat?" (86–87).

In the course of the story we are given two more examples of Pechorin's fatal effect on women. Not only does the Princess Mary fall unhappily in love with him, but Vera, a former lover still suffering, appears on the scene. However, it is in his contest with Grushnitski that Pechorin, without losing his ironic perspective, begins to assume more positive force as a hero. He insinuates himself between Grushnitski and the Princess, reducing his rival to a caricature in her eyes and

supplanting him in his putative heroic role. His friend
Werner tells him, "In her imagination you became a hero of a
novel in the latest fashion" (95). Pechorin goes on to goad his
adversary to the point of challenging him to a duel. Grushnitski plans the affair as a trap; he will make sure that his pistol
is loaded and Pechorin's is not. But as Pechorin overhears this
plan he is able to put the duel back into the realm of the im-
ponderable. The duel takes place at the edge of a cliff. Grushnitski fires first but only grazes Pechorin. Pechorin then asks
for his empty pistol to be loaded and kills Grushnitski in cold
blood. In doing so he kills the literary stereotype of the hero
and assumes himself a more terrifyingly demonic aspect.

After killing Grushnitski and before rejecting coldly the dis-
traught Princess Mary, Pechorin does reveal a capacity for suffering himself, however, a trait that humanizes his emerging
heroism. His love for Vera is revived when he discovers a
farewell letter from her. In chasing after her, riding his horse
to death, and sobbing in the grass, he reveals an emotional
depth rarely glimpsed in him. "If, at that moment, anyone had
seen me, he would have turned away in contempt," he remarks
(175). A moment of compassion qualifies our heroic awe. Yet
the blinds are immediately drawn across this psychological insight. "I returned to Kislovodsk at five in the morning, threw
myself on my bed and slept the sleep of Napoleon after Water-
loo" (176). The man with feelings hides behind the mask of the
world-historical individual. One may suspect the psychological
motives of Pechorin in the duel with Grushnitski, but as
Pechorin reflects upon himself—this is the only view we have
—personal motivation is finally a mystery. Before the fatal
outcome of the duel he analyzes his manipulations as the pursuit of sustenance for his heroic power—power reduced to its
raw essence.

> I look upon the sufferings and joys of others only in rela-
> tion to myself as on the food sustaining the strength of
> my soul. I am no longer capable myself of frenzy under
> the influence of passion: ambition with me has been sup-

pressed by circumstances, but it has manifested itself in another form, since ambition is nothing else than thirst for power, and my main pleasure—which is to subjugate to my will all that surrounds me, and to excite the emotions of love, devotion, and fear in relation to me—is it not the main sign and greatest triumph of power (123)?

The three stories of Pechorin's journal show a progression in the attainment of this power. In "Taman" the quest is largely a comic failure, as it leads Pechorin into the misadventures in the primitive folk world of the smugglers. His fatal effect, as we said earlier, was largely accidental. In "The Princess Mary" the power is more deliberately pursued and successfully achieved, yet it is still defined largely in social terms. Pechorin triumphs over a social rival and causes family unhappiness in the best of Russian society. In the final story, "The Fatalist," Pechorin achieves power in a more disinterested way, and in a more cosmic and metaphysical context. The *Heldenbildung* moves from the primitive folk imagination of "Taman" through the more sophisticated social world of "The Princess Mary" to the cosmological, philosophical level of "The Fatalist." The narrative point of view in the journal changes accordingly: in "Taman" Pechorin looks back on his past, in "The Princess Mary" he records his present, and in "The Fatalist" he tests his future. The closer we get to Pechorin himself, the more compelling his heroic otherness comes to seem.

"The Fatalist" is metaphysical in the way it addresses itself to the question of predestination, whether or not such a thing exists. The general topic is given a specific focus characteristic of the nihilistic strain in Lermontov, a focus on death: "Where are those reliable people who have seen the scroll where the hour of our death is assigned?" a skeptic asks (182). By effectively foreseeing the impending death of the officer Vulich, Pechorin proves himself to be such a "reliable" person, and by testing his own life against the murderous Cossack who has killed Vulich, he validates his insight with a personal act.

Vulich's death also provides an example of a pattern seen in Pechorin's cold-blooded triumph over Grushnitski's attempted hoax. The actual events in which the hero is involved transcend the artificial situation which would contain them. Vulich's attempted suicide grows out of the card game; he will test his fate in a classic example of Russian roulette. As he places the pistol, possibly loaded, to his head, he takes bets. Pechorin obliges and "seemed to decipher the imprint of death upon his pale face" (185) just before the pistol misfires. But Pechorin's fatal intuition is vindicated—as Vulich confesses with his dying gasp—when the latter is murdered by the drunken Cossack later that night. In the contrived situation of the pistol and the wager, chance is operative, but in the larger context of actuality, something like fate prevails. Pechorin is much more disinterested here than he was in the death of Grushnitski, and perhaps for this very reason he puts his own fate to the test. He breaks into the room where the Cossack has barricaded himself, and though he is grazed by a bullet he subdues the murderer. "After all this," he asks, "how, it would seem, can one escape becoming a fatalist" (193)?

Of course in philosophical terms this existential "proof" of fatality is completely spurious. Pechorin admits his rational doubts right away: "I have doubts, about everything." However, he goes on to say, "This inclination of the mind does not impinge upon resoluteness of character. On the contrary, as far as I am concerned, I always advance with greater courage, when I do not know what awaits me" (193–94). What Pechorin has done is translate the notion of an external fate into the inner resolve of the heroic character.[54] He has literally taken fate into his own hands. Earlier, in looking up at the sky, Pechorin has considered fate in the old, external, sense:

54. As John Mersereau notes, the term "fate" is freely and loosely used throughout the earlier stories and is defined more precisely here (*Mikhail Lermontov*, pp. 135–40). Mersereau's interpretation of "The Fatalist" as providing a rational explanation of Pechorin's earlier behavior seems to me quite wrong.

The stars shone calmly upon the dark-blue vault, and it amused me to recall that, once upon a time, there were sages who thought that the heavenly bodies took part in our trivial conflicts for some piece of land or some imaginary rights. And what happened? These lampads, lit, in the opinion of those sages, merely to illumine their battles and festivals, were burning as brightly as ever, while their passions and hopes had long been extinguished with them, like a small fire lit on the edge of the forest by a carefree wayfarer! But on the other hand, what strength of will they derived from the certitude that the entire sky with its countless inhabitants was looking upon them with mute but permanent sympathy! Whereas we, their miserable descendants, who roam the earth without convictions or pride, without rapture or fear (except for that instinctive dread that compresses our hearts at the thought of the inevitable end), we are no longer capable of great sacrifice, neither for the good of mankind, nor even for our own happiness, because we know its impossibility, and pass with indifference from doubt to doubt, just as our ancestors rushed from one delusion to another. But we, however, do not have either their hopes or even that indefinite, albeit real, rapture that the soul encounters in any struggle with men or with fate (188).

As a hero of our time, however, Pechorin achieves something of a resurrection of this archaic strength of will—without the least belief in the cosmology that supposedly sustained it. Like Byron's Lara, he "half mistook for fate the acts of will," [55] but Lermontov is more serious about this equation. Pechorin's heroically privileged insight into fatality is thrown into relief by the comic response of Maxim Maximich, who misses the modern view and mechanically reiterates the archaic one: " 'Yes, I'm sorry for the poor fellow. . . . Why the devil did he talk to a drunk at night! . . . However, this must have

55. "Lara," *Works*, 3 : 336.

been what was assigned to him at his birth,' " "Nothing more could I get out of him," Pechorin concludes, "he does not care, generally, for metaphysical discussions" (194).

There is a passage in Kierkegaard that is directly relevant to Pechorin's situation as a hero who has lost his belief in an external fate but not his existential resolve. The following is from the essay in *Either / Or* entitled "The Ancient Tragical Motif as Reflected in the Modern":

> The peculiarity of ancient tragedy is that the action does not issue exclusively from character, that the action does not find its sufficient explanation in subjective reflection and decision, but that the action itself has a relative admixture of suffering, passion [*passio*]. . . . In ancient tragedy the action itself has an epic moment in it; it is as much event as action. The reason for this naturally lies in the fact that the ancient world did not have subjectivity fully self-conscious and reflective. Even if the individual moved freely, he still rested in the substantial categories of state, family, and destiny. This substantial category is exactly the fatalistic element in Greek tragedy, and its exact peculiarity. The hero's destruction is, therefore, not only a result of his own deeds, but is also a suffering, whereas in modern tragedy, the hero's destruction is not really suffering, but is action. In modern times, therefore, situation and character are really predominant. The tragic hero, conscious of himself as a subject, is fully reflective, and this reflection has not only reflected him out of every immediate relation to state, race, and destiny, but has often even reflected him out of his own preceding life.[56]

There are many such ways in which Romantic criticism sought to relate the isolated condition of the modern hero to the less isolated condition of the heroes of the past: Kierkegaard is borrowing freely from Hegel here. It is his ability to act, in spite of his highly developed reflectiveness, that sustains Pechorin in his heroic role. As a hero, Pechorin fits quite well

56. *Either / Or*, 1 : 141.

the post-Romantic description of Maurice Blanchot, skeptical in its analysis of heroic substance: "Heroism is revelation, the marvellous brilliance of the act which unites essence and appearance. Heroism is the luminous sovereignty of the act. The act alone is heroic, and the hero is nothing if it is not a question of this. . . . As a result, heroic authenticity—if there is any—would have to determine itself as a verb, never as a noun." [57] Heathcliff is a very different kind of hero, a hero of the ancient mode. His heroic nature is substantive rather than active; there is always more to him, we are made to believe, than his acts reveal.

In the terms we have been using to describe the Romantic hero in his privileged status, Pechorin is a hero who has lost his metaphysical ground, although through a series of acts of increasing desperation, he remains a hero nonetheless. Lermontov is the most radical in his treatment of the hero in this regard, in that he presents the hero at his most uprooted. Pechorin is a hero whose only ground is a void. He is certainly denied a ground in nature, in spite of the numerous descriptions of the physical beauty of the Caucasus; the emphasis in all the descriptions is on the visual distance of the observer from the landscape. The ever-present mountains, in fact, are a natural correlative to the presence of "fate" in the novel—an archaic background which the modern self can never hope to be a part of. The visual clarity of Lermontov's landscapes, for which he is often praised, condemn the observer to the eye's unbridgeable distance.[58] Such a treatment of nature is in direct contrast to the way nature is used in *Wuthering Heights*, as a ground in which the hero can immerse himself almost at will.

Pechorin is similarly deprived when it comes to the idea of a metaphysical ground in social and political history. The title

57. "Le Héros," *Nouvelle Revue Française* 25 (1965) : 93 (my translation).
58. Cf. Geoffrey Hartman on the attempt of Romantic poets to escape "the tyranny of the eye," in *The Unmediated Vision* (New York, 1966), pp. 127 ff.

A Hero of Our Time is an echo of Musset's *Confessions d'un enfant de notre siècle,* the self-analysis and self-condemnation of a very unheroic protagonist, but it also echoes, ironically, the Hegelian idea of the hero in *The Philosophy of History.*[59] Hegel's world-historical individual was the political leader who would bring the emerging will of the people to consciousness. The Russian hero is denied this political-historical basis, Lermontov implies, specifically because of the severe repression that followed the Decembrist uprisings in 1825, but more generally because of the deep sense among Russian intellectuals, like Belinsky, that they lacked a history altogether in the European sense.[60] The hero of *our* time (and place), Lermontov implies, has lost any hope for a source of being in social history and has turned to destructive action as an end in itself. Thus he was judged harshly by Herzen: "Lermontov never learned how to hope and never sacrificed his own self, since nothing demanded of him such a sacrifice. He did not walk onto the scaffold with a proudly lifted head like Péstel and Ryléyev, because he did not believe in the reality of such a sacrifice; he stood aside of truth and perished without rhyme or reason." [61]

In denying the hero the common Romantic ground in nature or history, Lermontov is much like Kierkegaard, who attacked the immanent faith of Goethe and Hegel. But Kierkegaard's existentialism is based on a theism, as difficult as this God is to reach. Lermontov's existentialism is a nihilism, in its obsessive confrontations with physical death. An interesting contrast to both Kierkegaard and Lermontov is provided by

59. Lermontov would probably have absorbed Hegel through Belinsky rather than through his own study. Hegel was popular in the debating circles at the University of Moscow, but Lermontov did not belong to these groups when he was there. I am indebted to my friend Michael Holquist of the Yale Slavic Department for pointing out the connection with Hegel, and for much valuable guidance in my interpretation of *A Hero of Our Time.*

60. This thesis is developed at length in a forthcoming book by Michael Holquist on Dostoevsky.

61. Quoted by Lavrin, *Lermontov,* p. 56.

Dostoevsky, who finds the nihilism of the Romantic hero incompatible with Christian faith but deeply compelling nonetheless.

In *Notes from Underground* we are presented with "a representative of a generation still living," but an antihero rather than a hero of our time. His overdeveloped self-consciousness does deprive him of any resoluteness of character: the Underground Man is unable to act. "Now, I am living out my life in my corner, taunting myself with the spiteful and useless consolation that an intelligent man cannot become anything seriously, that only a fool can become something. Yes, an intelligent man in the nineteenth century must and morally ought to be pre-eminently a characterless creature; a man of character, an active man, is pre-eminently a limited creature." [62] *Notes from Underground* reads at times like a reply to *A Hero of Our Time,* where the narrator has devoured the heroic substance and plunged himself in impotent despair. Instead of exposing the literary clichés and then redeeming the idea of the hero existentially as Lermontov does, Dostoevsky shows a figure forever trapped in literary categories. The Underground Man has read Lermontov, and Pushkin, whose Silvio was a prototype for Pechorin; he dreams of "something in the Manfred style." [63]

But the idea of the hero was not so easily overcome by Dostoevsky. *Crime and Punishment* shows the attempted appropriation of the Napoleonic gestalt by a young man in despair of his own becoming, and though Raskolnikov cannot himself bear the burden of going beyond good and evil, we are given the image of someone who can, however self-destructively, in Svidrigaylov. It is in *The Devils* or *The Possessed,* in the figure of Stavrogin, that Dostoevsky gives the idea of the

62. *Notes from Underground and The Grand Inquisitor,* trans. Ralph Matlaw (New York, 1960), p. 5.
63. *Notes from Underground,* p. 51. In the Underground Man's "duel" with the officer there seems to be an ironic echo of Pechorin's duel with Grushnitski. Dostoevsky is, of course, taking on other literary adversaries besides Lermontov in this novel.

hero its most profound and exhaustive treatment, and it is in Stavrogin that Pechorin finds his true successor. (Lermontov and Pechorin are both mentioned in the novel as heroic proto types, along with Shakespeare's Prince Hal and Hamlet.) In fact, in the narrative technique of *The Devils* there is some thing of the meditative form, where Mr. G————v, the friend and confidant of Stepan Verkhovensky, acts as a first-person narrator of the extraordinary events. The narrator does not figure so prominently in the presentation of Stavrogin himself, however. Dostoevsky rather uses a series of alternate charac ters, who reflect and react to various aspects of the central heroic figure: Peter Verkhovensky, who worships Stavrogin as the "beautiful" embodiment of his nihilistic political hopes, who invented all his schemes, he says, while looking at Stavrogin; Kirilov, another Stavrogin-inspired emanation, who represents Stavrogin's atheistic will to power; and Shatov, who worships the Christ-like will to suffering and humiliation in this radically divided heroic self. The terrible irony of the novel is that although all these hero-worshipers and partial heroes have derived their visions from Stavrogin, he himself has gone beyond these visions to a point of empty indifference "From me nothing has come but negation, but with no magnanimity and no force," he writes in his final letter to Dasha.[64] His suicide is the gesture of a heroic will to power that in its total freedom achieves a total negation of humanity.

Like Stavrogin and Kirilov, Pechorin is the ancestor of the modern existential heroes of Gide, Camus, and Sartre, different in so many ways from the Romantic heroes of the nineteenth century. Lermontov, of course, has been much less influential in the development of modern European literature than Dostoevsky. For this very reason, in a rather different mode, it is interesting to find the young James Joyce writing to his brother Stanislaus about Lermontov while Joyce was in the midst of one of his own novels: "The only book I know like it is Lermontov's *Hero of Our Days*. Of course mine is much longer and Lermontov's hero is an aristocrat and a tired man

64. *The Devils*, trans. David Magarshack (London, 1953), p. 667.

and a brave animal. But there is a likeness in the aim and in the title and at times in the acid treatment." [65] The novel that Joyce is referring to is his *Stephen Hero,* the unsuccessful forerunner of *A Portrait of the Artist as a Young Man.* Joyce's notice of Lermontov may serve as an indication of the kinship between the meditation on the hero and the Bildungsroman proper, as well as a reminder of the curious byways of literary history.

65. *Letters of James Joyce,* vol. 2, ed. Richard Ellmann (New York, 1966), p. 111.

4

Melville: The Extended Hero and Expanded Meditation

It is unlikely that Melville read *Wuthering Heights,* either be
fore or after writing *Moby-Dick.* The similarities between
Heathcliff and Captain Ahab have often been noted,[1] but al
though Melville could conceivably have encountered Brontë's
novel on his trip to England in 1849, there is no evidence that
he did so. Melville did take home with him a copy of *Frankenstein,* as well as other Gothic novels, and it is from these common roots that the similarities between the two heroes seem to
proceed. "The gothic hero's most successful immediate heirs
are Heathcliff and Ahab," writes Lowry Nelson, Jr.[2]

The story of common roots only begins here. Melville was
also a Romantic reader of Milton's Satan and a student of
Byron's heroic poems and dramas. He was less heterodox than
Blake or Shelley on Satan in *Paradise Lost;* he insisted on the
lack of dignity in wickedness per se. But he argues that this inherent defect only increases our admiration of Milton's
achievement: "This takes not from the merit of our high priest
of poetry; it only enhances it, that with such unmitigated evil
for his material, he should build up his most goodly struc-

1. E.g. Lowry Nelson, Jr., "Night Thoughts on the Gothic Novel," *Yale
Review* 52 (1962): 251–56; James Justus, *"Wuthering Heights* and an
American Tradition," *Tennessee Studies in Literature* 5 (1960): 25–33;
F. O. Matthiessen, *American Renaissance* (Oxford, 1941), p. 457n.; and
Thomas Woodson, "Ahab's Greatness: Prometheus as Narcissus," *ELH*
33 (1966): 351–69.
2. "Night Thoughts," p. 251. Cf. Newton Arvin, "Melville and the
Gothic Novel," *New England Quarterly* 22 (1949): 33–48.

ure." As Henry Pommer has shown, there are in *Moby-Dick* numerous allusions to and echoes of *Paradise Lost* in general and Satan in particular.[3] The most obvious Byronic trait of Ahab is the mark of Cain, the scar that runs down his face, but there are echoes of Childe Harold and an incident from Byron's life as well. Traces of Goethe's *Faust* can be seen in Ahab's relationship with Fedallah, and in the dramaturgy of the chapter "Midnight, Forecastle," which resembles the *Walpurgisnacht* in *Faust,* Part 1.[4]

The importance of all these heroic prototypes pales, however, before the example of Shakespeare. It is from the heroes of Shakespeare's tragedies that Ahab is born and borrowed. The story is well known and needs only a brief rehearsal here. In 1849 Melville obtained a copy of Shakespeare's plays, which he read carefully for the first time because, he said, the print of the previous editions he had tried had been too small for his weak eyes. "Dolt & ass that I am I have lived more than 29 years, & until a few days ago, never made a close acquaintance with the divine William," he wrote to Evert Duyckinck in February of that year.[5] The impression Shakespeare made seems to have remained latent as far as his own writing was concerned through his travels in England and the beginning of his work on *Moby-Dick* in the summer of 1850. But when he read and met Hawthorne in July, the Shakespearean influence was catalyzed. The process is most evident in "Hawthorne and His Mosses," written in August, in which Melville compares Hawthorne's "power of blackness" with Shakespeare's and all but announces his own intention of taking on the mantle of the great English dramatist. "You must believe in Shakespeare's unapproachability, or quit the country," he complains.

3. Henry F. Pommer, *Milton and Melville* (Pittsburgh, 1950), pp. 81–104. Pommer gives the quote above, from *Redburn.*

4. See Edward Fiess, "Byron and Byronism in the Mind and Art of Herman Melville," (Ph.D. diss., Yale University 1951), pp. 152–54, and William F. Betts, Jr., "*Moby-Dick:* Melville's Faust," *Lock Haven Bulletin* 1 (1959): 31–44.

5. *The Letters of Herman Melville,* ed. Merrill R. Davis and William H. Gilman (New Haven, 1960), p. 77.

"But what sort of a belief is this for an American, a man who is bound to carry republican progressiveness into Literature, as well as into Life? Believe me, my friends, that men not very much inferior to Shakespeare are this day being born on the banks of the Ohio." [6]

It was in the hills of the Berkshires at this time, as far as scholars have been able to determine, that the Shakespearean character of Ahab was conceived. Although the evidence is not entirely conclusive, it seems that Melville had begun *Moby-Dick* without intending to give Ahab a major role. He had apparently written fifteen chapters of a first-person sea adventure, the mode of all his previous books, in which Ishmael, Queequeg, and perhaps the elusive Bulkington were all to play important roles. But when Ahab assumed his Shakespearean proportions in Melville's imagination, the book became structurally quite different from Melville's previous novels. Ishmael became the narrator and observer of Ahab's heroism through large portions of the book, even disappearing as protagonist from the last thirty chapters; Queequeg and Bulkington were similarly truncated.[7] It would be a mistake to see Ahab as solely the product of the Shakespearean influence. There are examples of the mysterious, demonic, dominating character in Melville's earlier works—Jackson in *Redburn,* who like the emperor Tiberius "endeavored to drag down with him to his own perdition all who came within the evil spell of his power," [8] and Taji in *Mardi,* who emerges in the quest after Yillah has been lost and ends the voyage in suicide. But there was not the overwhelming concentration on the single heroic figure, nor the indirect narrative form to pre-

6. "Hawthorne and His Mosses," in *Billy Budd and Other Prose Pieces,* ed. Raymond Weaver, *The Works of Herman Melville,* vol. 13 (London, 1924), p. 132.

7. This theory, advanced by Leon Howard, Charles Olson, Howard P. Vincent and others, receives its most convincing statement in George R. Stewart's "The Two *Moby-Dicks,*" *American Literature* 25 (1954) : 417–48.

8. *Redburn,* ed. Harrison Hayford, Hershel Parker, and G. Thomas Tanselle, *The Writings of Herman Melville,* Northwestern-Newberry Edition, vol. 4 (Evanston and Chicago, 1969), p. 276.

sent him, until the extranovelistic influence of Shakespeare had made itself felt. Only then did Melville conceive a full-blown meditation on the hero.

The Shakespearean dimensions of Ahab have been discussed in depth by F. O. Matthiessen and Charles Olson, and there is no need to repeat the numerous parallels in language, scene construction, theme, and archetype that both these critics have pointed out.[9] It is only in determining the meaning and significance of Ahab's Shakespearean qualities that I think Matthiessen's discussion can be improved on. Matthiessen claims that Melville's use of Shakespeare is not at all self-conscious: "An important contrast between such allusions and those of our own age of more conscious craft, those in *The Waste Land* or *Ulysses,* is that Melville did not intend part of his effect . . . to depend upon the reader's awareness of his source. Indeed . . . he seems to have been only partly aware of its pervasive presence. His attention was wholly taken up with the effort to pour this energy into a new mould of his own." [10] Such an analysis seems to me to apply much better to Emily Brontë's use of Shakespeare in *Wuthering Heights,* where the allusions are much less overt than in *Moby-Dick,* where occasional Shakespearean phrases, gestures, and situations reinforce the heroism of Heathcliff without calling attention to their allusiveness. The presence of Shakespeare behind Ahab is much more obvious: he is Hamlet in "The Quarterdeck," swearing his crew to revenge; Lear in outfacing the fire in "The Candles" and in his dialogues with Pip as Fool; Macbeth in his fatal reliance on Fedallah's prophecies at the end. Such obvious appropriation of dramatic devices, "the conspicuous Shakespearean archtypalism," as Julian Markels

9. Olson, *Call Me Ishmael* (New York, 1947); Matthiessen, *American Renaissance.* Other useful discussions of the Shakespearean elements in *Moby-Dick* include Julian Markels, *"King Lear* and *Moby-Dick:* The Cultural Connection," *Massachusetts Review* 9 (1968) : 169–76; Kenneth Lash, "Captain Ahab and King Lear," *New Mexico Quarterly Review* 19 (1949) : 438–45; and Julian C. Rice, *"Moby-Dick* and Shakespearean Tragedy," *Centennial Review* 14 (1970) : 444–68.

10. *American Renaissance,* p. 432.

calls it,[11] is hardly the result of unconscious influence. This i
not even to mention the language of *Moby-Dick,* which a
Matthiessen himself says, echoes Shakespeare on almost ever
page. Melville is less ironic than Eliot or Joyce but no les
aware of a particular literary past.

In fact, Matthiessen's approach to Melville through exten
sive comparison with Shakespeare plays right into Melville'
hands. The chapters on Melville in *American Renaissanc*
have the same artistically ennobling effect that Melville hac
tried to create for Hawthorne in "Hawthorne and His Mosses"
and was suggesting for his own work in progress. Shake
spearean tragedy is less an influence on Melville than an idea
for imitation, to be appropriated, transformed, and tran
scended. Shakespeare occupies somewhat the same position
for Melville that Milton held for the English Romantic poets
Harold Bloom speaks of "the Romantics' loving struggle witl
their ghostly father, Milton."

> The role of wrestling Jacob is taken on by Blake in hi
> "brief epic" *Milton,* by Wordsworth in *The Reclus*
> fragment, and in more concealed form by Shelley i
> *Prometheus Unbound* and Keats in the first *Hyperion*
> The strength of poetical life in Milton seems always t
> have appalled as much as it delighted; in the fearful vigo
> of his unmatched exuberance the English master of th
> sublime has threatened not only poets, but the value
> once held to transcend poetry.[12]

The fact that Melville discovers his ghostly father relativel
late in his career only makes the struggle more intense.

Melville does not feel in Shakespeare a threat to value
once held to transcend poetry, however. What Shakespeare'
tragic heroes mean to Melville imaginatively is indicated b
his remarks in "Hawthorne and His Mosses." Melville is see

11. *"King Lear* and *Moby-Dick,"* p. 169.
12. "Keats and the Embarrassments of Poetic Tradition," *From Sens*
bility to Romanticism: Essays Presented to Frederick A. Pottle, ed. Fred
erick W. Hilles and Harold Bloom (New York, 1965), p. 513.

ng Shakespeare through a tradition of Romantic interpreta-
ion that emphasizes Shakespeare's metaphysical vision at the
xpense of his aesthetic craft.[13] The passage is famous but
worth quoting at length:

> It is those deep far-away things in him; those occasional
> flashings-forth of the intuitive Truth in him; those short,
> quick probings at the very axis of reality;—these are the
> things that make Shakespeare, Shakespeare. Through the
> mouths of the dark characters of Hamlet, Timon, Lear,
> and Iago, he craftily says, or sometimes insinuates the
> things which we feel to be so terrifically true, that it were
> all but madness for any good man, in his own proper
> character, to utter, or even hint of them. Tormented into
> desperation, Lear the frantic king, tears off the mask, and
> speaks the [sane] madness of vital truth.[14]

Melville anticipates Nietzsche's dictum that we need art to
ave us from the truth. The tragic heroes are less important
n what they say outright than in what they hint at obliquely.
Melville carries this metaphysical overreaching to its logical
conclusion and leaves the plays behind in a leap of dark
aith: "In Shakespeare's tomb lies infinitely more than Shake-
peare ever wrote. And if I magnify Shakespeare, it is not so
much for what he did do, as for what he did not do, or re-
rained from doing." [15]

In making Ahab a composite Shakespearean hero, then,
Melville wants to invoke the meaning, not the name. He is
ess concerned with outdoing Shakespeare in the realm of art
han with using him as a kind of philosophical extension lad-
ler to the truth. Melville stands out among the writers of the

13. Leon Howard finds indications that Melville had read the Shake-
pearean criticism of Coleridge and Lamb (*Herman Melville: A Biography*
Berkeley, 1951], p. 165).

14. "Hawthorne and His Mosses," p. 130. I have followed Eleanor
Metcalf in emending "same" to "sane" on Melville's authority. See
Herman Melville: Cycle and Epicycle (Cambridge, Mass., 1953), p. 92.

15. "Hawthorne and His Mosses," p. 131.

American Renaissance in his desperate search for absolute
through his art, able neither to believe, as Hawthorne said
nor to be happy in his unbelief. Emerson's vatic optimism
seems shallow in comparison, and only Emily Dickinson ap
proaches Melville's metaphysical anguish at a Being so radi
cally transcendent as to defy the human imagination. It is in
this light, it seems to me, that the Shakespearean qualities o
Ahab are best understood. The creation of Ahab in the image
of Hamlet, Lear, Macbeth, and Timon (Melville rated *Timon
of Athens* higher than most critics) is an act of both artisti
faith and wish fulfillment, an attempt by Melville to appro
priate Shakespeare's terrible visionary power, however crudely
Through the mouth of Ahab we are meant to feel, Melville
"craftily says, or sometimes insinuates, the things which we
feel to be so terrifically true that it were all but madness for a
good man, in his own proper character, to utter, or even hin
of them."

Part of Ahab's burden as hero, then, is this Shakespearean
obligation to probe at the very axis of reality, to leave behind
the shifting world of the temporal and the finite. But Ahab
is not a pure Shakespearean hero; the heroic gestalt is im
posed on a lesser humanity. Thus Ishmael confesses after
building up Ahab by comparison with absolute monarchs
"But Ahab, my Captain, still moves before me in all hi
Nantucket grimness and shagginess; and in this episode touch
ing Emperors and Kings, I must not conceal that I have only
to do with a poor old whale-hunter like him; and therefore
all outward majestical trappings and housings are denie
me." [16] As Peleg puts it earlier, Ahab has his humanities
which maintain his sympathetic and egalitarian bonds with
others in spite of his heroic ascendance over them. At the end
of chapter 27, for example, Ahab responds to the warm breeze
with a smile, and in chapter 132, "The Symphony," these ordi
nary human emotions come to the fore as Ahab talks with

16. *Moby-Dick; or, The Whale,* ed. Charles Feidelson (New York, 1964
p. 199. In all further references to this novel, page numbers cited paren
thetically in text are from this edition.

Starbuck. But even in the demythologizing quote given above, Ishmael cannot resist a swing back in the other direction. "Oh Ahab!" he continues, "what shall be grand in thee, it must needs be plucked at from the skies, and dived for in the deep, and featured in the unbodied air." The heroic form is not simply denied, but internalized, rendered less visible.

This is one of the ways that, like so many Romantic heroes, Ahab is divided against himself. His transcendental Shakespearean self dominates but never completely obscures an empirical self that is natively American. This was never much of a problem for a writer like Emerson, who was less concerned with the tragic limitations of history than was Melville. "All these great and transcendent properties are ours," Emerson wrote in his essay "Heroism." "If we dilate in beholding the Greek energy, the Roman pride, it is that we are already domesticating the same sentiment." [17] For Melville, however, the empirical self is involved in the temporal, the finite, most of all in the contingent nature of mankind. Ahab's revolt against contingency is most evident in the way his desire for cosmic revenge proceeds from the loss of his leg to Moby-Dick. We hear rumors of previous acts of defiance and impiety from Elijah, but it is his physical dismemberment that drives Ahab to scorn his contingent selfhood in the desperate attempt to confront the eternal. There is a passage in *The Sickness unto Death* that provides a surprisingly apt description of Ahab's condition, which Kierkegaard would denote as despair:

> The more consciousness there is in such a sufferer who in despair is determined to be himself, all the more does despair too potentiate itself and become demoniac. The genesis of this is commonly as follows. A self which in despair is determined to be itself winces at one pain or another which simply cannot be taken away or separated from its concrete self. Precisely upon this torment the

17. *The Selected Writings of Ralph Waldo Emerson,* ed. Brooks Atkinson (New York, 1940), p. 256.

man directs his whole passion, which at last becomes
demoniac rage. Even if at this point God in heaven an
all his angels were to offer to help him out of it—no, no
he doesn't want it, now it is too late, he once would hav
given everything to be rid of this torment but was mad
to wait, now that's all past, now he would rather rag
against everything, he, the one man in the whole c
existence who is the most unjustly treated, to whom it i
especially important to have his torment at hand, im
portant that no one should take it from him—for thus h
can convince himself that he is in the right.

"This sort of despair is seldom seen in the world," Kierkegaar
adds, "such figures generally are met with only in the works c
poets, that is to say, of real poets, who always lend the
characters this 'demoniac' ideality (taking this word in th
purely Greek sense)." [18]

Kierkegaard's description reminds one that Ahab's demor
ism is initially conceived of as a defense of the contingen
self. It is not simply a desire to leave the temporal and th
finite behind that drives Ahab toward his transcendenta
goal, but a desire to defend a fragile human self against th
assault of the natural and the supernatural worlds. If Ahab i
like King Lear in his overt acts of defiance, he is finally unlik
Lear in his refusal to accept the pitiable nature of the bar
forked animal. Indeed, where Lear divests himself of his roya
trappings and discovers the lowest common denominator o
humanity, Ahab assumes Lear's mantle in an attempt to re
venge the commonly human in himself and in mankind gen
erally.[19] As Thomas Woodson puts it in one of the best in
terpretations of Ahab's heroism I have encountered, "To live
to create a substantial body for oneself, is to destroy th
other" in Melville's world: "man finds behind nature a com
peting mind and creative force; in order to become himsel

18. *Fear and Trembling and The Sickness unto Death*, pp. 205–06; th
parallel is also noted by M. O. Percival in *A Reading of Moby-Dick* (Chi
cago, 1950), pp. 34–35.
19. Cf. Lash, "Captain Ahab and King Lear," p. 443.

man must destroy this competing other." [20] This defense of
the self by destruction of the other has tragic consequences for
the self, a paradox I would like to reserve for later discussion.

Ahab's humanities are associated with the temporal as well
as the finite, just as Abraham's humanity is related to the moment of choice, Heathcliff's to family history, and Pechorin's
to the present age. "Forty years of continual whaling! forty
years of privation, and peril, and storm time! forty years on
the pitiless sea!" Ahab laments to Starbuck when his humanities are momentarily resurgent. "For forty years Ahab has
forsaken the peaceful land, for forty years to make war on the
horrors of the deep" (683). Like the forty years of the
Israelites in the wilderness, Ahab's heroic quest is measured
in time lost from common human living.

Ahab's identity is thus divided between time-bound and
time-transcending elements. He is unlike Abraham in that he
is willing to sacrifice his personal temporal humanity (leaving his young wife and child, for example) to accomplish his
transcendental purpose. He is unlike Heathcliff in that his
revenge is directed not at a temporality that has excluded him
but at an eternity that has insulted his temporality. But he is
more involved in the temporal world than a Byronic hero like
Manfred, with whom he is frequently compared and from
whom Melville probably drew some inspiration. G. Wilson
Knight has noted in an aside that Heathcliff and Ahab are,
like the Byronic hero, "personalities tugged by some strange
evil between time and eternity." [21] But Manfred is able to
turn his back on time with a much more cavalier disdain:

> Thinkst thou existence doth depend on time?
> It doth; but actions are our epochs: mine
> Have made my days and nights imperishable,
> Endless, and all alike . . . (II, i, 1–54).

> The Mind which is immortal makes itself
> Requital for its good or evil thoughts,—

20. "Ahab's Greatness," p. 355.
21. *The Burning Oracle* (Oxford, 1939), p. 203.

Is its own origin of ill and end—
And its own place and time . . . (III, iv, 129–32).[22]

Whereas Manfred retreats from human time to a private
eternity, Ahab sallies forth against an eternity that is alien to
him, an eternity that he is not even sure exists. Notice also how
Manfred echoes Satan in *Paradise Lost* here ("the mind is its
own place"). When Ahab echoes Satan it is with more of a
longing for what has been lost, less the defiant rhetoric than
the tormented musing: "This lovely light, it lights not me,
since I can ne'er enjoy. Gifted with high perception, I lack
the low enjoying power; damned, most subtley and most
malignantly! damned in the midst of Paradise!" (226).[23] The
paradise that Ahab has lost is a garden of earthly delights.

Ahab's divided selfhood is thus considerably more dynamic
than Manfred's. Its divisions are considerably more complex,
expressing themselves in different ways on different occasions, but always involving an active struggle between two
conflicting elements. A classic expression of Ahab's inner conflict is given in "The Chart," when Ishmael reports how
Ahab would burst from his cabin at night as though his bed
were on fire.

> For, at such times, crazy Ahab, the scheming, unappeas-
> edly steadfast hunter of the white whale; this Ahab that
> had gone to his hammock, was not the agent that so
> caused him to burst from it in horror again. The latter
> was the eternal, living principle or soul in him; and in
> sleep, being for the time dissociated from the characteriz-

22. *Works*, 4 : 100–01, 135.
23. Cf. *Paradise Lost*, 4 : 33–39, 73–74; 9 : 99–123. In the opening phrase
Melville is also invoking the pathos of the poet's invocation to Book III
ll. 40–42:

> Thus with the Year
> Seasons return, but not to me returns
> Day, or the sweet approach of Ev'n or Morn . . .

(*The Works of John Milton*, II, i, ed. Frank Allen Patterson, [New York
1931], p. 79).

ing mind, which at other times employed it for its outer
vehicle or agent, it spontaneously sought escape from
the scorching contiguity of the frantic thing, of which,
for the time, it was no longer an integral. But as the
mind does not exist unless leagued with the soul, therefore it must have been that, in Ahab's case, yielding up
all his thoughts and fancies to his one supreme purpose;
that purpose, by its own sheer inveteracy of will, forced
itself against gods and devils into a kind of self-assumed,
independent being of its own. Nay, could grimly live and
burn, while the common vitality to which it was con-
joined, fled horror-stricken from the unbidden and un-
fathered birth (272).

This passage has been singled out by some of Melville's more
sensitive critics; Paul Brodtkorb rightly emphasizes the tor-
tuous syntax and problematic epistemology of this description, but beneath the Ishmaelean uncertainties, as Thomas
Woodson notes, there is a basic sense of Ahab's classically
Romantic division of self.[24] The terms of this analysis are
important for still another reason, in that they suggest the
narrative structure of the book as a whole, the narrative form
that presents Ahab as hero. The demonic willfulness of the
hero is presented by a narrator who is shifting and evasive in
his categories, who is continually dissociating *his* eternal living
principle or soul from the intensity of his *hero's* characterizing
mind. What this passage suggests, in other words, is the logic
of the narrative form of *Moby-Dick,* the meditation on the
hero. It suggests that this form is to some extent a projection,
on a larger screen, of the conflict and tension within the
hero himself.

The central question for interpreters of *Moby-Dick* has
been whether to accept Ahab's view of man and the universe,
or whether to prefer the more balanced, unheroic view of
Ishmael. Is the issue "the power of blackness," or should we

24. Brodtkorb, *Ishmael's White World* (New Haven, 1965), pp. 62–66
and Woodson, "Ahab's Greatness," p. 361.

pay more attention to "Ishmael's white world"?[25] Many critics, of course, try to strike a balance between Ishmael and Ahab in their interpretations, but it is this very balance that constitutes the narrative structure of the meditation on the hero. Neither the narrator nor the hero can exist independently; only in their interaction does the story come to life. What makes *Moby-Dick* unique among the other meditations on the hero we have discussed is the way that the narrator and the hero reflect and complement each other. Ishmael meditates on Ahab directly at a number of points in his narrative, but he is also engaged in a quest of his own that runs parallel to the quest of Ahab. The full title of the book is *Moby-Dick; or, The Whale;* whereas Ahab hunts for a particular Leviathan, Ishmael tries to comprehend the species as a whole.

We might begin by considering the names of the narrator and hero. Both are biblical, both are given to characters who are Romantically revised versions of the Old Testament figures, but Ahab's is a given name whereas Ishmael's is assumed. "Call me Ishmael," the narrator invites us with colloquial ease, but he gives us no assurance that we are dealing with anything more than an alias; he assumes an identity from which he can escape if the need arises. Ahab's identity is more fixed and determined by his name. An old squaw at Gay Head "said that the name would somehow prove prophetic" (119), and so it does.[26] Another biblical identity, that

25. The phrases are taken from Brodtkorb and Harry Levin, *The Power of Blackness* (New York, 1958). The contrast between the Ahabians and the Ishmaelites can be seen in the difference between M. O. Percival's reading, which treats Ishmael largely as a prologue and epilogue to the story of Ahab and Edgar Dryden's approach in *Melville's Thematics of Form* (Baltimore, 1968), which focuses on Ishmael as author and argues that "Even Ahab, the character described by one critic as the book's 'Alpha and Omega,' owes his existence to the creative voice of Ishmael" (pp. 89–90).

26. Useful discussions of these names can be found in Natalia Wright, *Melville's Use of the Bible* (Durham, N.C., 1949), pp. 46–76; Dryden, *Melville's Thematics,* pp. 85–87; and Woodson, "Ahab's Greatness," p. 352.

of Jonah, seems to be shared by Ishmael and Ahab in its
different aspects. Father Mapple's sermon sees the Book of
Jonah as a "two-stranded lesson" (72). The second strand,
describing the figure of the confirmed prophet, obviously
looks ahead to Ahab: "Delight is to him—a far, far upward,
and inward delight—who against the proud gods and commodores of this earth, ever stands forth his own inexorable
self" (80). The first strand, however, describing Jonah's attempted flight from the Lord's command, has more applica-
tion to Ishmael.

Ishmael goes to sea for reasons that he leaves unclear, but
his voyage is in part one of flight. "Some years ago—never
mind how long precisely—," he says, withdrawing warily from
fixing his voyage in time. He is a picaresque traveler, whose
quest is for escape as well as for adventure. He goes to sea, he
says, to avoid a suicidal and homicidal depression: "This is
my substitute for pistol and ball." In this brief allusion to the
darker side of existence, delivered humorously enough, we can
see a kind of vestigial rebelliousness in Ishmael from which he
is in flight. Just as Ahab has his "humanities," which link him
to Ishmael and the others, so Ishmael has a trace of the fatal
Prometheanism of Ahab, which cuts him off from his mates
and which helps account for his sympathy for his hero. "I am
quick to perceive a horror, and could still be social with it"
(30). Ishmael is fascinated by the supernatural but resists the
spell it would fix upon him.

One of the broadest kinds of contrast between the narrator
and his hero involves the difference between a comic and a
tragic mode. Ahab is a tragic hero, if not according to the
classical definition, at least "the ancient tragical motif as reflected in the modern." [27] Ishmael is of a more comic disposi-
tion, finding humor in the incongruities between man and nature. His "genial, desparado philosophy," as he call it (303),

27. See Julian Rice, *"Moby-Dick* and Shakespearean Tragedy," and
Richard Sewell, *The Vision of Tragedy* (New Haven, 1959), pp. 92–105,
for discussions of *Moby-Dick* as tragedy.

emphasizes the geniality. The comic mode is directly involved
in meditating on the tragic hero, as when Ishmael indulges in
a mock-heroic catalogue of whale men:

> The more I dive into this matter of whaling, and push my
> researches up to the very spring-head of it, so much the
> more am I impressed with its great honorableness and
> antiquity; and especially when I find many great demi-
> gods and heroes, prophets of all sorts, who one way or
> other have shed so much distinction on it, I am trans-
> ported with the reflection that I myself belong, though
> but subordinately, to so emblazoned a fraternity (465).

By a characteristic stretching of definitions, Ishmael is able to
enroll Perseus, St. George, and Hercules in the ranks of
whalemen. The genuine, mysterious heroism of Ahab is
counterpointed by Ishmael's penchant for the tall tale.

In fact, Ishmael's mock-heroic meditations derive from
sources other than Shakespeare, Milton, and Byron. The
American folktale is one clear source, as when Ishmael calls
Hercules "that antique Crockett and Kit Carson" (468). The
heroes of these American legends, Max Eastman has noted,
are generally treated with a humorous exaggeration. "All
mythical heroes have been exaggerations, but they have been
serious ones. America came too late for that. Her demigods
were born in laughter." [28] Another hero in *Moby-Dick* from
these native American sources is Steelkit in "The Town-Ho's
Story," a "canaller" who may owe something to the legends
of Mike Fink.[29] "Freely depicted in his own vocation,"
Ishmael tells his audience at the Golden Inn, "the Canaller
would make a fine dramatic hero" (332). A second major
source of the mock-heroic in Ishmael's vision is Carlyle's
Sartor Resartus, which Melville had borrowed from Duyckinck
in the summer of 1850.[30] *Sartor Resartus* itself takes the form

28. Quoted by Matthiessen, *American Renaissance,* p. 640.

29. See Sherman Paul, "Morgan Neville, Melville, and the Folk Hero,"
Notes and Queries 194 (1949) : 278.

30. Merton M. Sealts, Jr., *Melville's Reading* (Madison, Wisc., 1951),
p. 120.

of a meditation on the hero, with the English editor presenting the life and opinions of the German philosopher Teufelsdröckh. While the mock-heroic elements of this literary hoax are ultimately subsumed by a more genuine note of social prophecy, Melville, like many other readers since, seems to have been more struck by the comically encyclopedic aspects of Teufelsdröckh's Clothes Philosophy than by his serious pretensions to heroic action.[31] Teufelsdröckh asserts that "the whole External Universe and what it holds is but Clothing, and the essence of all science lies in the PHILOSOPHY OF CLOTHES." [32] Ishmael attempts a similar encyclopedic vision of the world through an anatomy of whales and whaling. "From his mighty bulk the whale affords a most congenial theme whereon to enlarge, amplify, and generally expatiate" (579). There are, of course, many other sources for this habit of mind in Ishmael—Burton's *Anatomy of Melancholy* and Sir Thomas Browne's *Religio Medici*—but it is only in *Sartor Resartus* that this encyclopedism is associated with the idea of heroes and hero worship.

Thus we have Ishmael and Ahab not only as narrator and hero, but as two complementary forms of the quester. In most of the meditations on the hero we have been considering, the narrator has been adjectival to a substantive hero, significant primarily in the way he reflects on him. The major exception is Constantine Constantius, who engages in his own attempt to achieve repetition apart from his hero. But Ishmael's quest is not merely a "parody" of Ahab's, as Constantine's is of the young man's; it is a contrasting form of vision and mode of existence. Thomas Vogler's remarks on the narrators of *Wuthering Heights* see much more applicable here (see p. 111). Ahab's assault on the eternal and the infinite is clearly more heroic in its posture, but Ishmael's speculative, oblique approach is not without its own metaphysical ambitions, in-

31. My argument here runs counter to that of Leon Howard in his biography of Melville, who sees a more serious influence of Teufelsdröckh on Ahab (p. 171).

32. *Sartor Resartus,* ed. C. F. Harrold (New York, 1937), p. 74.

dependent of those of the hero himself. As a narrator, Ishmael has considerable independence from his hero, and can even be seen as something of an alternate self.

Once this contrast between Ishmael and Ahab is grasped as a structural principle, a good deal of the apparent formlessness of *Moby-Dick* is resolved. For example, there is the question of the dramatic chapters in the book, where the first-person narrator disappears and the characters speak their lines, with stage directions, as in a play. Some critics have felt this to be a clumsiness on Melville's part, but it can more profitably be seen as a rendering of the tension between the narrator and the hero in this expanded version of the meditative form. At one extreme is the kind of direct address to the reader that we find in the opening chapter, where Ishmael assumes a name, but immediately identifies himself with his audience, shifting to the second person: "Circumambulate the city of a dreary Sabbath afternoon. Go from Corlears Hook to Coenties Slip, and from thence, by Whitehall, northward. What do you see" (24)? Ishmael is subjectively though unobtrusively present as a companion and guide. At the other extreme is the dramatic objectivity of the chapters in which Ahab exerts his influence on the crew. Chapter 40, "Midnight, Forecastle," dramatizes the revels of the crew after Ahab has pledged them to his revenge. All information except the speeches and songs are supplied by stage directions. It is only at the beginning of the next chapter that the first-person narrative reasserts itself: "I, Ishmael, was one of that crew; my shouts had gone up with the rest" (239).

As Glauco Cambon has noted, the shifts back and forth from narrative to dramatic mode are "skillfully modulated." "Because of its strategic collocation and of its intense tone, that initial phrase, 'I, Ishmael, was one of that crew' rivals the felicitous opening of the whole narration: 'Call me Ishmael.' " [33] It is also worth noting that the dramatic or theatrical intrusions into the narrative mode occur only by degrees. In chap-

33. "Ishmael and the Problem of Formal Discontinuities in *Moby-Dick,*" *Modern Language Notes* 76 (1961) : 518.

ter 29 the first dramatic element appears merely in the title of the chapter, which is a stage direction: "Enter Ahab; to Him, Stubb." In the following chapter, "Cetology," Ishmael reasserts his presence as narrator more forcefully; he offers a curious classification of whales as though they were printed volumes. "By naming the main divisions of his cetological construct 'Folio,' 'Octavo,' and 'Duodecimo' and calling the smaller units 'Chapters,' he turns whales into books." [34] The authorial self-consciousness of the device resists the pull toward the dramatic, but a few pages later Ahab renews his magnetic attraction: "But Ahab, my Captain, still moves before me in all his Nantucket grimness and shagginess" (199). Ishmael's disclaimer, "In this episode touching Emperors and Kings, I must not conceal that I have only to do with a poor old whale-hunter," suggests a continuing resistance on his part to Ahab's dramatic potential, but the drama of Ahab reemerges in the proto-dramatic form of "The Quarterdeck," where more stage directions are given. As Matthiessen notes, there are reminders of Hamlet and the Ghost forcing the others to swear.[35] The four following chapters finally attain full dramatic form—the soliloquies by Ahab, Starbuck, and Stubb, then the midnight chorus of the sailors. Ishmael is no longer the presiding consciousness but "one of that crew."

The contrast between the narrator and the hero is thus not a passive kind of parallelism but an active struggle between two different visions and the respective fictional modes that these visions entail. The "formal discontinuities," where a dramatic form intrudes upon the narrative, are not merely isolated incidents; they are reflections of a larger pattern in *Moby-Dick,* a dialectic of narrative meditation on the mysteries of the ocean and dramatic action taken against them. We noted in the first chapter Goethe's distinction between the hero of the novel and the hero of the drama, and the distinction seems particularly applicable to the overall form of *Moby-Dick:*

34. Dryden, *Melville's Thematics*, p. 94.
35. *American Renaissance*, p. 432.

> In the novel, it is chiefly *sentiments* and *events* that are
> exhibited; in the drama, it is *characters* and *deeds*. The
> novel must go slowly forward; and the sentiments of the
> hero, by some means or another, must restrain the
> tendency of the whole to unfold itself and to conclude.
> The drama, on the other hand, must hasten, and the char-
> acter of the hero must press forward to the end; it does
> not restrain, but is restrained.[36]

Although, as I have already suggested, Ishmael is engaged on
a metaphysical quest of his own, his approach is not one of
confrontation but one of delay. Ishmael goes to sea to escape
the confinement of the land. When he finds himself a part of
Ahab's revenge, his shouts go up with the rest under Ahab's
immediate influence, but he is continually digressing from
the forward progress of the voyage in an attempt to expand
his narrative consciousness. He is more concerned with sentiments than events, in Goethe's terms. Fascinated by Ahab's
presence, he would also escape from it.

The sense of escape can be felt in the many chapters in
Moby-Dick in which Ishmael restrains the forward motion of
Ahab's hunt. For example, he freezes the temporal flow of the
narrative to give the reader a clear visual picture in the
present tense: "It must be borne in mind that all this time we
have a Sperm Whale's prodigious head hanging to the
Pequod's side. But we must let it continue hanging there a
while till we can get a chance to attend to it. For the present
other matters press, and the best we can do now for the head,
is to pray heaven that the tackles may hold" (420). There is
literally a suspension of the progress of the chase here.
Ishmael can move backward in time before the Pequod's
voyage to describe his view of a whale's skeleton in "A Bower
in the Arsacides." In "The Town-Ho's Story," he makes a
temporal leap forward. Here Ishmael makes his most successful gesture of escape from Ahab's hunt: he creates a narrative
within the narrative, offering an interpolated tale in "the

36. *Wilhelm Meister,* trans. Carlyle, pp. 288–89.

style in which I once narrated it at Lima, to a lounging circle of my Spanish friends, one saint's eve, smoking upon the thick-gilt piazza of the Golden Inn" (322). The after-dinner context and the interruptions of the friends remove the tale to a realm of relaxation and entertainment. The story of Radney and Steelkilt, which Ishmael offers as a twice-told tale, is like *Moby-Dick* itself a tale of revenge. It is as though Ishmael were retreating to a fictional mode where he could reassert his absolute narrative control.

Thus in the figure of Steelkilt we are given an alternative version of the hero. As a canaller, "a fine dramatic hero," Steelkilt is an Ahab of the inland waterways. And by a coincidence worthy of *Tristram Shandy*, Ishmael manages to introduce into his tale Moby-Dick himself. Since Moby-Dick acts here as the instrument of Steelkilt's revenge, seizing the first mate Radney in his jaws, Ahab's story is stood on its head. Instead of a hero's revenging himself on Moby-Dick, Moby-Dick acts as the hero's agent of revenge.[37] In this narrative tour de force, Ishmael demonstrates his superiority to and independence from the main events of the book. One feels the strength of his comic invention as a teller of tall tales.

Ishmael would thus arrive at a sense of life's mysteries not by frontal assault but by indirection and surmise. As Geoffrey Hartman has observed, the surmise, a persistent questioning of natural fact, is an important strategy in the supernatural vision of Romantic poetry.[38] But the avoidance of confrontation, the negative capability in Ishmael, leads to a loss of self. He is less a fully developed character in the book than a consciousness divorced from concrete existence. There is little or no sense of an inner selfhood behind his assumed name and rambling discourse. His identity is continually losing itself, in the way that he describes in "The Mast-Head": "Lulled into such an opium-like listlessness of vacant, unconscious reverie

37. Cf. Harry Levin, *The Power of Blackness*, p. 215: "Moby-Dick seems to be a *deus ex machina* for the Town-Ho; on the Pequod he will become a *diabolus ex machina*."

38. *Wordsworth's Poetry, 1787–1814* (New Haven, 1964), pp. 8–12.

is this absent-minded youth by the blending cadence of waves
with thoughts, that at last he loses his identity" (214). At several points in the voyage Ishmael describes such a loss of self
on his part: at the masthead, gazing into the ocean; at the
tiller, gazing into the fire of the try-works; at the tubs of
sperm, squeezing the substance from solid to liquid form. His
consciousness flows out into the world around him until some
event recalls it, often with a shock, to the self from which it
went forth.

Ahab, on the other hand, is a character whose existence has
deliberately cut itself off from such expansive consciousness.
He represses any awareness of himself in the larger contexts of
nature or humanity. Ahab has moments of self-recognition
and remorse, but his identity is continually contracting itself
into a single-minded will to one thing. Hence the passage in
which Ishmael describes Ahab's thoughts creating an independent being within him: "God help thee, old man, thy
thoughts have created a creature in thee; and he whose intense thinking thus makes him a Prometheus; a vulture feeds
upon that heart forever; that vulture the very creature he
creates" (272). The centripetal force of Ahab's thinking pre-
cipitates within him a more archetypal heroic identity, complete with its attendant suffering.

The relationship of Ishmael's speculative consciousness to
Ahab's active existence may be further understood in the terms
provided by the geometrical metaphor of the circle that runs
throughout the book. Ishmael lives at the circumference of
human experience while Ahab lives at its center. At one point
Ishmael envisions life as a series of circlings through the ages
of man, a cyclical movement which only ends in death (624).
In another context he compares the ocean on which he is voy-
aging to the unknown regions of the mind that surround an
individual's identity. "For as this appalling ocean surrounds
the verdant land, so in the soul of man there lies one insular
Tahiti, full of peace and joy, but encompassed by all the
horrors of the half known life. God keep thee! Push not off

from that isle, thou canst never return" (364). Ishmael has
pushed off from that isle, and thus looks back on it nostal-
gically as a point of peace and joy. But Ahab, who lives at the
center of the circle of human experience, finds this center a
tragic point:

> In an instant's compass, great hearts sometimes condense
> to one deep pang, the sum total of those shallow pains
> kindly diffused through feebler men's whole lives. And
> so, such hearts, though summary in each one suffering;
> still, if the gods decree it, in their life-time aggregate a
> whole age of woe, wholly made up of instantaneous in-
> tensities; for even in their pointless centres, those noble
> natures contain the entire circumference of inferior
> souls (695).

Ahab's tragic heroism is the concentrated center of the tragic
element in mankind as a whole. This figure is realized more
literally as well. On the first day of the chase of Moby-Dick,
Ahab's boat is destroyed and the white whale swims around
the boat in "ever-contracting circles." The other boats can
only stand by and watch: "With straining eyes . . . they remained on the outer edge of the direful zone, whose centre
had now become the old man's head" (694).

The imagery of circle and center is pervasive in *Moby-Dick*.
Although at times it is merely invoked as a passing analogy, it
also appears as an organizing pattern of the action. In the
chapter "The Grand Armada" Starbuck's boat enters into a
charmed circle in the middle of the herd of whales, a circle
that protects the mother whales and their newborn young. As
in the image of the "insular Tahiti," the center of this circle
suggests peace and joy—until the circumference begins to close
in and the whaleboat is almost crushed. In the chapter "The
Doubloon" various characters surround the gold coin, itself a
circle, with their different interpretations of its meaning. At
the end of the book the Pequod goes down in a vortex and
out of the center springs Queequeg's coffin, the life buoy on

which Ishmael survives. As hero, Ahab stands at the center of the circle, drawing the attention of those on the periphery toward him. As narrator, Ishmael moves on the circumference, drawn to the center but resisting the pull of that fatal point.[39]

Since the relationship of Ishmael and Ahab is a dynamic one, however, it might be more useful to say that Ishmael's meditation is centrifugal, Ahab's action centripetal. But Ishmael's retreat from the center is not merely a negative impulse; it is also symptomatic of his desire to present his story to an audience, to *com*-municate in the full sense of the word. Ishmael is by nature a raconteur, and his favorite narrative situation, as he reveals in recounting the Town-Ho's story, is the after-dinner anecdote. This situation might be called a symposium in the original Platonic sense. It is a gathering where speech is mixed with food and drink and discourse is a shared experience. It is a situation where there is a close relationship between the speaker and his audience and a considerable distance between the speaker and the serious truth of his tale. Ishmael expresses his narrative stance in the opening chapter: "Not ignoring what is good, I am quick to perceive a horror, and could still be social with it" (30). The desire to socialize the horror of his story is a fundamental motive with Ishmael. It expresses itself in his comradely, confiding tone and in his particular concern with social ceremonies involving food and / or drink.

From Ishmael's social perspective, Ahab's centripetal thrust seems itself a flight, an escape from human relationship. Where Ishmael prefers a relaxing drink among companions, Ahab assumes the role of a priest at Mass when he offers the crew a round of grog after swearing them to his revenge. Ahab insists on maintaining ascendancy over the minds and

39. Cf. Georges Poulet, *The Metamorphoses of the Circle,* trans. Carley Dawson and Elliott Coleman (Baltimore, 1966). Poulet's discussion of Schopenhauer (pp. 109–10) seems particularly relevant to the circular motif in Melville. See also Emerson's essay "Circles" in *Essays: First Series.* John Seelye's "ironic diagram" for Melville involves the interaction of circle and line; our geometrics overlap but are not congruent (*Melville: The Ironic Diagram* [Evanston, 1971], pp. 6–10).

bodies of his crew, and he does so even over the mind of Ishmael. Where Ishmael digresses in the context of the symposium, Ahab compels attention through a narrative situation of his own. The mode of discourse peculiar to Ahab is more oratorical than narrative in the strict sense, and it may be identified as the mode of the sermon.

Ahab acts and speaks like a Shakespearean tragic hero, but he also behaves like a preacher in the tradition of American Puritanism. Given Melville's view of Shakespeare as a visionary and prophet, these two modes are not so much in conflict as they might appear. Beneath the Shakespearean gestures and diction is the sensibility of a Puritan, and the Puritanism manifests itself particularly in Ahab's sense of an audience. Perry Miller has written of the congregational aspect of Puritanism in a way that describes quite well Ahab's rhetorical stance. "Puritanism in the early seventeenth century, the Puritanism that settled New England, was more properly symbolized, not by the secluded individual, but by the social tableau of the covenanted church and the public discourse. . . . Puritan life, in the New England theory, was centered upon a corporate and communal ceremony, upon the oral delivery of a lecture." [40] Ahab is a Puritan preacher in the way that his social effect is dependent, paradoxically but according to theory, on his spiritual isolation. Like the Reverend Dimmesdale in *The Scarlet Letter,* his private anguish makes his public delivery the more compelling.

The stage is set for Ahab's sermonic effects, of course, by the actual sermon of Father Mapple. Some critics have felt that the content of Father Mapple's performance is important; W. H. Auden, for example, claims that it gives "the moral

---

40. *The New England Mind: The Seventeenth Century* (New York, 1939), pp. 297–98. On the "sermon-form" in *Moby-Dick* see Walter E. Bezanson, "*Moby-Dick:* Work of Art," in *Moby-Dick Centennial Essays,* ed. Tyrus Hillway and Luther S. Mansfield (Dallas, 1953), pp. 50–52. Benzanson is more concerned with the internal structure of the sermon, which he finds examples of throughout the book; he does not identify the sermon particularly with Ahab.

presuppositions by which we are to judge the speeches and actions of Ahab and the rest." [41] It seems to me rather that the form of his delivery is more significant. Father Mapple isolates himself for dramatic effect when he climbs up to his pulpit and pulls the rope ladder up behind him. He addresses his pastoral "shipmates" in the name of a higher truth. And the spiritual form if not the spiritual content of his peroration points directly ahead to Ahab:

> Delight is to him—a far, far upward, and inward delight —who against the proud gods and commodores of this earth, ever stands forth his own inexorable self. Delight is to him whose strong arms yet support him, when the ship of this base treacherous world has gone down beneath him. Delight is to him, who gives no quarter in the truth, and kills, burns, and destroys all sin though he pluck it out from under the robes of Senators and Judges (80).

Although we must postpone a close consideration of Ahab's conception of the absolute, we can see how closely the preferred Puritan attitude corresponds to Ahab's attitude toward the powers responsible for his injury. One might say that Father Mapple's God has retreated from Ahab's universe and that Ahab is left to grapple with the proud gods and commodores by the light of his own sense of justice. In his attitude toward the crew of the Pequod he follows Father Mapple's lead. He isolates himself from the crew and engages in what Carlyle would call "deceptive dramaturgy" to bind them to his purpose. [42] He addresses them as a congregation whom he must convert to a higher law, even though this higher law is simply the law of his own revenge. (The biblical Ahab was a king who set up a false god for worship.) Melville's Ahab acts as the preacher of a God conspicuous by his absence.

41. *The Enchafèd Flood; or, The Romantic Iconography of the Sea* (New York, 1950), p. 122.
42. *On Heroes and Hero-Worship,* p. 201.

Thus Ahab conducts his own inverted religious ceremony on the quarterdeck. Where Ishmael tries to relate the "horror" of his tale to the social norms of his audience, Ahab tries to convert his audience to the horror of his private revenge. It is always a question as to how much of Ahab's behavior is deceptive dramaturgy and how much is genuine self-expression. But the overall effect of Ahab's fire-and-brimstone utterances to the crew—on the quarterdeck, when he makes his initial announcement, or in the storm of "The Candles," when he holds the lightning rods in his hands and defies the gods—is to raise their sight above the common material vision to something transcendent. Like many Puritan visions, Ahab's preaching is closely involved with notions of sin and evil. It is true that Ahab has no thought for the welfare of the souls of his crew, but it is also true that as a literary character he is most fully himself in his public utterances. His silences and soliloquies are adjuncts of this rhetorical effect.

Once we have recognized the sermon and the symposium as the verbal modes of the hero and his narrator, we can see how these modes also operate apart from Ahab and Ishmael themselves and extend, symbolically, the influence of each. For example, Ahab's sermonizing is picked up by Stubb: "Stubb's exordium to his crew is given here at large, because he had a rather peculiar way of talking to them in general, and especially in inculcating the religion of rowing. But you must not suppose from this specimen of his sermonizings that he ever flew into downright passions with his congregation" (293). Other characters, such as the captain of the Samuel Enderby, echo Ishmael's conviviality with strangers and his sociability with a horror:

> Yes, caught me just here, I say, and bore me down to Hell's flames, I was thinking; when, when, all of a sudden, thank the good God, the barb ript its way along the flesh—clear along the whole length of my arm—came out nigh my wrist, and up I floated;—and that gentleman

there will tell you the rest (by the way, captain—Dr.
Bunger, ship's surgeon: Bunger, my lad,—the captain).
Now, Bunger boy, spin your part of the yarn. (561)

The captain of the Samuel Enderby has been savagely attacked
by the white whale, but he recounts it in the manner of
Ishmael rather than in the manner of Ahab. The sermon and
the symposium occur in combination as well as apart, extend-
ing symbolically the interaction of narrator and hero. "The
Captain's Table" shows Ahab turning dinner into a hierarchi-
cal occasion rather than a convivial one. "The Gam" shows
how even the lonely whaling ships have a social intercourse,
while "The Pequod Meets the Jereboam" shows the social occasion of the gam being interrupted by the sermonic ravings
of Gabriel, the mad Shaker prophet. In the chapter entitled
"Stubb's Supper" there is a particularly explicit mixing of the
two basic modes. Stubb the epicure is feasting on a steak cut
from a captured whale. He instructs the cook to deliver a
sermon to the sharks, in order to convert them from their
animal ravenousness to more civilized behavior. The cook
preaches that "all angel is not'ing more dan de shark well
goberned" (367) but concludes also that Stubb, in his gour-
mandise, is more shark than the shark himself. The chapter
burlesques the narrative modes of the book, but in doing so
it conducts a dialectical inquiry into human nature, examin-
ing where on the scale between the angels and the beasts man
belongs. In fact, the chapter brings out the contrasting
philosophies of man implicit in the symposium and the
sermon. The symposium sees no essential conflict between the
bodily and the spiritual appetites, while the sermon emphasizes the conflict to such an extent that there often seems no
middle ground possible for human nature: man is either all
angel or all shark.

The after-dinner colloquies of Ishmael and the hellfire and
damnation sermons of Ahab, therefore, involve two conflicting
views of the human self. Kierkegaard would call these two

views the aesthetic and the religious,[43] and although he is much more rigorous than Melville in his definitions, it is interesting to remember that Kierkegaard associates the aesthetic view with the form of the symposium. In both authors one can see the tension between Hellenistic and Hebraic modes that Matthew Arnold was to codify some years later. But Melville's dialectic looks back as well as foreward. Behind the meditation and the action of *Moby-Dick* there is an implicit essay on man, a Romantic version, writ large, of the kind of Enlightenment dialectic one finds in a poet such as Alexander Pope. Beneath man's feet is the swirling, chaotic world of nature, the ocean, and the natural appetites. Above his head is the realm of the gods, who may not exist in actuality, but whose possibility continues to haunt the human mind. In the detached and reflective consciousness of Ishmael these dialectical opposites achieve an uneasy synthesis in the cheerful, colloquial attitude that turns away from despair. In the committed and immediate existence of Ahab, the natural physical world must be subdued in order to free the godlike potential of the human spirit, in order to bring man and the gods face to face.

To some extent, then, *Moby-Dick* is more than a meditation on the *hero*, as a good deal of meditation is not on Ahab at all. Ishmael speculates at length not only on the central heroic figure but also on a series of human and natural phenomena. As I suggested in the first chapter, Melville's obsession with Shakespeare and the tragic hero is balanced by his debt to Jonathan Edwards and the "images, or shadows of divine things." There is a sense in which the hero is only the most commanding of these images that Ishmael meditates on in his own pursuit of the ultimate. Yet one might also reverse the assertion and say that the images and shadows that occupy Ishmael are alternatives or substitutes for the hero who, when

43. Brodtkorb, *Ishmael's White World*, p. 138, makes this same point; he suggests that Starbuck can be seen as Kierkegaard's ethical stage, teleologically suspended.

all is said and done, dominates the book, especially at the end. The latter seems to be the case at least with Ishmael's meditations on the whale, which often treat the animal as if it were human, as if it were a mysterious hero whose nature needed special interpretation.

Melville had signaled such an analogy between whale and hero in a letter to Duyckinck written in 1849 after hearing one of Emerson's lectures. "I love all men who *dive*," he wrote. "Any fish can swim near the surface, but it takes a great whale to go down stairs five miles or more; & if he don't attain the bottom why, all the lead in Galena can't fashion the plummet that will. I'm not talking of Mr. Emerson now—but of the whole corps of thought-divers, that have been diving & coming up again with bloodshot eyes since the world began." [44] As in his approach to Ahab, Ishmael would use the whale as such a visionary agent, a presence outside himself through whom he might glimpse the supernatural realm. He himself is not a deep diver—"All this to explain," he says at one point, "would be to dive deeper than Ishmael can go" (251)—but he is drawn to such efforts on the part of others. When Ahab is not present as hero, he turns to the whale, the hero's antagonist, in his vicarious visionary quest.

Thus in "The Praire" Ishmael subjects the head of the sperm whale (generally considered) to a phrenological analysis. He compares the whale's brow to the high foreheads of such human geniuses as Melancthon and Shakespeare. "But in the great Sperm Whale, this high and mighty god-like dignity inherent in the brow is so immensely amplified, that gazing on it, in that full front view, you feel the Deity and the dread powers more forcible than in beholding any other object in living nature" (447). The whale is less a natural object here than a humanized figure seen against a metaphysical ground. In "The Tail," Ishmael tries to read the character of the whale from the other end. He falls into an exclamation of ignorance characteristic of the narrator before his hero ("Abraham I cannot understand . . . "): "The more I consider this mighty

44. Davis and Gilman, eds., *Letters*, p. 79.

tail, the more do I deplore my inability to express it. At times there are gestures in it, which, though they would well grace the hand of man, remain wholly inexplicable. . . . Dissect him how I may, then, I go but skin deep; I know him not, and never will" (486).

There are many similarities between Melville and Hawthorne in the way they subject certain phenomena to symbolistic speculation; one major difference between them is the nature of the phenomena they choose to treat as symbolic. Hawthorne, as I suggested in the first chapter, focuses more often on artifacts or objects than on human selves. The mysteries he is concerned with are psychological, and he uses the object or emblem (Hester Prynne's scarlet letter, Governor Endicott's red cross, Minister Hooper's black veil) as a means of exploring the mysteries of the enigmatic human heart. Melville is more concerned with the metaphysical mysteries of the enigmatic cosmos; the means he uses to approach these mysteries are exotic phenomena of the natural world and the heroic conception of character. Thus in Hawthorne the study of character is often an end in itself, while in Melville it tends to be a means to another end. The difference can be best appreciated by a comparison of Ahab with the Hawthorne character who most resembles him, Ethan Brand.

Melville read "Ethan Brand" in May of 1851,[45] and *Moby-Dick* was completed in July of that year, so the actual influence of Hawthorne's main character on Melville's could not have been very great. There are many features that the two heroes share in common, most notably the demonic isolation from their fellow men and their mysterious quests.[46] But

45. Jay Leyda, *The Melville Log*, 2nd ed. (New York, 1969), 1 : 412.
46. See Sherman Paul, "Hawthorne's Ahab," *Notes and Queries* 196 (1951) : 255–57, and James E. Miller, "Hawthorne and Melville: The Unpardonable Sin," *PMLA* 70 (1955) : 91–114. The only element specific enough to be called a borrowing that I have been able to find is the discussion of Ahab's artificial leg retaining its feeling (Chap. 108) and the same phenomenon, not in Ethan Brand himself but in a minor character named Giles: "Yet, though the corporeal hand was gone, a spiritual member remained; for, stretching forth the stump, Giles stead-

Ethan Brand is a hero whose ultimate object, "The Unpardonable Sin," is of his own making and lies within himself. His heroism collapses in solipsism as he burns in the lime-kiln; his story is "A Chapter from an Abortive Romance." In searching for the Unpardonable Sin, Brand is seeking to divorce himself from God, and—according to Hawthorne's more liberal theology—from the community of nature and mankind. The supernatural, natural, and social communities provide what little "ground" there is for Brand as hero, but he is deliberately withdrawing from them. It is clear from the stylized way that Hawthorne presents "nature" and "human brotherhood" in the story that these realities have been seriously eroded for the author as well as for his hero. After Brand's death, the author evokes the landscape: "Stepping from one to another of the clouds that rested on the hills, and thence to the loftier brotherhood that sailed in air, it seemed almost as if a mortal man might thus ascend into the heavenly regions. Earth was so mingled with sky that it was a day-dream look at." Nature is artificial and suspect, like the pictures in the diorama presented by the Jew of Nuremberg. Brand's suicide is not a gesture of defiance but a surrender to the emptiness of his emotional isolation. His skeleton lies "in the attitude of a person who, after long toil, lies down to long repose." [47]

"Was the fellow's heart made of marble?" one of the survivors exclaims.[48] Hawthorne is providing an obvious moral to the tale—that Brand was simply too selfish—yet as in so many of Hawthorne's stories the very obviousness of the conclusion calls into question the ethical certainty it would reflect. Ethan Brand has found the Unpardonable Sin, we are told, yet the author gives us no sense of a secure frame of reference from which judgment can be passed on him. As

---

fastly averred that he felt an invisible thumb and fingers with as vivid a sensation as before the real ones were amputated" (*Complete Novels and Selected Tales*, ed. Norman Holmes Pearson [New York, 1937], p. 1190).

47. Pearson, ed. *Novels and Tales*, p. 1195, 1196.
48. Ibid., p. 1196.

with Hester Prynne, Brand's "sin" is the psychological condition of modern man rather than a religious or ethical offense
against a traditional God. Like Melville, Hawthorne could not
believe but was able to avoid the metaphysical anguish of his
unbelief. This does not make him any less brilliant a writer
than Melville, but it does create an uncongenial atmosphere
for the figure of the hero. In their discussions with one another
in the relatively brief period of their close friendship Melville and Hawthorne talked of "ontological heroics," as Melville put it.[49] It is the lack of the ontological, it would seem,
that causes Hawthorne's Romantic hero to abort.

The concern with confronting this "ontological mystery,"
as Erich Heller has called it,[50] is what distinguishes Melville
from Hawthorne. It is a concern that Ishmael and Ahab share
within *Moby-Dick,* yet one that they express in opposing ways.
Their different approaches raise the question of the hero's—
and in Melville's case, the narrator's—relation as a figure to
the ontological ground.

Ahab is a Calvinist in his search for truth in radical transcendence of the world. Ishmael is a Transcendentalist with
more faith in immanence, who feels with Emerson that "We
live amid surfaces, and the true art of life is to skate well on
them." [51] Ahab's heroic stance toward the world requires that
he strike through the mask, but Ishmael, in his meditative
approach, multiplies his surmises on the concealing surfaces of
things. After explaining in one chapter "what the white whale
was to Ahab," he explains with characteristic tentativeness in
the following chapter ("The Whiteness of the Whale") "what,
at times, he was to me" (252). Characteristically, it is the
surface of the whale that fascinates Ishmael, the whiteness of
his skin. Ishmael argues in circles trying to isolate the essence
of this whiteness, the specific quality of its appearance that so
affects the imagination. What happens in the course of this
chapter is characteristic of his mental processes. As he multi-

49. Quoted by Paul, "Hawthorne's Ahab," p. 256.
50. "Goethe and the Idea of Scientific Truth," *The Disinherited Mind*
(Cleveland, 1959), p. 17.
51. "Experience," *Selected Writings,* p. 350.

plies the examples in support of his argument that whiteness
per se is terrifying, his logic becomes less and less convincing;
he is forced to rely more and more on rhetorical questions.
The closer he gets to the essence of whiteness, rather than to
any accidental qualities associated with it, the more unsure
his analysis becomes. At the end of the chapter he has both
expanded and reduced his explanation to the point that he
can see beneath the white surface only a void.

> And when we consider that other theory of the natural
> philosophers, that all other earthly hues—every stately or
> lovely emblazoning—the sweet tinges of sunset skies and
> woods; yea, and the gilded velvets of butterflies, and the
> butterfly cheeks of young girls; all these are but subtile
> deceits, not actually inherent in substances, but only laid
> on from without; so that all deified Nature absolutely
> paints like the harlot, whose allurements cover nothing
> but the charnel-house within; and when we proceed fur-
> ther, and consider that the mystical cosmetic which pro-
> duces every one of her hues, the great principle of light,
> for ever remains white or colorless in itself, and if oper-
> ating without medium upon matter, would touch all ob-
> jects, even tulips and roses, with its own blank tinge—
> pondering all this, the palsified universe lies before us a
> leper; and like wilful travellers in Lapland, who refuse
> to wear colored and coloring glasses upon their eyes, so
> the wretched infidel gazes himself blind at the monu-
> mental white shroud that wraps all the prospect around
> him (264).

What the white whale means to Ishmael is finally the vision
of a metaphysical void. He collapses the distinction between
the noumenal and the phenomenal categories, which results
in a vision of Being as Nothingness.[52]

This vision of nothingness is not to be taken as the im-

---

52. Cf. Seelye, *Ironic Diagram*, p. 64, and Brodtkorb, *Ishmael's White
World*, pp. 137–39, on Ishmael and Nothingness.

plicit metaphysics of *Moby-Dick* as a whole, however, for it is
a result of Ishmael's habits of thought, peculiar to him. Instead of attempting to fix, define, and analyze a particular
phenomenon, Ishmael prefers to surround it with a series of
analogies. "There is no quality in this world that is not what
it is merely by contrast," he says. "Nothing exists in itself"
(86). The argument by analogy is logically a weak form of
argument; it is what a character in *The Confidence-Man* calls
punning with ideas.[53] What this fondness for analogy indicates in Ishmael is a desire *not* to resolve ambiguities, but
rather to multiply them, to catch the ontological mystery in a
net of significant relationships. "What could be more full of
meaning?" he asks of Father Mapple's pulpit (69), and of the
whale itself he says with apparent satisfaction, "So there is no
earthly way of finding out precisely what the whale looks
like" (352). To look at an object is to fix it in one's physical
vision. Ishmael prefers the metaphor as a way of multiplying
visual possibilities. Hence his three-chapter excursus on the
iconography of the whale: "Of the Monstrous Pictures of
Whales," "Of the Less Erroneous Pictures of Whales, and the
True Pictures of Whaling Scenes," and "Of Whales in Paint;
in Teeth; in Wood; in Sheet; in Iron; in Stone; in Mountains;
in Stars." The visual emphasis here leads us further and further from the limits of the object itself, an expansion ad
infinitum.

Periodically, however, Ishmael's "expanded meditation"
(183) overextends the relational meanings it perceives among
things and the analogical structure collapses. In the chapter
"Fast-Fish and Loose-Fish", for example, Ishmael is discussing
a legal distinction pertaining to the ownership of captured
whales. He begins on a literal level, citing a court case involving a whale, but he soon extends the distinction to other areas
as well.

53. " 'But is analogy argument? You are a punster.' / 'Punster, respected
sir?' with a look of being aggrieved. / Yes, you pun with ideas as another
man may with words" (*The Confidence-Man: His Masquerade,* ed. Elizabeth S. Foster [New York, 1954], pp. 140–41).

But if the doctrine of Fast-Fish be pretty generally applicable, the kindred doctrine of Loose-Fish is still more widely so. That is internationally and universally applicable. . . .

What are the Rights of Man and the Liberties of the World but Loose-Fish? What all men's minds and opinions but Loose-Fish? What is the principle of religious belief in them but a Loose-Fish? What to the ostentatious smuggling verbalists are the thoughts of thinkers but Loose-Fish? What is the great globe itself but a Loose-Fish? And what are you, reader, but a Loose-Fish and a Fast-Fish, too? (510).

The analogy is stretched to cover the whole earth, and collapses, characteristically, into authorial self-consciousness.

Against Ishmael's conception of the world as an analogical idea, however, is juxtaposed Ahab's sense of the world as logical will. Both characters are symbolists, but Ishmael's symbolism tends toward allegory in the Romantic distinction, whereas Ahab's tends toward existential engagement. Although he occasionally entertains the idea that being is nothingness ("Sometimes I think there's naught beyond" [221]) Ahab's whole quest for revenge depends on his assumption that the noumenal substance behind the phenomenal world is active and must be met with force. "All visible objects, man, are but as pasteboard masks. But in each event—in the living act, the undoubted deed—there, some unknown but still reasoning thing puts forth the mouldings of its features from behind the unreasoning mask. If man will strike, strike through the mask!" (220). Ahab's conception of the ontological ground involves two important assumptions: its rationality and its active force. The noumenal "thing" is "unknown but still reasoning." Where Ishmael revels in veiled meanings and ambiguities, Ahab demands direct and open revelation. "That inscrutable thing is chiefly what I hate," he says (221), and later, "Omen? omen?—the dictionary! If the gods think to speak outright to man, they will honorably speak outright;

not shake their heads, and give an old wives' darkling hint"
(697). But the ontological mystery, according to Ahab, is revealed in action rather than in speech—"in the living act, the
undoubted deed." Ahab's revenge imitates what it takes to be
the incarnation of the absolute in the act of the White Whale
by incarnating Ahab in an act of his own. The hero would
engage the metaphysical ground in direct confrontation. He
would do so, it is worth noting, not through Ishmael's encyclopedic diversity but through a single-minded concentration on a single natural object. His impiety of heart is to will
one thing.

In terms of the book as a whole, Ahab's aggressive attack
on Being emerges as the alternative to Ishmael's tentative in-
terrogation of it. While it is possible to prefer Ishmael's
agnostic curiosity, Ahab's faith is clearly the heroic attitude.
In comparison with the heroes of Brontë and Lermontov,
Ahab appears as a hero who posits his own ground. If the
gods did not exist, Ahab would have had to invent them, and
Melville provides no real assurance that such is not the case.
Like Pechorin, Ahab can be seen as "the ancient tragical motif
as reflected in the modern," the hero whose tragedy emanates
from his character alone rather than from his interaction
with something substantive outside himself. But Ahab is
unaccepting of this modernity and would re-create a substantive world to rebel against. His heroism is in this respect
archaic. On the other hand, he is not as archaic as Heathcliff,
who lives in immediate association with the ground of his
being, whose heroic autonomy is ultimately swallowed up by
the natural world that supports it. Ahab's metaphysics is not
necessarily the implicit metaphysics of the book as a whole
either, but it is the imaginative hypothesis against which his
heroism becomes possible.

One of the ways in which Melville posits this hypothetical
ground for his hero is in his adaptation of Shakespearean diction. Matthiessen comments on the language of a passage in
"The Candles," where Ahab defies the fire of the corpusants:
"Melville has now mastered Shakespeare's mature secret of

how to make language itself dramatic. He has learned to de
pend more and more upon verbs of action, which lend thei
dynamic pressure to both movement and meaning." Thoma
Woodson arrives at a similar conclusion: "The style convert
naming words (nouns, adjectives) into actions (verbs, adverbs)
trying to bring every object to life, desperately projecting ani
mation into 'things' and fighting the 'blankness' it sense
within itself." [54] Thus Ahab says of Moby-Dick, "He tasks me
he heaps me' (221), transforming the burden of his sufferin
into the active antagonism of the world. (A comparison witl
Heathcliff's speech in *Wuthering Heights* reveals the lack o
any such active verbal energy and a much greater dependenc
on adjectives and the verb "to be.")

Another Shakespearean element important in evoking ;
sense of the world as substantive will is Ahab's use of "thee'
and "thou." Melville makes this plausible in Ahab by refer
ring in advance to "the stately thee and thou of the Quake
idiom" (111), and there are biblical associations as well a
Shakespearean ones. The archaic second person singula
evokes a more personal sense of nature, as in Ahab's address tc
the corpusants: "Oh! thou clear spirit of clear fire, whom or
these seas I as Persian once did worship, till in the sacra
mental act so burned by thee, that to this hour I bear the scar
I now know thee, thou clear spirit, and I know that thy righ
worship is defiance" (641). Ahab's own words best explain
the significance of his rhetoric: "In the midst of the person
ified impersonal, a personality stands here." This intense, non
reductive personification, completely unlike the comic, anthro
pomorphizing of nature Ishmael indulges in, is accomplishec
by Ahab as a means of engaging a living natural world. [55]

The hero's relation to his ground is particularly precarious
in *Moby-Dick,* however, for the simple reason that the hero i
in open rebellion against that ground. Ahab is attempting not
only to confront the ontological mystery face to face, but to

54. Matthiessen, *American Renaissance,* p. 430, and Woodson, "Ahab's
Greatness," p. 363.

55. Cf. Harold Bloom's discussion of Shelley's evocation of nature as a
Burberian 'Thou' in *Shelley's Mythmaking* (New Haven, 1959).

subdue it, directly or indirectly: "Be the white whale agent, or be the white whale principal, I will wreck that hate upon him," he says (221). Gabriel, the mad Shaker prophet on the Jereboam considers the White Whale the Shaker God incarnate; Ahab is less a Fundamentalist and certainly not a prophet of this putative deity. If Ahab's Shakespearean language evokes the living godhead, his American technology subdues it, turning the living god into a dead universe. Carlyle's Teufelsdröckh underwent a conversion from the mechanism of the Everlasting No to the vitalism of the Everlasting Yea in his perception of the universe. Ahab vacillates between spiritual affirmation and mechanistic denial with an increasing emphasis on the latter.

Paradoxically, Ahab's preoccupation with the technology of striking through the mask depersonalizes the hero as a personality. He would make fast and secure what Ishmael regards as "the ungraspable phantom of life" (26). "The path to my fixed purpose is laid with iron rails, whereon my soul is grooved to run," Ahab says to himself (227). Instead of humanizing nature, his technical imagination naturalizes man. When Ahab traces out courses on his charts it seems as if some invisible hand is tracing out courses in the lines of his forehead. When Ahab is ordering a new leg from the Pequod's carpenter, he fancifully orders a complete mechanical man. The carpenter himself is an example of the man who has become his technology; "He was a pure manipulator; his brain, if he had ever had one, must have early oozed along into the muscles of his fingers. He was one of those unreasoning but still highly useful, *multum in parvo*, Sheffield contrivances, assuming the exterior—though a little swelled—of a common pocket knife; but containing, not only blades of various sizes, but also screw-drivers, cork-screws, tweezers, awls, pens, rulers, nail-filers, counter-sinkers" (596).

It is part of Ahab's heroism that he avoids this kind of technological dehumanization;[56] he dehumanizes others in this way more than himself. "To accomplish his object Ahab

56. Cf. Woodson, "Ahab's Greatness," pp. 356–59, for an argument that parallels mine.

must use tools; and of all tools used in the shadow of the moon, men are most apt to get out of order" (284). As he nears his goal, Ahab becomes increasingly impatient with technological aids. He throws the quadrant overboard; he seizes the lightning rods in his bare hands. He tempers his specially forged harpoon in blood, making it a sacramental object instead of a mechanical implement. But in Fedallah's prophecies technology comes back to haunt him: the Pequod turns out to be the hearse made of American wood and the whale line the hemp that will hang him.

In our last vision of him, Ahab is bound by his own technology to his adversary, but even before this literal convergence of hunter and hunted there is a symbolic representation of it in what many critics have noticed and one has called the "duplicate imagery" of the book: that is, the series of images that are common to Ahab and Moby-Dick—they both have a wrinkled brow, for example.[57] As Lewis Mumford said long ago, Ahab "becomes the image of the thing he hates."[58] In pursuing so relentlessly the object of his quest, Ahab personifies its impersonality, but virtually dehumanizes himself. Like Heathcliff, Ahab is a hero who is in the end immersed in the ground of his heroism, but in *Moby-Dick* the ontological status of that ground is finally in doubt. In attempting to raise his heroism to the level of more than human being, Ahab ends by disappearing into an ambiguously intermediate realm of nature.

Thus the figure of the hero is finally quite precarious in *Moby-Dick*. Melville praises "The rare virtue of interior spaciousness" in man (410), but when Ishmael attempts to look into Ahab's inner self, he frequently finds himself looking at a landscape or at an architectural ruin:

> This is much; yet Ahab's larger, darker, deeper part re-
> mains unhinted. But vain to popularize profundities, and

57. Sister Mary Ellen, I. H. M., "Duplicate Imagery in *Moby-Dick*," *Modern Fiction Studies* 8 (1962–63): 252–64.
58. *Herman Melville* (New York, 1929), p. 186.

all truth is profound. Winding far down from within the very heart of this spiked Hotel de Cluny where we here stand —however grand and wonderful, now quit it;—and take your way, ye nobler, sadder souls, to those vast Roman halls of Thermes; where far beneath the fantastic towers of man's upper earth, his root of grandeur, his whole awful essence sits in bearded state; an antique buried beneath antiquities, and throned on torsoes! (249)

Through much of the book, Ahab maintains the integrity of his heroic selfhood, but as the end of the chase approaches, the divisions between his human self and his heroic role become more pronounced. The Promethean "creature" that Ishmael saw created within him becomes virtually autonomous and self-sufficient; "I am the Fates' lieutenant," he proclaims (707), forgetting that all along his character has been his fate. "Is Ahab, Ahab? Is it I, God, or who, that lifts this arm?" he asks (685). The reification of Ahab's purpose is accompanied by a resurgence of his "humanities," those common human sympathies he had previously suppressed. It is as though his purpose had gone on ahead of him, projecting itself into Moby-Dick, and had left room within him for other qualities of mind. In an act of sympathy Ahab adopts Pip, the crazed cabin boy, as his companion. He seems to see in Pip a loss of self similar to his own. In "The Symphony" he expresses to Starbuck a longing for the companionship of others, sentiments that are surprisingly reminiscent of Ishmael.

A further sign of Ahab's alienation from himself is the increasing emphasis in the narrative on the double, or doppelgänger. "How dost thou know that some entire, living, thinking thing may not be invisibly and uninterpenetratingly standing precisely where thou now standest; aye, and standing there in thy spite?" Ahab asks the carpenter (600). In adopting Pip, Ahab appoints him to fill a vacancy he feels in himself: "Do thou abide below here, where they shall serve thee, as if thou wert the captain. Aye, lad, thou shalt sit here in my own screwed chair; another screw to it, thou must be" (525). At the end of "The Symphony," when Ahab has denied his sympathetic feelings aroused by Starbuck, he gazes over the side of the ship and discovers Fedallah's eyes reflected in place of his own. If Pip is the double to Ahab's humanities, Fedallah is the double of his demonic resolve.

To point out the diminishment of Ahab as a heroic figure toward the end of *Moby-Dick* is not to deny his heroism altogether. It is rather to show the dialectical tensions the Romantic hero is involved in here becoming too severe to be held in equilibrium. The heroic resolve of Ahab is thrust beyond his selfhood toward the ambiguous ground of his being. The common human sympathies, on the other hand, are pulled in the direction of the witness of his heroism. Part of him is already with the inhuman savagery of Moby-Dick, part of him looks back toward the humanizing spirit of Ishmael. This is how I interpret the fact that Ishmael all but disappears as a narrative presence from the last thirty chapters of the book, not that this is a deliberate device on Melville's part but that the strain which Ahab puts upon his heroic identity becomes too great for any mediating figure to intervene. Ahab's enforced delay of his revenge earlier gave Ishmael considerable scope and freedom for his meditations in the cetological center of the book, as Howard Vincent has called it, but as the hero nears his goal, all digression is countermanded by the increasing urgency of his quest. Ishmael becomes merely "one of that crew" again, surfacing only as the substitute oarsman in Ahab's whaleboat. Thus in the last section of *Moby-Dick*, there is a collapse of the meditation on the hero from without, which is replaced by the rendering of a more immediate struggle within. The imaginative synthesis of the meditative form, in other words, is pulled apart by the increasing split within the hero himself, the split between his cosmic ambitions and his human frailty.

It seems to me that the seeds of Melville's subsequent crisis and decline as a writer are present in his masterpiece. Driven by literary ambition, as well as economic need, he plunged im-

nediately into *Pierre,* writing to Hawthorne only a month
ifter *Moby-Dick* had been published, "Lord, when shall we
ie done growing? As long as we have anything more to do we
iave done nothing. So now, let us add Moby-Dick to our
ilessing, and step from that. Leviathan is not the biggest fish;
—I have heard of Krakens." [59] Melville's visionary impulse is,
f anything, greater; his new hero will go further than Ahab in
irobing at the very axis of reality. But Melville made a crucial
ihift in the goal of the hero's quest in his next novel—a shift
irom an ontological mystery in the natural cosmos to an
intological mystery in the human psyche. "Not yet had he
dropped his angle into the well of his childhood," the author
writes condescendingly of Pierre, "to find what fish might be
there; for who dreams to find fish in a well?" [60] Melville's own
problem was that he was fishing in a well for a sea monster
larger than Moby-Dick.

To put it in terms more familiar to readers of this study,
Pierre is Melville's attempt to present a hero and his quest in
the form of the Bildungsroman. As we saw in the first chapter,
the Bildungsroman is a complementary form of the meditation on the archaic hero, and in many ways Pierre is a diminished mirror image of Ahab. *Pierre* owes a good deal to
Hamlet—Melville focuses on this earlier Shakespearean tragedy quite explicitly—but the idea of a Hamlet of our time had
already been used by Goethe in the original Bildungsroman,
Wilhelm Meister. Melville borrowed a copy of Goethe's novel
from Duyckinck in 1850. Where Wilhelm outgrows the model
of Hamlet in his quest for a self in harmony with the world,
Pierre ends by playing out the Shakespearean role with melodramatic excess; the stage at the end is littered with corpses.
As in "Hawthorne and His Mosses," Melville attempts to play
down his worship of Shakespeare, and he appeals to the story

59. Davis and Gilman, eds. *Letters,* p. 143.
60. *Pierre; or, The Ambiguities,* ed. Hayford, Parker and Tanselle, in
The Writings of Herman Melville (Evanston and Chicago, 1971), p. 284.
In all further references to *Pierre,* page numbers cited parenthetically in
text are from this edition.

of Memnon and Aurora as an archetype of Shakespeare's
drama: "For in this plaintive fable we find embodied the
Hamletism of the antique world. . . . And the English Tragedy is but Egyptian Memnon, Montaignised and modernized;
for being but a mortal man Shakespeare had his fathers too'"
(135). Melville thus implies that he is only following Shakespeare's example in his own modernizing of *Hamlet.*

Like Hamlet, Pierre is forced to fit an unheroic adolescent
self to an older heroic role. The ghost gives Hamlet his role
as revenger. Hamlet must find a way to make this archetype
(or stereotype) his own. Pierre's father gives Pierre more ambiguous directions, but in his fierce championing of Isabel,
Pierre seems to be following his father's romantic example.
There are also his two heroic grandfathers; all three male
Glendinnings bear the same name. The grandfathers were
military heroes, the father a hero (apparently) in love, the son
is to be a hero in a more abstract and absolute realm of "Life."

> For Pierre is a warrior too; Life his campaign, and three
> fierce allies, Woe and Scorn, and Want, his foes. The wide
> world is banded against him; for lo you! he holds up the
> standard of Right, and swears by the Eternal and True!
> But ah, Pierre, Pierre, when thou goest to that bed, how
> humbling the thought, that thy most extended length
> measures not the proud six feet of thy grand John of
> Gaunt sire! The stature of the warrior is cut down to
> the dwindled glory of the fight. For more glorious in
> real tented field to strike down your valiant foe, than in
> the conflicts of a noble soul with a dastardly world to
> chase a vile enemy who ne'er will show front (270–71).

In comparison with Ahab, Pierre is dubiously heroic. Alan
Lebowitz puts it succinctly: "Ahab is the hero burdened with
his humanity; Pierre is a man overwhelmed by his assumption
of a hero's duty." [61]

But it is important to see that the concept of heroism is not

61. *Progress into Silence: A Study of Melville's Heroes* (Bloomington,
Ind., 1970), p. 165.

itself rejected. It is an ideal toward which Pierre is aspiring, which his author holds out for him even as Pierre fails to appropriate it. What Pierre shows, in fact, is a deepening of the divided selfhood of Ahab, where the hero's temporal development is now foremost, his eternal gestalt at such a distance that it makes impossible a unified personality. In the coach on his way to the city Pierre discovers the pamphlet "Chronometricals and Horologicals," which reflects a mocking image of his schizoid condition—in terms, I might emphasize, of its ambivalent temporality. The chronometrical self is attuned to eternity, the horological self is attuned to the local time of the world. Pierre's problem is that he is imperfectly attuned to both. Plotinus Plinlimmon, author of the pamphlet, is able to defend the horological as the appropriate mode of temporality for the mass of men, but Pierre, as hero and putative Christ, cannot accept such a pragmatic compromise.

"The tale of moral or psychological growth is one of the major productive conventions of nineteenth-century fiction," Warner Berthoff has written, "but when Melville undertakes it directly, as in . . . *Pierre,* he appears, formally, at his weakest." [62] *Pierre* is indeed an abortive Bildungsroman. But the reason for this failure has to do with the nature of time itself in the novel. It is the intimation of eternity that renders futile the productions of time. All value is eternal value, and time is the medium of loss, not of meaningful growth. "Oh, what quenchless feud is this, that Time hath with the sons of Men" (8). Pierre is awakened to a sense of the eternal out of his youthful naïveté, but only becomes increasingly aware of his alienation from it.

> In the midst of the merriments of the mutations of Time, Pierre hath ringed himself in with the grief of Eternity. Pierre is a peak inflexible in the heart of Time, as the isle-peak, Piko, stands unassaultable in the midst of waves (304).

62. *The Example of Melville* (Princeton, 1962), pp. 102–03.

The phenomenon that *Pierre* presents is not the *deus* but the *heros absconditus,* the disappearance of the heroic archetype from human view. The closer Pierre gets to the Truth in his quest, the more the truth eludes him and the less heroic he becomes. The most powerful evocation of the hero in the book is the dream vision of Enceladus at the end. The author describes this natural phenomenon of the landscape near Saddle Meadows:

> You saw Enceladus the Titan, the most potent of all the giants, writhing from out the imprisoning earth;— turbaned with upborne moss he writhed; still, though armless, resisting with his whole striving trunk, the Pelion and the Ossa hurled back at him;—turbaned with upborne moss he writhed; still turning his unconquerable front toward that majestic mount eternally in vain assailed by him, and which, when it had stormed him off, and heaved his undoffable incubus upon him, and deridingly left him there to bay out his ineffectual howl (345).

The vestiges of Ahab are unmistakable here, but for Pierre this is only a hallucination. Two things are noteworthy about this heroic vision. The first is that it is not a true human form, but a geological formation that only to the fanciful eye resembles the mythical deity. The second is that it is presented not through the consciousness of Pierre but through the detached reportage of the author. When we return to seeing the vision through Pierre's eyes at the end of the passage, we see "his own duplicate face and features" projected onto the Titanic form. "With trembling frame he started from his chair, and woke from that ideal horror to all his actual grief" (346).

The loss of heroic substance also involves a loss of the dialectics of the meditative form. Pierre is an abortive hero who, like Ethan Brand, can find no relation to a ground beyond himself. The ontological mystery of *Moby-Dick,* sustained by Ahab's demonic act of faith, collapses into psychological ambiguity in *Pierre.* That Melville still would achieve a cosmological vision is indicated by his juxtaposition of the *Inferno* with *Hamlet* as a literary model for his novel. Enceladus recalls the half-buried giants in Canto 31 of Dante's work. But the external cosmos which Ahab tried to assault becomes a landscape within the self:

> Yet now, forsooth, because Pierre began to see through the first superficiality of the world, he fondly weens he has come to the unlayered substance. But, far as any geologist has yet gone down into the world, it is found to consist of nothing but surface stratified on surface. To its axis, the world being nothing but superinduced superficies. By vast pains we mine into the pyramid; by horrible gropings we come to the central room; with joy we espy the sarcophagus; but we lift the lid—and no body is there!— appallingly vacant as vast is the soul of a man! (285).

"Hark ye yet again—the little lower layer," Ahab said in the beginning of his speech on the pasteboard masks of reality (220). There is no "unlayered substance" in *Pierre,* and the imagination turns from the emptiness of the world to the emptiness of the self. We find the hero sliding here from the plenitude of Ahab's vision toward Ishmael's void.

Similarly, the hero loses touch in *Pierre* with the narrator, who can only admire, love, and rejoice in him. Instead of Ishmael's parallel consciousness, we have the exacerbated omniscience of the Victorian "Author," which in the first half of the book all but annihilates its subject with its dark and ironic foreboding. "Ay Pierre," the Author addresses his young hero, "now indeed thou art hurt with a wound, never to be completely healed but in heaven; for thee, the before undistrusted moral beauty of the world is forever fled; for thee, thy sacred father is no more a saint; all brightness hath gone from thy hills, and all peace from thy plains; and now, now, for the first time, Pierre, Truth rolls a black billow through thy soul!" (65).

The narrator is continually anticipating his hero's discoveries, in his own impatience, and must periodically rein himself in: "But the thoughts we here indite as Pierre's are to be very carefully discriminated from those we indite concerning him" (167). The Author knows too much that Pierre doesn't know, but, as he himself confesses, "Easy for man to think like a hero; but hard for man to act like one" (170).

In the second half of the novel, much more symmetrical in its ambiguity than *Moby-Dick,* the Author begins to dissociate himself from his hero. The overidentification becomes a rejection; the melodrama turns into burlesque, as Melville takes on the literary fashions of his time. With little or no indication of Pierre's literary ambitions in the first half of the book, he unaccountably becomes an aspiring author. There is much pathos in Pierre's driving himself at his prematurely attempted mature work, and much of Melville's own increasingly bitter experience as an American author lies behind this portrait of the artist. But the Author has withdrawn from his attempt to see the dark truth through Pierre and contents himself with commenting bitterly on Pierre's increasing ability to discover the truth as author himself. "For the more and the more that he wrote, and the deeper and the deeper that he dived, Pierre saw the everlasting elusiveness of Truth" (339).

Pierre manages to act out the role of Hamlet, departing in a litter of corpses. But what has happened in the course of the novel is that he has moved from the position of a hero who confronts the ontological mystery to the position of a narrator who speculates on a series of more artificial ambiguities. As with Kierkegaard's *Repetition,* though in a much more somber mood, the meditation on the hero has become a portrait of the artist as a young man. A passage close to the end of the book is telling in its forecast of Melville's own disillusionment with the visionary powers of the literary artist. Pierre has begun to doubt that Isabel is really his sister, to consider that his heroic enthusiasm has been based on a delusion:

> Of late to Pierre, much more vividly than ever before, the whole story of Isabel had seemed an enigma, a mystery, an imaginative delirium; especially since he had got so deep into the inventional mysteries of his book. For he who is most practically and deeply conversant with mysticisms

and mysteries; he who professionally deals in mysticisms and mysteries himself; often that man, more than any body else, is disposed to regard such things in others as very deceptively bejuggling; and likewise is apt to be rather materialistic in all his own merely personal notions (as in their practical lives, with priests of Eleusinian religions), and more than any other man, is often inclined, at the bottom of his soul, to be uncompromisingly sceptical on all novel visionary hypotheses of any kind. It is only the no-mystics, or the half-mystics, who, properly speaking, are credulous. So that in Pierre, was presented the apparent anomaly of a mind, which by becoming really profound in itself, grew sceptical of all tendered profundities; whereas, the contrary is generally supposed (354).

With the loss of the hero in Melville's imagination, the narrator or author becomes a kind of confidence man, offering skepticism instead of profundity. This skepticism culminates finally in *The Confidence-Man: His Masquerade*, where the figure of the narrator, the Ishmaelean purveyor of benevolence and ambiguities, all but crowds the hero out. The only vestiges of the demonic heroism of Ahab are found in the figures who oppose the Confidence-Man, and these distrustful antagonists are almost always overcome. Colonel Moredock, the Indian-hater, is reminiscent of Ahab, but he can only appear in an ambiguously interpolated tale. *The Confidence-Man* proved to be Melville's farewell to the art of fiction, and in chapter 44 he laments the passing of the hero, "the original character," from his own imaginative world.

The character sheds not its characteristic on its surroundings, whereas, the original character, essentially such, is like a revolving Drummond light, raying away from itself all round it—everything is lit by it, everything starts up to it (mark how it is with Hamlet), so that, in certain minds, there follows upon the adequate conception of such a character, an effect, in its way, akin to that which in Genesis attends upon the beginning of things.[63]

63. *The Confidence-Man*, p. 271.

Melville mentions Hamlet, Don Quixote, and Milton's Satan as examples of the original character; he is surely thinking of Ahab as well. The Confidence-Man is no such original. In his fragmented nature he has lost what Kierkegaard would call the unifying power of personality. He puts out the light at the end of the book in an effect akin to Apocalypse, the herald not of the beginning of things but of their end.

Thus the Romantic hero, with his Shakespearean and Miltonic heritage, slowly disappeared from Melville's imaginative universe. It would be an oversimplification to see his entire literary career as a single-minded search for heroes, but it is hard to ignore the way Melville makes the possibility of literary creation itself, literary creation on the grand scale of *Moby-Dick,* depend on the presence of a powerful heroic figure. As heroism such as Ahab's continued to elude Melville after *Moby-Dick,* he came to despair of the visionary powers he had once projected for himself. He settled for the lesser achievement of his tales and poems, fine enough in their own right but hardly of the scope of his Great American Novel and burdened with a sense of defeat. Once he had conceived the meditation on the hero, it became for Melville not so much a technical, formal device as the vital sustenance of his literary ambition. The success of an American Shakespeare depended on a hero of our time.

5

Concluding Unscientific Postscript: The Twilight of the Hero and the Meditative Form

The six texts we have been mainly concerned with in this study were all published within twelve years of one another, from *A Hero of Our Time* in 1840 to *Pierre* in 1852. Although Kierkegaard, Lermontov, Brontë, and Melville were isolated from one another by barriers of language and geography, they were all responding to the literary culture of Romanticism that had flourished in the previous generation (they were all born within six years, from 1813 to 1819). The preoccupations these authors share are occasionally specific, such as the fascination with Byron in Brontë and Lermontov, or the interest in Shakespeare's tragic heroes and Milton's Satan. But they are better seen as general—an interest in the figure of the Romantic hero per se, a "polemical emphasis on heroism," to borrow a phrase from Georg Lukács.[1]

What we find in their works, as diverse as they are, is a similar formal expression of a common imaginative concern: can the figure of the hero, belonging to an earlier age and / or to a different literary mode, be dealt with by a modern writer of prose fiction? Could there be a hero of their time and their way of writing? To each of these authors the hero meant different things, psychological as well as aesthetic, as I have occasionally indicated in my brief forays into biography. But they all arrived at the similar solution of subjecting the heroic presence to a process of meditation. A narrative presence is

1. *The Theory of the Novel*, trans. Anna Bostock (London, 1971), p. 44.

differentiated from the hero, introducing a dialectical complication in the way this figure is presented; other dialectical complications are entailed. The wholeness and immediacy of the hero are tested by a divisive reflection, and this testing takes precedence over the more common interest of the traditional story or plot.

What happened to the meditation on the hero after the mid-nineteenth century? Does this imaginative form disappear, or is it somehow transformed and continued? We have seen some evidence of survivals in Kafka and Dostoevsky, and there are others. In fact, this book might be expanded considerably if it were to treat such later novels as Conrad's *Lord Jim*, Faulkner's *Absalom, Absalom!* and Mann's *Doctor Faustus,* all of which approach a central heroic figure through the indirection of a narrator or narrators. The concern with the Romantic hero and with the complicating presence of the skeptical hero-worshiper does carry over into the twentieth century. One might even say that the form itself becomes more central to the traditions of the modern novel, with authors such as Conrad, Faulkner, and Mann, than it was to the traditions of the novel in the mid-nineteenth century, to which the works of Kierkegaard, Brontë, Lermontov and even Melville remained peripheral. And yet, even as the meditation on the hero becomes a more common and recognizable genre (Turgenev's *A King Lear of the Steppes*, Fitzgerald's *The Great Gatsby,* and other Conrad novels, *Under Western Eyes* and *Heart of Darkness,* could be added to the list), it is clear that the hero himself is increasingly threatened in the modern age. In this last chapter I shall only consider these later developments briefly.

One can perhaps best appreciate the changing status of the hero by considering Melville's *Billy Budd,* the unfinished work written during the period of his public abdication as a novelist. As evidence from the manuscript shows, the story began as a short poem, a dramatic monologue with a prose headnote, and only the figure of Billy Budd. Gradually Melville added new characters and new points of view. "All along, Melville's dramatizations had the effect . . . of dissociating

the narrator from commitments he had earlier made or positions that Melville might wish to insinuate without endorsing,"
report Harrison Hayford and Merton Sealts.[2] It is as though
the meditative stance emerged willy-nilly, as though Billy
Budd's fate insisted on an increasing complexity of interpretation. The omniscience of the author who relates the story becomes what one commentator calls "omniscient ambiguity," [3]
a knowledge that advertizes its own limitations. "Forty years
after a battle it is easy for a non-combattant to reason about
how it ought to have been fought. It is another thing personally and under fire to have to direct the fighting while involved in the obscuring smoke of it" (114).

In his youthfulness and naïveté, Billy Budd is hardly a hero
in the Romantic tradition. But the fact that the fate of the
hero is the underlying concern of the story is indicated early
on, when the author defends Lord Nelson's military heroics
against the "Benthamites of war," the scientific rationalists
who would deny heroic values altogether. "If thus to have
adorned himself for the altar and the sacrifice were indeed
vainglory, then affectation and fustian is each more heroic line
in the great epics and dramas, since in such lines the poet but
embodies in verse those exaltations of sentiment that a nature
like Nelson's, the opportunity being given, vitalizes into acts"
(58). In fact, Billy Budd is a rather weak defender of epic
heroism, and this is very much to the point. He is presented as
a type, "the Handsome Sailor," and his character can be
clearly read from his appearance. In his simplicity he is frequently compared with animals, and his killing of Claggart
seems an instinctive act of self-defense. Thus Billy's heroism
seems too much of the surface, and Melville was compelled to
extend his meditation to other figures. Claggart is introduced,
a villain, but one whose villainy is much more profound than

2. Editors' Introduction to *Billy Budd, Sailor* (Chicago, 1962), p. 38. In
all further references to this novel, page numbers cited parenthetically
in text are from this edition.

3. Edward A. Kearns, "Omniscient Ambiguity: The Narrators of *Moby-
Dick* and *Billy Budd*," *Emerson Society Quarterly* 58 (1970) : 117–20.

Billy's goodness. "But for the adequate comprehending of Claggart by a normal nature these hints are insufficient. To pass from a normal nature to him one must cross 'the deadly space between.' And this is best done by indirection" (74). Yet even with Claggart's "mystery of iniquity" we are hardly out of our depths. If these were the only two figures in the story (as they were in an earlier version) there would be little to argue about. We would have a fairly straightforward conflict of good and evil. But Melville chose to add the character of Captain Vere, and it is over his decision to have Billy executed that most of the critical debate about this tale has been waged. Was Vere making an ethical choice or was he merely acting as a cog in the military machine? Here Melville is the most deliberately ambiguous, as the meditation moves from the hero to the villain to the would-be arbiter of the case.

Melville's strategy in this tale is similar to the strategy Kierkegaard uses in *Fear and Trembling:* he withdraws the narrative consciousness from the hero, focusing it on alternate figures in order to preserve the integrity of that heroism. Yet though Billy Budd may be a Christ figure—this is one hypothesis among many that the story offers—he is hardly a religious hero like Abraham. He is the victim rather than the heroic sacrificer, and in a curious coincidence Melville appeals to the story of Abraham and Isaac as he simultaneously describes and avoids describing Vere's last interview with Billy Budd. "The austere devotee of military duty, letting himself melt back into what remains primeval in our formalized humanity, may in end have caught Billy to his heart, even as Abraham may have caught Isaac on the brink of resolutely offering him up in obedience to the exacting behest" (114). There is no question here of an assault on the ontological mystery such as Ahab carried out. The heroic existence is a much more fragile thing. Only by adopting the posture of meditation is the author able to protect the hero, to keep alive the hope for a hero of our time.

One can observe a similar protective attitude against the hero's seemingly inevitable self-destruction in Conrad's *Lord*

Jim. Jim commits an initial act that is clearly unheroic, his leap of bad faith from the Patna, and it is from his all-too-human weakness that his potential for heroism must be rescued. Marlow, the narrator, is the most concerned to rescue Jim from the shame and anonymity into which he has plunged himself. Conrad arranges it so that we see Jim from an increasing distance as the novel unfolds, first from the point of view of an omniscient author, then from Marlow's perspective in his oral account, then through Marlow's reconstruction of events two years later in a letter. It is of course unclear whether Jim really becomes the hero, with whose image he deluded himself earlier in his career, but Marlow, as meditator, is able to leave this question in luminous doubt.

> And that's the end. He passes away under a cloud, inscrutable at heart, forgotten, unforgiven, and excessively romantic. Not in the wildest days of his boyish visions could he have seen the alluring shape of such an extraordinary success! For it may very well be that in the short moment of his last proud and unflinching glance, he beheld the face of that opportunity which, like an Eastern bride, had come veiled to his side.[4]

In *Heart of Darkness* the heroic image is completely shattered, the corruption of the heroic ideal more fully exposed. In *The Great Gatsby*, with which both these Conrad novels are often compared, the corruption and the magnificent potential seem to coexist. Gatsby is a confidence man, but he has the creative energy of Melville's "original character, . . . raying away from itself all around it." Nick Carraway, Gatsby's narrator, acts like Marlow in defending the ideal even as he deplores its failure. "One of the few honest people that I have ever known," as he calls himself,[5] Carraway is a kind of moral insulator against the reader's natural indignation toward his hero.

Thus the meditation on the hero in its later manifestations takes the form of a problematical defense of heroism, a lament

4. *Lord Jim* (London, 1923), p. 416.
5. *The Great Gatsby* (New York, 1925), p. 60.

over its corruption and demise, or both together. "Our world, today, is less sure of itself, more modest, perhaps, since it has renounced the omnipotence of the person, but more ambitious, too, since it looks beyond," writes Robbe-Grillet. "The novel seems to stagger, having lost what was once its best prop, the hero." [6] The gradual loss of the hero and his unifying power of personality is of course part of a more widespread decline of character in modern art and should be seen against this background. "We have had a pendulum shift in the view of character over the last hundred years," Martin Price observes.

> Victorian critics found character more absorbing than the structures it inhabited—the plots of plays or novels, whether Sophocles and Shakespeare or the work of their own age—and created in turn that ultimate tribute to the mysteries and subtleties of character, the dramatic monologue. But in that form alone we can see a movement through Pound and Eliot towards a symbolist mode, where character becomes at most the constellated form of image patterns, historical allusions, philosophical themes. . . . The creation of character is a form of art as well as moral exercise and the symbolist novel seems to have abjured this art for others, much as painting has shattered the portrait and disposed of its elements in new ways.[7]

I should like to argue, in fact, that in the case of the Romantic hero it is not simply a case of decline or eclipse or overshadowing by the antihero (all along, the ironic critique of heroes continues to coexist with more positive treatments, as in the case of Julien Sorel or the Underground Man). Rather I would say that the image of the Romantic hero is shattered in the modern novel, and its elements are disposed

6. "On Several Obsolete Notions," *For a New Novel,* trans. Richard Howard (New York, 1965), p. 29.

7. "The Other Self: Thoughts About Character in the Novel," in *Imagined Worlds,* ed. Maynard Mack and Ian Gregor (London, 1968), pp. 290–92.

of in new ways. The elements are dispersed in one of two directions, either backward into the substratum of myth (from which the human heroic form originally emerged) or forward, as it were, into the multiple ambiguities of the narrator who celebrates the hero's achievement. Unable to maintain his precarious middle ground—precarious even in the mid-nineteenth-century meditations—the Romantic hero in the twentieth century is absorbed into the background and / or the foreground that he originally tried to stand apart from. As the structure of thought of the age changed in myriad and complex ways, the imaginative form of the meditation on the hero underwent a basic transformation.

The beginnings of the hero's fade-out into the background of myth can be seen in Victor Hugo, whose *William Shakespeare* (1864) discusses the heroes of literature as a series of ideal types rather than as single beings. The drama, Hugo claims, "creates living types. A lesson which is a man; a myth with a human face so plastic that it looks at you and that its look is a mirror." The mythical type, of which each hero is an example, is by no means a secondary abstraction from reality. "These types are beings," Hugo says. "They exist with an existence more intense than that of any creature thinking himself alive there in the street. These phantoms are more substantial than man." Hugo defends the hero, but his defense entails a pluralism that denies the integrity and autonomy of the single heroic figure. "As we said before," he continues, "as many types, as many Adams. The man of Homer, Achilles, is an Adam: from him come the species of the slayers; the man of Aeschylus, Prometheus, is an Adam: from him come the race of the wrestlers; the man of Shakespeare, Hamlet, is an Adam: to him belongs the family of the dreamers." [8] The individual identity of each hero is implicitly denied as he is placed on this evolutionary tree. We are not far here from the mythical "Hero with a Thousand Faces" of Campbell and Jung, the hero with no face of his own.

8. *William Shakespeare,* trans. Melville B. Anderson (London, n.d.), pp. 174–75, 176.

The furthest extent of this imaginative dissolve occurs in a novel like Hesse's *Steppenwolf,* which with its lengthy editorial preface to the hero's journal has itself some semblance of the meditative form. Hesse ironically explodes the Faustian dialectic of the *zwei Seelen,* the tension at the heart of the Romantic hero's identity.

> When Faust, in a line immortalized among schoolmasters and greeted with a shudder of astonishment by the Philistine, says: "Two souls, alas, do dwell within my breast!" he has forgotten Mephisto and a whole crowd of other souls that he has in his breast likewise. The Steppenwolf, too, believes that he bears two souls (wolf and man) in his breast and even so finds his breast disagreeably cramped because of them. The breast and the body are indeed one, but the souls that dwell in it are not two, nor five, but countless in number. Man is an onion made up of a hundred integuments, a texture made up of many threads. The ancient Asiatics knew this well enough, and in the Buddhist Yoga an exact technique was devised for unmasking the illusion of personality.[9]

Harry Haller has seen himself as "the Steppenwolf," but he discovers this critique of his Romantic identity in an anonymous pamphlet. It marks a stage in his belated *Bildung,* his education away from the outmoded Goethean ideals toward a merging of his single selfhood with the metaphysical ground. The ultimate dissolution of his character comes with his entry into the Magic Theater, where reality and fantasy blend in a dreamy *jenseits von gut und böse,* a realm of mystical laissez-faire.

The name "the Magic Theater" betrays a certain ambiguity about the ontological status of this ground of all being into which the hero has disappeared, however. The quest for myth in modern literature often leads through fiction and illusion, and it is debatable in many instances whether the mythical realm that is invoked still retains its original religious sub-

9. *Steppenwolf,* trans. Basil Creighton, rev. Joseph Mileck and Horst Frenz (New York, 1971), p. 69.

stance. The fiction- and myth-making of Joyce is a case in point. Joyce's novels, from *Stephen Hero* to *Finnegans Wake,* show an increasing fragmentation of the single "heroic" personality into a plurality of mythical archetypes. Stephen Dedalus' name alludes modestly to the mythical artificer; Leopold Bloom's compendious identity contains more numerous and more obvious roles; HCE is almost completely submerged in a sea of allusion. Joseph Campbell and others have argued that the mythical dimensions of Joyce are strong and deep,[10] but it is at least equally valid to insist on the fictive, synthetic quality of Joyce's complex vision. Rather than plunging into the collective unconscious, Joyce often seems to be collecting the consciousness of his race.

Indeed, one might argue that the very concept of myth is suspect in modern literature, that it is an ideal that literature invoked to lend itself substance at a time when literary values seemed increasingly threatened.[11] This brings us to the other side of the dialectic in which the Romantic hero was originally involved, to the narrator, the speculative purveyor of fictions, who uses the hero as the solid basis for his own powers of invention. Unlike Johannes de Silentio, the narrator may decide that he *can* do what the other does; he may usurp the hero's preeminence and authority. We have already observed this tendency on the part of the narrators in *Repetition* and *Pierre.* "Literature, heroism, accomplices and dupes of one another, exchange their gifts," Maurice Blanchot wryly observes. "The song gives glory and assures the name of its renown; the singer himself is obscure and he remains anonymous. Then the hero becomes *his* hero; the artist, in his turn, lays claim to immortality, no longer indirectly but directly. . . . "[12] The meditator on the hero becomes, by this logic, the hero as artist.

10. Cf. Joseph Campbell and Henry M. Robinson, *A Skeleton Key to Finnegans Wake* (New York, 1944), pp. 13–21.

11. This theory of myth has been proposed to me by my colleague Alvin Kernan, formerly of Yale, now of Princeton University.

12. "Le Héros," *Nouvelle Revue Française* 25 (1965), p. 104, my translation. There is a useful summary of the idea of the artist–hero in Edith Kern's *Existential Thought and Fictional Technique,* though the treatment of Kierkegaard in terms of this tradition is questionable.

This countergenre of the artist as hero arises in the early nineteenth century, about the same time as the meditation on the hero. In the twentieth century the artist tends to become a hero—or vice versa—to such an extent that the hero himself, the active, unselfconscious, often inarticulate figure, is virtually excluded from the scene. The most subtle form of this usurpation seems to me to occur in Nietzsche's *Thus Spake Zarathustra*. There is no meditation as such, only an extended series of prophecies presented by an omniscient author. Zarathustra is not himself the hero; he is rather the celebrator of the Übermensch to come. But as this heroic ideal is continually projected into the future, and as Zarathustra seems relatively free of the debilitating weaknesses of the unheroic age, the prophet effectively assumes the hero's place.[13]

In Faulkner's *Absalom, Absalom!* a similar process of narrative takeover seems to occur, though in a much more pathetic vein. There are a series of narrators in this novel. Their meditations form a sequence that moves from the religiously charged vision of Rosa Coldfield, who sees Sutpen as profoundly demonic, through the more balanced but decadent classicism of Mr. Compson, who thinks in terms of the heroes of Aeschylus, to the frankly speculative and much more tentative collaboration of Quentin and Shreve, who think in terms of themselves.[14] In each successive vision of him as hero, Sutpen loses something of his centrality and his heroic aura. In each successive vision the narrators are more clearly revealed as the makers of the heroic figure they meditate upon. Thus Quentin and Shreve are eventually seen as "the two of them creating between them, out of the rag-tag and bob-ends of old tales and talking, people who perhaps had never existed at all anywhere, who, shadows, were shadows not of flesh and blood which had lived and died but shadows in turn of what were (to one of them, at least, to Shreve) shades too, quiet as

13. Cf. Albert LaValley, *Carlyle and the Idea of the Modern* (New Haven, 1968), pp. 107–13.

14. See Robert Adams, *Faulkner: Myth and Motion* (Princeton, 1968), pp. 181–93.

the visible murmur of their vaporizing breath." [15] The historical existence of the hero gradually loses its importance for the historians. The key "fact" of Bon's Negro blood, for example, is merely a hypothesis on the part of Quentin.[16] As in Melville's progress from *Moby-Dick* to *Pierre* we move in *Absalom, Absalom!* from a meditation on the hero to a portrait of the artist whose sensitivity, we know from *The Sound and the Fury*, dooms him to suicide. Like Pierre also, Quentin is a Hamlet unable to imitate the archaic example before him.

It is in the context of this modernist transformation of the active Romantic hero into the hero as artist that one can best appreciate Mann's *Doctor Faustus*. Adrian Leverkühn maintains his heroic preeminence—he is never threatened by his narrator's taking over—but his artistic vocation places him in a less original relation to the universe than his Romantic predecessors had enjoyed. Goethe's Faust, in particular, would tolerate no such mediation in his quest to participate in Reality. It is true that as a musician Leverkühn gets closer to the deep wells of being than a mere man of letters could. Hesse's comment in *Steppenwolf*—"In the German spirit the matriarchal link with nature rules in the form of the hegemony of music to an extent unknown in any other people" [17] —is apropos. But it is also true that this modern Faustus, even in his culminating work, *The Lamentation*, can only deal in echoes of the natural: "The echo, the giving back of the human voice as nature-sound, and the revelation of it *as* nature-sound, is essentially a lament—Nature's melancholy 'Alas!' in view of Man, her effort to utter his solitary state." [18] Mann's Faust has in him much more of Mephistopheles, the spirit who denies, than Goethe's ever did. It is worth noting also that Leverkühn was intended as a portrait of the author

15. *Absalom, Absalom!* (New York, 1936), p. 303.
16. See Adams, *Faulkner*, p. 199, for a convincing argument on this disputed point.
17. *Steppenwolf*, p. 154.
18. *Doctor Faustus*, trans. H. T. Lowe-Porter (New York, 1948), p. 486. In all further references to this novel, page number cited parenthetically in text are from this edition.

of *Zarathustra* as well, not the ideal figure of the superman
but the writer, finally insane, who dreamed of the heroic
future.

In fact, one might say that *Doctor Faustus* is essentially a
parody of the earlier meditation on the hero, an ironic imitation which reevaluates the Romantic values from a modernist
perspective. "Why must I think that almost all, no, all the
methods and conventions of art today *are good for parody
only,*" Leverkühn asks (134), and his complaint reflects a
problem Mann faces in all his writing. And yet Mann does not
conceive of the conflict as simply one between Romanticism
and Modernism; rather it is one between the children of the
spirit and the children of nature, as he puts it in an essay on
Goethe and Tolstoy. For the children of the spirit, such as
Schiller, Dostoevsky, and Nietzsche, human value and dignity
are enhanced by a solitary opposition to the natural; for the
children of nature, Goethe, Tolstoy, and to some extent Mann
himself, human value and dignity are enhanced by a harmo-
nious acceptance of the natural, in all its contradiction and
plenitude. The children of nature are thus more closely allied
with the realm of being, but their visions, according to
Mann, are decidedly lacking in the human heroic form. The
children of the spirit are heroic opposers, but they are doomed
to alienation and disease.

Thus in *Doctor Faustus* Mann presents a spiritual hero, but
places this heroism in a more natural perspective. For example, the artist's demonic inspiration is carefully grounded in
the physical nature of his syphilitic infection, although we
are invited—challenged, in fact—to believe that there occurs
a "metastasis into the metaphysical" (232). Or as Zeitblom puts
it later on, "Genius is a form of vital power deeply experienced in illness, creating out of illness, through illness creative" (355).[19] We are never allowed to separate the spiritual

19. Cf. Mann's "Goethe and Tolstoy": "It may be going too far to say
that disease *is* spirit, or, which would sound very tendentious, that spirit
is disease. Still, the two conceptions do have very much in common"
(*Essays*, trans. H. T. Lowe-Porter [New York, 1957], p. 96).

heroism of Leverkühn from its natural origins. Nor are we
able to focus on his heroism in isolation, as Zeitblom continues to give us a broad panorama of the social decline and
corruption leading to the Third Reich, the illness of an
"outer world," which touches only peripherally on the life of
the hero.

Thus *Doctor Faustus* subjects the figure of the hero to a
series of revisions. He is an artist, with more ironic self-
consciousness than the traditional Romantic hero, whose only
actions are the creation of an art that questions the relationship between man and the universe. At the same time his
heroic genius is closely tied to the progress of a physical
disease. Finally, we might note that the heroic role of Faustus
given him by the title of the novel is never something that he
acquires directly in the book. Mann carefully researched the
Faust legend in the course of writing the novel, but this
archaic gestalt is never something that is brought into the
hero's own awareness, any more than Leopold Bloom realizes
himself as Odysseus in Joyce's *Ulysses*. Just as Leverkühn's
Lamentation is presented as the negation of the heroic
humanism of Beethoven (and Schiller) in the Ninth Symphony, *Doctor Faustus* is Mann's attempt to free the German
imagination from its fatal fascination with the figure of the
hero, from "the grim deposit of saga in the soul of the nation" (481).[20]

One of the reasons Mann adopts the form of the meditation
on the hero in *Doctor Faustus* is that the once-unpolitical
German had been forced to acknowledge, for a whole century
of aesthetic hero-worshipers, the horrors of hero-worship in its
political form. "The hero with the folkish banner," as Hitler
was called by Eric Bentley, had reminded Western culture in
the most forcible way since Napoleon of how artistic fictions
can be corrupted into political myth. It is worth noting that

20. In *Thomas Mann's Doctor Faustus: The Source and Structure of
the Novel,* trans. Krishna Winston (Chicago, 1969), Gunilla Bergsten notes
that Mann conspicuously avoids alluding to Goethe's *Faust;* she sees this
as evidence that the novel is a retraction of Goethe's Romantic drama.

Leverkühn has no direct connection with the political; he is not a world-historical individual in the Hegelian sense. "I will only add that the word 'historic' fits with a far more sinister emphasis the time [i.e. 1944] in which, than about which, I write," Zeitblom observes (252). It is the narrator who provides the link between the aesthetic sublimity of the Romantic hero and its political and military degradation.

There is marked contrast between the way Mann relates the artistic and the political manifestations of Romantic heroism and the way Carlyle, with much less self-awareness, relates the Hero as Man of Letters with the Hero as King. As we saw at the beginning of this study, Carlyle had tried to assert, in *On Heroes and Hero-Worship,* that heroism was stable and unchanging, "eternal adamant" in the turmoil of history. But against this mythical permanence was working a more historical sense of decline and fall; thus Carlyle moved from "The Hero as Divinity" to "The Hero as Prophet," finally to the radical split between knowledge and power in the two peculiarly modern forms of heroism, the man of letters and the "king." Carlyle was suspicious of Napoleon's claims to such kingship, and he tried to minimize the tension between the acknowledged and the unacknowledged legislators of the world, but the conflict had already driven him away from sympathy with heroism in its literary form.

Mann, on the other hand, explores the terrible differences and similarities between the two figures of artistic and political power. Hitler, of course, is barely mentioned in the novel, but this is itself significant; the holocaust of World War II is declared beyond the range of aesthetic vision. Where Carlyle ultimately rejects the aesthetic dimensions of heroism and falls into a more blinded worship of political power, Mann is able to find some redeeming value in a hero who looks back to his audience as well as ahead to his mythical goal. Mann put it most succinctly in an essay contemporary with the writing of *Doctor Faustus,* appropriately entitled "Dostoevsky—in Moderation."

Life is not prudish, and it is probably safe to say that life prefers creative, genius-bestowing disease a thousand times over to prosaic health; prefers disease, surmounting obstacles proudly on horseback, boldly leaping from peak to peak, to lounging, pedestrian healthfulness. Life is not finical and never thinks of making a moral distinction between health and infirmity. It seizes the bold product of disease, consumes and digests it, and as soon as it is assimilated, it is health. An entire horde, a generation of open-minded, healthy lads pounces upon the work of diseased genius, genialized by disease, admires and praises it, raises it to the skies, perpetuates it, transmutes it, and bequeaths it to civilization, which does not live on the home-baked bread of health alone. They all swear by the name of the great invalid, thanks to whose madness they no longer need to be mad. Their healthfulness feeds upon his madness and in them he will become healthy.[21]

It may be that we have not seen the last of the revivals of the Romantic hero, in literature or in politics. But *Doctor Faustus* may stand as the meditation on the hero to end all such meditations, an attempt to comprehend, to sympathize with, and to atone for the best and the worst in human nature. In Mann's greatest novel, the meditation on the hero attains to its most tragic expression; the tone of the meditation changes from awe to lament. There are humbling truths here that Kierkegaard, Brontë, Lermontov, and Melville perhaps foresaw in their more reflective moments but that they foreswore in their common search for a champion of individual human integrity, a hero who could withstand the leveling of society and the ravages of thought endemic to our time.

21. Preface to *The Short Novels of Dostoevsky* (New York, 1945), pp. xiv–xv. Cf. *Doctor Faustus*, p. 242, where Mephistopheles echoes this paragraph.

Index